D1446697

THE
SAVAGE PILGRIMAGE

THE
SAVAGE PILGRIMAGE

A NARRATIVE OF

D. H. LAWRENCE

BY

Catherine Carswell

WITH A MEMOIR OF THE AUTHOR BY

John Carswell

It has been a savage enough pilgrimage. . . . We keep faith. I always feel death only strengthens that — the faith between those who have it.

D. H. LAWRENCE, 1923

CAMBRIDGE UNIVERSITY PRESS

CAMBRIDGE

LONDON   NEW YORK   NEW ROCHELLE

MELBOURNE   SYDNEY

Published by the Press Syndicate of the University of Cambridge
The Pitt Building, Trumpington Street, Cambridge CB2ᵉ IRP
32 East 57th Street, New York, NY 10022, USA
296 Beaconsfield Parade, Middle Park, Melbourne 3206, Australia

Copyright 1932 by Catherine Carswell
Introduction © Cambridge University Press 1981

First published by Chatto and Windus 1932
Reissued by the Cambridge University Press with
a memoir of the author by John Carswell 1981

Printed in Great Britain at the University Press, Cambridge

Library of Congress catalogue card number: 81-3891

British Library Cataloguing in Publication Data
Carswell, Catherine
The savage pilgrimage.
1. Lawrence, D. H.—20th century—Biography
2. Authors, English—20th century—Biography
I. Title
823′.912   PR6023.A93Z
ISBN 0 521 23975 3 hard covers
ISBN 0 521 28386 8 paperback

INTRODUCTION

Nearly fifty years after it was written and thirty-five after the death of its author, the story of the author and this book can be told in context.

D. H. Lawrence dreamed from time to time of ideal communities and exerted an extraordinary magnetism on those he met, but he did not surround himself with like-minded people. Rather, he took people as he found them in his stormy life, preached at them, exalted them, quarrelled with them, and put them into his books. He married a German aristocrat, to whom he was inviolably faithful, endured a complicated attachment with a blue-coat boy from Camberwell, depended on a sombre and excitable Russian Jewish refugee, admired an ambitious short-story writer from New Zealand, and enjoyed the company of numerous Americans. He also had an enduring friendship with the literary woman from Glasgow who was the author of this book. This friendship was characterised by the most absolute trust.

Catherine Carswell, originally Catherine Roxburgh Macfarlane, was born in Glasgow in March 1879, some five years earlier than Lawrence, into the family of a god-fearing benevolent business man and his unworldly, deeply religious wife, as their second child. She has herself described the strict but loving atmosphere of her home in another book.*

In the last twenty years of the nineteenth century Glasgow was a vigorous, outward-looking, imperial city, in spite of its poverty, slums, drunkenness, and oppressive Presbyterianism. Its intellectual life was strong. Gilbert Murray was teaching

* *Lying Awake* (Secker and Warburg 1950).

at its university, and it had an Art School which was shortly
to produce Charles Rennie Mackintosh. Its paper, the *Glasgow
Herald*, was no doubt forbidding and conventional, but there
was nothing inward-looking about its massive columns. The
barriers against natural development of the individual,
especially of women, were still strong, but it was an invigorating climate for those with talent.

Catherine undoubtedly had talent. She read widely and
enthusiastically, she was musical, and she had a personal
charm which remained with her all her life. She was tall and
well-made with brown hair and strong features. Though not
in a conventional sense pretty, her face was extremely fine,
and was never seriously marred by age. When she was still in
her teens she was allowed to travel to Italy, where her family
had cousins, and also to Germany, where she studied at the
Frankfurt Conservatorium. All her life she spoke both
Italian and German reasonably well.

This was not the limit of the educational opportunities she
obtained from her earnest parents. She attended the Glasgow
School of Art and, though in those days she could not be
formally enrolled, the University of Glasgow, where she
followed the degree course in English Literature. As a result
of attending these two institutions she met Maurice Greiffen-
hagen, the painter, who became head of the Life Department of the School of Art in 1906, and Walter Raleigh,
Professor of English Literature, then at Glasgow, later at
Oxford.

During that time she refused at least one conventional but
eligible suitor, but in 1902, when she was not quite twenty-
three, and beginning to write reviews of novels for the *Glasgow
Herald*, she met and within a few weeks married a young
man called Herbert P. M. Jackson, who had recently
returned from fighting in the Boer War. They had been
introduced to one another by the Raleighs, and Jackson was
in fact Mrs. Raleigh's brother.

The marriage was a tragedy for all concerned. On the Italian honeymoon it became apparent that her husband was suffering from progressive paranoia. During the journey out he confided that the government had set spies to watch him, and before their return he was accusing her of infidelity with passers-by. When a child was conceived he declared it was none of his, and very soon he was threatening her life. After a struggle in which he had to be deprived of a pistol he was taken to a mental hospital from which he was never to emerge.

By the conventions of that time Catherine should have accepted husbandless marriage at the age of twenty-three. The law offered no relief by way of divorce. Insanity was not a ground.

Nevertheless she embarked on what must have seemed a hopeless struggle for release by way of an action for annulment of the marriage on the unprecedented ground that at the time of the ceremony her husband had not fully understood the contract he was undertaking. If such a plea succeeded, making her marriage no marriage at all, her child Diana would be illegitimate; and the action was strongly defended, even though the husband on whose behalf it was fought was by then too ill to give evidence. Against all odds she won her freedom and the case of *Jackson* v. *Jackson* (1908) was a leading case in matrimonial law until the reforms of the 1930's.

My mother rarely talked about this episode, and Diana, the unhappy child at its centre, died when she was only nine years old in 1912. The long-drawn-out tragedy did not spoil Catherine's serenity nor sap her energy, and she later made a happy and enduring second marriage, besides going on to considerable literary achievement. But it destroyed her youth and altered her attitude to society. She continued to respect and even venerate the simple virtues of her Glasgow childhood, and as she once said to me she could never reject the conviction that 'underneath were the everlasting arms'; but from being a Glasgow girl who seemed to have all before her, a favourite of professors, a centre of attention, she came to shrink from the world of success and security and the compromises that living in it demanded. She did not become a bohemian, and many of her literary friends regarded her as austere and conventional; but after her battle with her first husband's family she and the professional and academic world were at arms' length from each other.

Women were just beginning to enter the professions and make their own lives, and during the years between her marriages many of Catherine's closest friends were career women. Among my early 'aunts' were a woman medical officer of health, a professional musician, a sculptor whose sister married a Spanish railway engineer called Salvador de Madariaga. Catherine established herself in a cottage in Hampstead, which in those days was a cheap place to find such things, and steadily worked on the piles of novels now regularly sent to her for review by the *Glasgow Herald*.

At that time the *Herald* carried a full column of fiction reviews every Thursday. There were five, six, or even seven short pieces each week, and since none of them were signed it is impossible to say how many were by Catherine. But certainly a great many were, and among them was a notice of D. H. Lawrence's first novel *The White Peacock*, which appeared in 1911.* The novel deeply impressed the reviewer. She felt it spoke with a new voice.

About 1911 an impulsive girl, rather younger than Catherine, had come to live almost next door in Hampstead. She was called Ivy Low, and had rebelled against her family, written a novel, and taken a job as a clerk with the Prudential Assurance Company. Her later extraordinary adventures are here irrelevant, but she was a voracious reader of novels, and

* *Glasgow Herald*, 18 March 1911, p. 12.

particular admirer of D. H. Lawrence. When *Sons and Lovers* appeared in 1913 she and Catherine entered into correspondence with him, with results described in the opening pages of *The Savage Pilgrimage*. Lawrence was then living in Italy with Frieda, to whom he was not yet married, and Ivy presented herself at Fiascherino in the spring of 1914 as a kind of joint ambassador from herself and Catherine. She stayed a month: rather longer than Frieda cared to have her.

In June 1914 Lawrence and Frieda returned to England to get married, and Catherine first met him. In a vivid passage, she herself describes that first meeting and the powerful impression it made on her. The full circumstances that surrounded the meeting must be taken into account if the nature of the friendship that followed is to be fully understood.

Lawrence met Catherine (who was then thirty-five) as an established critic who had come to admire him through his work, not as a disciple approaching a man already famous. What is more, she met him as a man on the very point of marriage, and she herself had come to a critical point in her emotional life from which her own marriage was to follow only six months after Lawrence's.

After her parting from Jackson she had become involved in a long and hopeless affair with the painter Maurice Greiffen-hagen, whom she had come to know in Glasgow. Though he was some seventeen years older, it was a deep passion; and my father, normally the most tolerant of men, could not bear to hear the name of Greiffenhagen mentioned. As a child I was once taken to see him, then old and ill, in his house in St. John's Wood, and still retain the picture of a dim, invalidish figure wrapped in a dressing gown, and the secretive hush about my mother.

But this affair was over before she met Lawrence, and she was already considering marriage to a man who for some years—perhaps ever since they had edited the Glasgow University Magazine together—had offered her steady devoted love. This was my father, Donald Carswell, and in September 1914 she accepted him.

No one who reads *The Savage Pilgrimage* can doubt that Catherine's affection for Lawrence, almost from the moment she met him, was deep and lasting. But she never allowed it to override either her own family commitment or her commitment to being an author in her own right. Moreover, unlike most of those who fell under his influence, she did not seek to become part of his life, or to influence it reciprocally. If it had been otherwise, the long and unbroken friendship that subsisted between them for the rest of Lawrence's career, and the confidence he showed in her, would have been impossible. 'Something makes me state my position when I write to you'—words from a letter in 1916—comes close to defining their relationship. 'We are glad to hear you are going to marry Donald Carswell', he wrote. 'Your life will have a stable pivot then. I only want to know people who have the courage to live.'

At the time she met Lawrence she had for some time been working on a novel which emerged six years later under the title *Open The Door!*, and the earliest of the letters between them concern this work. She sent him her manuscript with a request for comments, and it is a pity it no longer exists because he returned it with copious suggestions for its improvement. The accompanying letter, though in no way crushing, was very much the kind an experienced writer sends to one less experienced in whom he perceives some ability: 'it is all there but it needs more organization'. Soon they were going over the manuscript together.

Lawrence was not one who spared even his friends when in a black mood. Yet one can search through the whole of his correspondence without finding a wounding reference to

Catherine, or any sign that she brought out his cynical, mis-
anthropic side. From 1914 to 1919 they met frequently, and
even after Lawrence set out on his travels their correspondence
continued almost to the time of his death. Altogether there
are more than two hundred letters to her from him, and there
may have been others which have not survived. When he
returned from America to England in 1923 he stayed at the
house she was living in at Hampstead, and on his last brief
trip to England in 1925 he travelled down to Buckingham-
shire, where she was then living. At least one of his books—
Women in Love—he sent to her in manuscript for comment:
a thing he did not often ask of any of his friends.

In other words, he trusted her judgement, both as a
creative writer and as an objective critic. Although he sometimes tried to include her (and even Donald) in his utopian
schemes, his offers were regularly refused, and one suspects
he knew they would be—that despite her admiration for him
she was determined to live her own life. Her friendship was
neither possessive nor servile.

They also shared a veneration for the religious feeling, and
she, with a Presbyterian background which was not altogether
conformist,* must have been one of the few among his friends
who were neither shocked nor embarrassed by Lawrence's
evangelicalism. Above all, she had in her character a kind of
championship which appealed to him because it took no stock
of personal consequences and advantages. Though she was a
highly practical person she was not a calculating one, and this
chimed with one of the most important sides of Lawrence's
temperament. This absence of any storm-cloud between them
over sixteen years is very evident in her book.

Early in 1915 Catherine married Donald Carswell, as she
had told Lawrence she would in the autumn of the previous

* The Macfarlane family were 'Wee Frees', and Mrs. Macfarlane was
also a British Israelite. Mr. Macfarlane was, in politics, a Liberal.

year. They were almost exact contemporaries and had met long ago in Glasgow where Donald's father was a doctor employed by the City Corporation, and one of the earliest public health doctors to specialise in psychiatry. He had married a woman from the Western Isles, a Gaelic speaker, and there was more than a trace of the Celt in Don's make-up.

From Glasgow University he had gone on to the political staff of the *Glasgow Herald* and in 1912 moved to London as a sub-editor on *The Times*. The paper was then in its prime as the greatest newspaper in the world, a solid bank of information from correspondents located almost like ambassadors in every major capital, and of magisterial comment, all arranged in an unvarying, impressive procession of columns in which a single misprint was regarded as an outrage that filled the post-bag for a week.

Don loved and understood *The Times*, and he was well suited to working on a paper of record. His range of information was wide, and his enquiring, well-stored mind systematically took in history, philosophy, political structure, the world of letters and the world of crime. There were few serious books he had not read, and he retained enough Latin and Greek to coach me in both those languages to what would now be thought a quite advanced level. He was the least combative of men; a gentle, learned journalist who wrote slowly and beautifully, preferably with a tankard of beer beside him to help the words to come. But he was also a rebel against the conventional Glasgow in which he had been brought up—perhaps more of a rebel than Catherine. There was in him a streak of irony and a strong scepticism which was wholly foreign to her. He had totally rejected the religion and the idealistic philosophy which had dominated the pulpits and lectures to which he had been exposed as a young man. He had become a Liberal, and with that political faith (personified for him by Mr. Asquith) he was led to political ambitions for which he was temperamentally unqualified.

As a writer, he was lucid, skilful, imaginative, correct, a master of the various moods of style; but he needed facts, and writing from imagination alone was not in him. He could never have written a novel, and did not read many, though he wrote an excellent historical drama, often performed. The only verse he ventured into was cast in the mannered forms of villanelle and ballade. He could be surprisingly waspish on paper, but personal dispute distressed him, and his refuge was in petulance and obstinacy, not retaliation. He enjoyed walking, and could ride (or at least was obliged to learn through service in the Horse Artillery) but otherwise he disliked outdoor pursuits. He rarely played games of any kind.

Catherine teased him and was often to despair of him as a breadwinner, but she had unbounded faith in his literary judgement, and everything serious that she wrote was subjected to his comment. The result was certainly to make her style more economical and more correct. It may also have made it flow less freely. For him his marriage was the triumph of his life, and she found in him someone from whom she never wanted to part—someone who added to her adventurousness not only devotion but system and wisdom, yet demanded the protection of her more decisive character.

Very soon after their wedding, there arrived a test of her championship of Lawrence which was also a test of her marriage. In September 1915 Methuen published *The Rainbow*, on which Lawrence had been working for some time, as Catherine knew, though he does not seem to have shown her the manuscript. As soon as it appeared it was attacked with the most furious drum-beats from the principal critics. Clement Shorter in *The Sphere* declared it contained stronger meat than anything in Zola. James Douglas filled a whole column of *The Star* which ended with the ringing claim that such a book had no right to exist. The police were set in motion. It had also, of course, appeared among Catherine's pile for the *Glasgow Herald*.

This was the situation when Catherine's review appeared at the top of the fiction review column in the *Herald* for 4 November. It was not uncritical, but even so she had taken the precaution of contriving that it should go straight to the composing room and escape editorial scrutiny. She referred to 'what most people will find revolting detail of a passion fruitful in a sense but bitter and terrifying at the core' and then went on:

The modern world, according to Mr. Lawrence, is mad and sick and sad because it knows not how to love. Further, in this book at any rate, he does not go. There is no cure offered, nothing but a merciless, almost gloating description of the disease which will be strongly offensive to most readers. It is a pity too that the impassioned declaration is marred by the increasingly mannered idiom which Mr. Lawrence has acquired since the writing of *Sons and Lovers*. The worst manifestations of this at present are a distressing tendency to the repetition of certain words and a curiously vicious rhythm into which he falls in the more emotional passages.

But the praise was far stronger and more generalised. The book 'showed the hand of a master writer' and 'must rank with the best work done by great novelists in any age'. It was 'so rich in emotional beauty and in the distilled essence of profoundly passionate and individual thinking about human life, that one longs to lavish on it one's whole-hearted praise'. The verdict was that the book's fault lay not in its impropriety or the style of its emotional passages, but in its bitterness and lack of any constructive aim.

The authorities of the *Herald* could not overlook such a review, nor, still worse, the contrivance by which it had been slipped past the eye of Robert Bruce, then still Assistant

Editor, but soon, and for many years, to be editor. Her reviewing was stopped at once, and she made, in Bruce, a lasting foe. A few days later the *Herald* had the mournful satisfaction of giving prominence, under the headline 'A Questionable Book' to the proceedings at Bow Street which ended in a decision that the remaining 1,011 copies of *The Rainbow* should be destroyed. The publishers humbly pleaded guilty and regretted they had not scrutinised the book more carefully—a failure the magistrate said he found it hard to understand in a firm of such high repute as Messrs. Methuen. However they escaped with the loss of the edition and an enforced contribution of £10 towards the costs of the prosecution.

This incident placed a seal on the rapidly developing friendship between my mother and Lawrence. There is a curious gap in the surviving correspondence between January 1915 and late November of that year when the letters resume on a much more familiar note than before. There are probably missing letters, and there were certainly meetings. Between 1915 and 1919, when Lawrence left for Italy, there were not only many meetings, but more than fifty letters from Lawrence.

Dismissal from the *Glasgow Herald* did not seriously interrupt Catherine's journalistic career, which she soon resumed as second string to St. John Ervine covering dramatic criticism for *The Observer*. Despite the War it was one of the happier and busier periods of her life, and I can remember her enthusiastic description of returning in an air raid from a theatre to her home at Hollybush House at the top of Hampstead, writing her notice in the small hours of Friday, and putting it aside for the copy boy who would be there for it at half past six on Saturday morning.

She was also working hard on her novel, still without a title, and most of the letters from Lawrence in the next few

years contain references to it and to *Women in Love*, which
was steaming ahead simultaneously. By now the Lawrences
were in Cornwall, where my parents more than once went to
see them, and Lawrence was the victim of swinging moods of
black depression, temporary elation, fury against the mobilisa-
tion of society brought about by the War, and desperation to
express the paradoxes he felt he was born to expose—perhaps
to resolve.

'I think you are the only woman I have met', he wrote to
her in April 1916, 'who is so intrinsically detached, so
essentially separate and isolated, as to be a real artist and
recorder. . . I believe your book will be a real book, and a
woman's book: one of the very few.' Reading between the
lines of the letters it is possible to see her replying that she
swung between productiveness and exhaustion, and his
encouragement continued. 'I think that is fairly well bound
to be', he wrote in June 1916, 'because I think your process
of life is chiefly exhaustive, not accumulative at all.' He asked
after the novel again—'I think that is very important'—and
described his own progress.

That year was the closest of their friendship, with at least
thirteen letters in each direction, and several meetings. They
argued about Christianity, about attitudes to the War, about
his circle of friends, about the mixture of aggression and
merging implied in sex. By September he was writing 'I feel
really eager about your novel, I feel it is coming under the
same banner as mine. The "us" will be books. There will be
a fine little squadron soon. . . I thought of calling this of mine
Women in Love.' Suggestions soon followed for the title of her
novel (none of which was adopted) and on 21 November
he sent her the manuscript of *Women in Love*—'*please
make any corrections necessary, and tell me any discrepancy.
Don't let anybody else read it*. I want to know what both of
you think of it. *I* think it is a great book.'

Her novel was not finished until nearly a year afterwards, and she sent Lawrence the manuscript in the autumn of 1917. The response was cryptic—'Yes, I think it is very good... but it shakes me badly—with a kind of nerve-wracking pain.' Since it is an autobiographical novel with a happy ending, and Lawrence had read much of it before, the comment is unexpected, but his mind was elsewhere. The letter goes on to describe his plans for escaping from England with a chosen few once the War was over.

He did not yet know that at the age of thirty-eight she was expecting another child. The novel, now christened *Open The Door!*, was submitted to Duckworth in the spring of 1918 and rejected on grounds of length. I was born in May.

Lawrence sent a poem about the baby and commiserated about the novel—'absurd of Duckworth to expect you to cut down the novel so ridiculously'. Frieda sent a cot-cover, and Lawrence described the flowers he had gathered on the Derbyshire hills in a letter which is almost a poem to take the place of the flowers it was impossible Catherine should see. In August Catherine and Donald, carrying me in a sling, joined Lawrence for a walking tour in the Forest of Dean. It was the longest continuous period they ever spent together with him, but throughout the remainder of Lawrence's stay in England, until he left for Italy in November 1919, they remained in close touch.

Very soon after Lawrence's departure *Open The Door!* found a publisher and more. It had been submitted for a prize offered by the firm of Andrew Melrose, and won it. The prize itself was considerable for those days—£250—and no first novel had won it before. 'We'll carry the field yet', Lawrence wrote from Italy when he heard the news, 'You see if we don't.' She offered him part of the prize, which he refused.

Naturally she now set to work on another novel, and in 1922 Chatto and Windus published *The Camomile*. It is cast in the form of letters and is a lighter and subtler work than its predecessor—perhaps because it had shaken off autobiography and escaped Lawrentian advice. He did not see it till proofs were sent to him in Australia, whence his comment was—'good: slighter than *Open The Door!* but better made ...sometimes very amusing, and really wonderfully well written.' The American edition of *Aaron's Rod* which had just appeared was sent in return, and thereafter Secker was under orders to send Catherine a copy of each of Lawrence's books on publication.

A further novel was planned, but never written. It exists only as a sketch which Lawrence prepared during his brief stay in England during the winter of 1923–24 for them to write together. The theme was to be Scottish and Catherine was to write 'the woman and the Scotchy part' and Lawrence was to provide the chief male character: a Scottish chief 'of about forty-five, rather small, dark-eyed, full of energy, but has been a good deal knocked about'.

That winter of 1923–24 was marked by the crisis in Lawrence's life which came to a head at the celebrated dinner party at the Café Royal, vividly described on pages 205–13 of this book. The background to that episode, as is now well known, was the suspicion shared at any rate by Lawrence and Catherine that Frieda (who had preceded Lawrence to England) was having an affair with Middleton Murry, who was also present. We now know that the affair, though real enough, was not consummated, and was resumed only after Lawrence's death. This latter fact goes far to explaining the scorn and bitterness in the references to Murry with which *The Savage Pilgrimage* ends—references which led to its withdrawal.

No two people could have been more different than Catherine and Murry. He was competitive and ambitious. He wrote with extraordinary rapidity and considerable professional skill. Catherine was uncompetitive and a slow composer. Murry's manner was evangelical and evasive, Catherine's austere and blunt. Her friendship for Lawrence, though strong, made no exclusive claims and was in no sense self-interested. She felt Murry's was both, and although she had written for Murry's *Adelphi* she had not found it easy to forgive him for having (as she considered) shown his professions of admiration for Lawrence to be insincere by his review of *Women in Love* in *The Athenaeum*—a notice which, in her words was 'murderous'. She did not like Murry, indeed she came to detest him, but it would be quite wrong to regard their quarrel as a dispute between two claimants to an exclusive interpretation of Lawrence. It was a dispute by her that anyone had such a claim.

After January 1924 Catherine met Lawrence only once more, when he visited England in the autumn of 1925, but their correspondence continued. Life was now difficult for the Carswell family. Donald had decided to read for the Bar while still with *The Times*, and had been called at the Middle Temple in 1916; and instead of returning to the paper after a brief and unhappy period of service in the Royal Horse Artillery, he had launched himself into a legal career which contained more than a tinge of Liberal politics. He obtained few briefs, and even if he had (as he hoped) been adopted as a Liberal candidate the destruction of the Liberal Party at the polls in successive elections would have prevented his ever reaching Westminster (a place for which his bookish talents would in any case have unfitted him). So by 1925 we were living in a small cottage near Great Missenden on the earnings of free-lance journalism.

My parents were not, however, without plans. Taken as a whole, these amounted to a reassessment of the Scottish literary inheritance, encrusted as it still was by a heavy Victorian overlay, and guarded by a powerful establishment of academics and clergy. At the time of Lawrence's visit in 1925 Donald was at work on a collection of essays about nineteenth-century Scotsmen which was published as *Brother Scots* in 1927. The essays are written with great economy and wit, and are unsparing not so much of their subjects (many of whom are treated with sympathy, unlike Strachey's) but of the society in which they lived. In a preliminary essay he exposed, in a few pages, the profound historical differences in the development of Scotland and England which made Scotland so much less comfortable a country.

At about the same time Catherine had formed the plan of writing a full-scale biography of Scotland's national poet, Robert Burns. This book, which is the most important she ever wrote, is significantly dedicated to both Donald and Lawrence.

No serious life of Burns had been attempted for many years, and his life and work alike were buried in a deposit of institutionalised sentiment presided over by those who controlled the Burns Federation. His career cried out for a refreshing biography; but it was a reckless, rebellious undertaking, and for a woman most imprudent. In 1927 the plan was revealed to Lawrence, who strongly approved. Burns appealed to him, and he warned that 'if Cath is condescending to Burns I disown her'.

By then he was engaged on his most celebrated, but not his most successful work. 'I want a little help' he wrote to Catherine in January 1928. 'I wrote a novel last winter... and its very *verbally* improper... will you find me some decent person who'll type it for me at the usual rates?' So in the middle of research on Scotland's bard she became involved in finding broadminded amateur typists among her friends. 'What title' asked the covering letter with the first batch of manuscript—'*Lady Chatterley's Lover*, *My Lady's Keeper*, *Tenderness*, which do you prefer?'

Lawrence never kept letters, so we do not know which choice she made. But he grew impatient over the return of the script and for the only time in their acquaintance began to show signs of moving into a mood of fury, in which the novel was his weapon against his persecutors. The persecutors were far from imaginary, as was shown by the fate of his pictures, raided in the Warren Gallery in 1929. Don's legal advice was on that occasion called upon for the last time, and Catherine's last letter from Lawrence is dated 12 August 1929. He died seven months later in an atmosphere clouded by publicity over the Warren Gallery raid and rumours about *Lady Chatterley*.

'I am glad,' that last letter had said, 'you are getting along with the Burns. What a thrill when the book is finally done.' It was virtually finished by the time she received this letter, and appeared in 1930 with the dedication 'Without D. H. Lawrence, my friend, and Donald Carswell, my husband, this book could not have been. I therefore inscribe it to them both.'

The Life of Robert Burns stands today, half a century after it was written, as a major work and a decisive return to the record of the man as he lived and wrote. It established Catherine as an author. Far from being a Stracheyan essay in debunking, it is sympathetic, even enthusiastic about its central figure. It drew out a new side of Burns as a poet whose peculiar gift it was to conceive poems in a musical setting that was present in his mind as he wrote, so that they were already Lieder without the aid of Schubert or Wolf. His adventures in love, which the Burnsians of the time had reduced to a kind of phlizz,* were described without either prurience or censure. She had to steer, as she said in her preface, between

---

* 'It's called a Phlizz.' 'And how do you make a Phlizz, Bruno?' 'The Professor taught me how', said Bruno. 'First oo takes a lot of air—' (Lewis Carroll, *Sylvie and Bruno*, vol. 1, p. 285).

'the established Burnsians, who guard their idol with a jealousy not unmixed with fears, and the . . . ordinary reader, whose indifference is too often tinged with a distaste for which I fear that we Burns worshippers must bear some of the blame . . . My sustaining faith has been faith in my subject, which has increasingly appeared to me as far above calling for the condescensions of excuse or suppressions of partial representation, however well meant.' This was a glance at certain sources which had been denied to her. 'In matters of deduction,' she continued, 'without which no living narrative can be constructed, I have relied upon my own conception of Burns formed by years of unremitted study and upon what knowledge I have of life through my own experience.'

This frank and sympathetic book about Scotland's national poet caused an uproar. Its author was denounced and praised. She received numerous anonymous letters—one of which contained a bullet—was denounced in the *Glasgow Herald*, praised by Arthur Bryant, congratulated by John Buchan, and preached against in Glasgow Cathedral by the Rev. Lauchlan Maclean Watt.

In the same year Donald Carswell produced *Sir Walter, A Four-Part Biography* on which he had been working for several years—a vivid, but to some unacceptable, set of portraits of Scott and his circle. Buchan, who saw the book's strengths and weaknesses, was to draw heavily on it for his own more massive biography a few years later. The total effect was to make the Carswells, in the eyes of many Scots, despoilers of all that Scotland held most dear.

Donald was no doubt startled by the consequences of his intellectual rebellion, but Catherine was a fighter, though she was very far from being a skilled controversialist. The current of her life steered her towards battles, though she did not seek them, and I have no doubt that the death of Lawrence a few

months before the Burns was published confirmed her in the
idea that direct attack in the cause she believed to be right
was a matter of conscience. Deviousness was not in her.
Lawrence's outlook had blended with her own austere and
simple Glasgow upbringing to produce a woman who was
quite fearless and capable of almost infinite endurance. At
that critical time she truly believed one should take no
thought for the morrow, for the morrow shall take thought
for the things of itself.

The Life of Robert Burns was in the press when Lawrence
died early in March 1930. The obituaries were almost
uniformly unsympathetic, and dwelt on recent controversies.
His death was treated as the disappearance of a figure news-
worthy for the scandals he caused, not as that of a significant
literary man.* On 16 March she protested against them in a
letter printed on that date in *Time and Tide*, which contains
the essence of the book that was to follow two years later:

Sir,

The picture of D. H. Lawrence suggested by the obituary notices of
'competent critics' is of a man morose, frustrated, tortured, even a
sinister failure. Perhaps this is because any other view of him would
make his critics looks rather silly. Anyhow to those who knew him
(and I knew him since 1914 as friend, hostess, and guest in varying
circumstances, often of the most trying kind, at home and abroad)
that picture would be comic if it were not in the circumstances
disgraceful.

Lawrence was as little morose as an open clematis flower, as little
tortured or sinister, or hysterical as a humming-bird. Gay, skilful,
clever at everything, furious when he felt like it but never grieved
or upset, intensely amusing, without sentimentality or affectation,
almost always right in his touch for the *content* of things or persons, he
was at once the most harmonious and the most vital person I ever saw.

---

* An exception was Murry's notice (necessarily in those days anonymous) in *The Times Literary Supplement*. Later, however, he changed his
views.

As to frustration, consider his achievement. In the face of formidable initial disadvantages and life-long delicacy, poverty that lasted for three quarters of his life and hostility that survives his death, he did nothing that he did not really want to do, and all that he most wanted to do he did. He went all over the world, he owned a ranch, he lived in the most beautiful corners of Europe, and met whom he wanted to meet and told them that they were wrong and he was right. He painted and made things, and sang, and rode. He wrote something like three dozen books, of which even the worst page dances with life that could be mistaken for no other man's, while the best are admitted, even by those who hate him, to be unsurpassed. Without vices, with most human virtues, the husband of one wife, scrupulously honest, this estimable citizen yet managed to keep free from the shackles of civilization and the cant of literary cliques. He would have laughed lightly and cursed venomously in passing at the solemn owls—each one secretly chained by the leg—who now conduct his inquest. To do his work and lead his life in spite of them took some doing, but he did it, and long after they are forgotten, sensitive and innocent people—if any are left—will turn Lawrence's pages and will know from them what sort of a rare man Lawrence was.

I am &c

Catherine Carswell

That letter claims no particular relationship and aims at no particular critic. But in June 1930 *The Adelphi* began to publish Murry's *Reminiscences of D. H. Lawrence* which lasted for several numbers and already contained elements of the 'destructive hagiography' that was to follow under the title of *Son of Woman* in the spring of 1931. 'The one object of my book', Murry wrote later,* 'was that it takes a great man to be wrong as Lawrence was wrong.'

Catherine's copy of Murry's *Reminiscences* is copiously annotated on matters of fact and opinion, and the idea of writing about Lawrence at greater length was already in her

---

* *The Adelphi*, December 1931, p. 238.

mind; but until *Son of Woman* it was probably limited to the
series of articles in reply to Murry which *The Adelphi* (by
now under the editorship of Richard Rees) began to print in
the autumn of 1931. It was *Son of Woman*, with its implication that Murry declared himself not only Lawrence's
literary heir but as one charged with the mission of repre-
senting him as a kind of fallen angel, a ruined genius, a man
tortured by internal conflicts which it was Murry's duty to
anatomise, that precipitated *The Savage Pilgrimage*.

The book was written in a white heat of enthusiasm and
indignation during the autumn and winter of 1931. In
writing it she had access not only to her own letters from
Lawrence and her personal recollections but to a considerable
range of Lawrence's correspondence. She was in close touch
with Aldous Huxley (who was already engaged on collecting
Lawrence's letters for the edition of 1932), with Koteliansky
(who had quarrelled irreparably with Murry many years
earlier) and with Lawrence's agent, Pinker, for which last
reason *The Savage Pilgrimage* is very informative about
Lawrence's literary finances.

The book was published by Chatto and Windus, who had
also published the Burns, in June 1932, and a writ for libel
was at once served by Murry in respect of the slurs cast on
him in the last ten pages, which throw bitter scorn on his
motives in seeking a deathbed reconciliation with Lawrence
after several years of estrangement. The book was withdrawn from circulation (though not before a good many
copies had been sold) amid headlines and outcries. A copy, of
course, had been sent to Frieda, who responded with this
(undated) letter:

Dear Catherine,

I have just swallowed your book! It's awfully 'well done', but of
that I am no competent judge—It really thrills me and *explains* my
own life to me, which is so *odd*, and then it's all so impersonal as if

I were reading about 'Elizabeth and Essex'. It's all just a wonder this whole show called 'life'—And somehow I am *grateful* to you for L's sake and my own and 'our' sake. You make me rather too 'splendiferous' a female, oneself is so much more aware of one's quivering, unsure, miserable feelings than of anything else! You have done *much* for him and wouldn't *he* be glad! Your own generosity is so obvious too in that book! It will also amuse you, that I always thought *you* so awfully elegant *and* original and felt a perfect *lump* beside you—I always feel *hideous* in a town anyhow!—

I am sure your book will get a connexion with the public, so necessary for later on.—

My Lawrence is again another one—the demon, the dynamic new thing on the face of the earth—the demon that it was my fate and my responsibility to struggle with—and so we all had our part in his destiny. *Your* Lawrence interests me so much, so does *your* Frieda. But of course the mystery of 2 people is always a mystery, even to themselves—and I *know* we don't bear each other a grudge, he and I! And don't forget that he thought women were more powerful than men, which is strange!

And now Ada wrote to me, 'the homage paid to D.H.L.'s widow goes to your head like wine' and 'a little humility is a good thing'— As if anything could go to my head after L's love for me!! About that I am conceited. . .

And so one thinks and speculates and that small, intense space of life is over and yet I feel he loves me still and forever and whatever I do—Your book *did* move me.

Yrs F.

There was no question of publication being abandoned. A second publisher was found who offered to bring it out with a preface by Murry which he was willing to volunteer, but this suggestion was not unnaturally refused. Eventually a third publisher, Secker, issued it early in 1933 with the last ten pages toned down and a few other changes. The present text follows the original edition.

The controversy between Catherine and Murry did not by any means end there, either in public or in private corres-

pondence which clearly displays the issue between them, and
Murry's subtle, almost theological approach to it.

These people [he wrote to Catherine on 26 September 1932] feel
the dissatisfaction with *Son of Woman* which (I think) you really feel.
And the point, as between you and me, is that your *expression* of that
dissatisfaction in S.P. was false. The feeling was true: but you
indulged in the easy way against me as a person.

In reply she sent him an article she had recently written
about Lawrence, and on 21 December he answered that it
was 'much better than anything in SP . . .'

Of course I still don't think you face up to the contradiction in
Lawrence. . . it is the conflict between the individual and the social
man. I don't *blame* L for not resolving that conflict. But how you
could have believed that any living man could have *followed* L is
beyond my comprehension. Moreover L himself would have been
the first to resist such 'following'.

. . . Lawrence was himself, and that's enough you may say. And of
course from one point of view it is enough—more than we deserve.
But. . . (1) L did not believe himself that it was enough and (2) this
attitude involves some obligation of coming to some final conclusion
on what he himself really was. The two go together. And I stick to
my point: that you shirk them. There's no reason why you should
not. But at the same time you shouldnt condemn me for not shirking
them, even if my conclusion was quite wrong. I attempted to do
something which has to be done—and something which your
Huxleys and your Nicolsons will never do. This Huxley–Lawrence
idyll of the last years is terribly false, as you represent it. L's isolation
in those last years was a magnificent and splendid thing. . . It is this
falsity of *tone* which I resent.

It was the implied claim to moral superiority—almost im-
munity—that she found hardest to bear, but she replied once
more in defence of the book: his answer, which ended the
correspondence, is dated January 19 1933.

I don't at all resent your making me the Judas, *provided* that you
admit the nature of the drama. That you won't do. You want me to

be Judas, and L to be one to whom Judas didn't matter. And that is what makes your book inwardly so false. Not that it matters...

I don't see that there is much good in our debating with one another. We look at things too differently: our 'values' are too heterogeneous. Thus you produce as your trump card the fact that Virginia Woolf said yours was the only book which had enabled her to understand Lawrence. That to *me* is a concise and perfect statement of my case *against* your book: that it did precisely that—enable the V.W.'s of this life to believe that they understood Lawrence.

And that again, to you, will seem a kind of nonsense. So we should never, never get anywhere.

I see, and freely admit, that you are perfectly sincere in your belief in my 'human betrayal' of Lawrence. And it doesn't matter to me. Wherever I may be, I am somewhere where such accusations are meaningless. And when you say: 'why single him out and compare him with yourself as *the* divided man of his generation?' it just shows how utterly at cross purposes we are talking. As though there were a greater thing to be than *the* divided man of an epoch! As though I do compare him with myself!

But there you are. It's no good. So long as we agree to treat each other honourably, I am quite content.

Yours sincerely

J. Middleton Murry

Later, in 1933, he published his *Reminiscences of D. H. Lawrence* in book form along with a detailed reply to *The Savage Pilgrimage* in which he printed most of the passages from it which he had insisted should be withdrawn.

Half a century later *The Savage Pilgrimage* appears as what it was intended to be: a biography in straightforward narrative form written by a close personal friend very soon after its subject's death. As such it has an evidential value and gives a personal portrait which can never be obliterated. It is neither critical nor analytic, and avoids any systematic interpretation of his life and work. Murry's perception that there

INTRODUCTION   xxix

were inconsistencies and depths in Lawrence with which *The Savage Pilgrimage* does not deal was correct; but not his claim that the book was false in tone. That claim was founded on a special position he asserted for himself.

The controversy surrounding the publication of *The Savage Pilgrimage* arose because the book disputed that special position. But the book is not about Murry—still less is it designed to assert another special claim. The picture so often drawn of Lawrence's friends squabbling over his inheritance is in this instance wide of the mark.

Factually the book has stood the test of time and the availability of a great deal of evidence that was not at the disposal of its author. In only one respect has it been subject to a correction of that kind. Some years ago Dame Rebecca West pointed out that the passage on pages 25–26 relating to Mrs. Belloc Lowndes's meeting with Lawrence is unjust to Mrs. Lowndes. She did not have influence in a literary fund which might help Lawrence, and did not consider she ever suggested she had.

The Life of Robert Burns and *The Savage Pilgrimage*, which were published on both sides of the Atlantic (and in the case of the Burns came out also in a shortened form) gave Catherine a place in the literary world which her novels had not secured for her, and she now had many friends—Vita Sackville-West and Harold Nicolson; Naomi Mitchison; Storm Jameson; Rose Macaulay; Gerhardi—many of whom had been drawn to her side during the controversy with Murry. Vita Sackville-West in particular gave support and advice at the height of the crisis, and their correspondence lasted for ten years or more. With Scottish authors such as Edwin Muir and his wife Willa (who lived near at hand), James Bridie and the extraordinary Hugh Macdiarmid she and her husband were on even closer terms.

But although she had many friends, and Vita and Margaret

Storm Jameson became very close to her, Catherine formed
in particular two friendships with men in the early thirties
which had a decisive influence on her work and on the rest of
her life. At a first glance one would say no two men could
have been more different in their interests or in the worlds in
which they moved; but they had affinities of character and
early struggle which illustrate what Catherine sought in
people, and what she found in Lawrence.

Daniel George Bunting, later more celebrated as Daniel
George, came into her life soon after the publication of *The
Savage Pilgrimage*, and was then only at the very beginning
of his literary career, though he must have been about forty.
The son of an ordinary merchant seaman from Portsmouth,
he had left school at thirteen and very soon afterwards had
served in the ranks of an infantry regiment in France throughout the First World War without, amazingly, suffering any
physical harm. At the time my mother met him he had risen
to be manager of Messrs. Ewart's Geysers in the Euston
Road. Thence he returned in the evening to Mill Hill and
a house that was crammed with books. He had entered the
literary world by becoming a friend of the veteran bookman
Holbrook Jackson, who happened to live nearby.

Very few men of our time can have had so wide, and at the
same time so exact a knowledge of English literature from the
sixteenth century onwards as Daniel. Misquotation and false
ascription could not escape him, and he was familiar with the
by-ways as well as the highways; yet there was nothing about
him that suggested the pedant or even the scholar. He was
spruce, neat, genial, fond of company and wine. There was
something of a rustic burr about his speech and it was spiced
with epigrams. There was another side to him. He was
beginning to express himself in poems which have a kind of
trenchant bitterness that perhaps has more in it of Roy
Campbell than any other contemporary. Sometimes he

suffered from migraine, and when he was resolved to work he fled from company.

In 1932 a hand was held out to Catherine from a very different quarter of the literary and social world. John Buchan, then M.P. for the Scottish Universities, had been impressed by Donald's work on Scott, and (although he must have choked rather over Lawrence) by Catherine's *Burns*— 'a really great book, which will be a classic long after the common Burnsite has ceased to exist', he wrote to her when it was published. Initially he must have represented, for her, the Scottish system against which she had crusaded; but on the single occasion when they lunched together, which she has described in a vivid essay,* she was utterly converted.

These two men had a lasting effect on the latter part of Catherine's life and work. With Daniel George she collaborated in more than one literary enterprise, notably two of the many anthologies he compiled, *A National Gallery* and *The English in Love*. She venerated him, and indeed gave him her heart. Her joy when he made the transition from manager of Ewart's Geysers to literary adviser to Jonathan Cape was unbounded. Perhaps she was a little saddened when he soared like a rocket into the world of literary cocktail parties and weekly journalism.

Buchan's world was not hers in many ways. Parliament, the General Assembly of the Church of Scotland, the business of influence, were outside the scope of her nature. Yet she saw the adventurer in his nature—not only the adventurer who had written the Hannay novels, but the one who climbed and disciplined himself to cram so much into his life. He too admired her gallantry, as his letters bear witness, and it was not chance that caused his widow, after his death, to choose Catherine to work on his papers and help

---

* 'John Buchan, A Perspective', included in *John Buchan by his Wife and Friends* (Hodder and Stoughton 1947), p. 148.

in the production of the two memorial volumes, *The Clearing House* and *John Buchan by his Wife and Friends*.

After 1932 and the battle with Murry, Catherine wrote little about Lawrence, whose career and reputation, as so often happens, passed into comparative eclipse for a decade during which his flame was kept alive, rather dryly, by the stern Leavis almost alone. 'Oh why is Lawrence dead?' she wrote to a friend in November 1930; and during the Second World War, in her fragmentary autobiography *Lying Awake*, she reflected that 'if Lawrence had lived to be sixty, he would have been admirably dry and moderate. But he would have repudiated nothing except the small mistakes of the past.' That he would take a place among the great figures of English literature she never doubted.

She turned to other work. With Donald she produced an excellent short study of the Abbey Theatre, *The Fays of The Abbey Theatre*, and a Scottish anthology *The Scots Weekend*. And in the midst of this and a considerable amount of journalism she produced a further major biography, *The Tranquil Heart*: the title suggests, perhaps, a contrast to *The Savage Pilgrimage*.

It was a life of Boccaccio—at first sight a strange choice, for a great deal of fresh reading was required, and the period was far from any she knew well. It was consciously put forward as a woman's book about a subject hitherto written about only by men. 'No writer before him', she says in her preface, 'dreamed of writing avowedly for women readers... Again and again Boccaccio repeated that he wrote for women's instruction and delight, yet none but men have written about him.' In that, and indeed all her work, she was very consciously a feminine writer who considered that as a woman she had a vision denied to men. At the same time she felt a disparity which excluded rivalry. 'The woman', she reflected towards the end of her life, 'because she is a woman must as an artist suppress what the man as artist or as man is entitled to reveal.'

As the pre-war decade ended with her sixtieth birthday one small gleam made its appearance in our family circumstances, and was then quickly quenched. Donald got a regular post in the Home Office to deal with the flood of naturalisation applications caused by Hitlerite persecution. Then came the War—the second in her adult life-time—and very soon after its outbreak Donald was killed in a street accident as he left the office in the evening.

She was now very much alone, and in some ways, I think, shrank from such literary company as existed in the black-out of the war years: not that she was unsociable. In a tiny flat in Camden Town which she held on condition of stoking the boiler, she would give dinner to particular friends, many of them younger than she was. She had a gift for making the most unpromising interiors attractive with very modest possessions picked up in Gospel Oak or Kentish Town for a few shillings. She rarely kept them for long. Others took their places. She was not, as Lawrence pointed out, an accumulator.

She also wrote a great deal, and her autobiography, later published as *Lying Awake*, was half finished at the time of her death: only the parts about her childhood and her last years had been finally formed, and it is questionable whether she would ever have attempted the part which lay between. She kept very few papers, and much must have gone into the fire in her repeated moves. One more major biography was planned, and there are copious notes for it among such papers as she left behind.

It was to be a life of Calvin, a man whose thought had dominated the years of her childhood, and against whom she had reacted so strongly. In her sixties she became increasingly tolerant, and so distrustful of ready-made solutions, including those she had adopted so eagerly in her youth. Her advice was much sought for its wisdom—all the more so because, as one of her close friends said after her death, she was wise having at some times in her life been unwise.

Writing was the centre of her life, and she could not exist without it, yet she was rarely satisfied:

A second-rate effort [she wrote] may make a strong appeal; especially at first it may carry one away. But it does not carry with it and illumine the separate world. What I am trying to express has nothing to do with interpretation, still less with illustration. There is no deliberate connexion. The reaction comes about. That is all.

A few months after the end of the War she died, shortly before her sixty-seventh birthday.

Her books have endured. Both the Burns and the Lawrence were republished in the nineteen-fifties, though the Lawrence was perforce still in the form acceptable to Murry. They have had the flattery of frequent piracy in the public domain of the United States. *The Savage Pilgrimage* has the passion and partiality of polemic, but the few passages in which the heat is here restored are not the most important parts of the book. Its significance lies in providing a picture of an extraordinary man and his career based on long personal friendship and direct observation. It might never have been written at all but for the challenge Murry threw down, but its value transcends that occasion of its writing.

That there was something quixotic in her cannot be denied, and an account of her in the context of *The Savage Pilgrimage* is bound to notice it. But it was far from being the most important side of her nature, and it was not, from his letters to her, what Lawrence valued her friendship for. He, and many others, saw in her a prudent, practical figure, someone to be turned to in moments of difficulty or debt, neither a bohemian nor a careerist: someone to whom one felt somehow one should 'state one's position.' Her advice to the aspiring and idealistic was often of the grittiest kind, evoking the examples of those who had devoted themselves to effort and triumphed over difficulty and opposition. '*There are only two ways of succeeding with writing*' she once wrote to an aspiring author: 'The first and best is because you want to write, drawing from your own heart and brain, and trusting to your own talent being discovered and sought after in time. The other way—if you are compelled to make money at once by your pen—is to study *the styles* of different magazines. Find out what they want for their public and how they like it done. Then do it as they like it, and let them have it. Many honest enough incomes are made in this way.' She believed in effort, but in her heart did not value success. This deep trait in her, combined with a powerful critical instinct, put her in a position to write this direct and lasting life of D. H. Lawrence.

Berins Hill. 3 January 1981

PREFACE

BARRING some youthful poems, D. H. Lawrence had just
twenty years of writing life. Throughout these years—
which included and were in a special way harried by the
incidence of the War—he was severely encumbered by
circumstances. He had to reckon with poverty, with illness,
with the misapprehension of friends and the malice of
strangers. None the less we find that, besides wresting from
the most unpromising elements a life that was rich and
adventurous, he was a prolific writer. Indeed, if we allow
for the various nature of his output and take for comparison
the twenty most productive years of any other accepted
author, he would appear to have been the most prolific
writer our country has had since Sir Walter Scott. In
addition to a dozen full-length novels he wrote short stories,
essays, translations, pamphlets, books of travel and of philosophy, plays and many poems. Over the same period his
correspondence, whether measured by interest or by bulk,
bids fair to rival the correspondence of our most communica-
tive English men of letters. Readers will be able to judge
of this for themselves to a reasonable extent in the coming
autumn, when Messrs. Heinemann will publish a selection
of the letters, edited by Mr. Aldous Huxley and running
to some eight hundred pages. As time goes on—though
of necessity not for some years—we shall see in print the
remaining letters that have survived, and which, by all
accounts, will engage several more stout volumes. It is
worth noting that from the very beginning most of
Lawrence's correspondents have had the instinct to preserve

what he wrote to them, and it may be safely predicted that his letters will have to be included with his more formal works in a particular sense that is faintly paralleled only in the case of Keats. They will be found to contain a free expression of his findings about life in the very accents he was accustomed to use in speech—accents that are fresh and inimitable. With their richness of human admission they will do away with the charge of morbidity as with the contention that there was a sad or bad discrepancy between the man and the writer. Further works—poems, essays and stories—still await print. For Lawrence as a writer it will then be seen that all things have worked together for good. The very difficulties of publication during his lifetime will justify, now that he is dead, his early and confident adoption of the phoenix as his emblem. Meanwhile he is like Joey in the Punch and Judy show. He will not ' stay put,' but bobs up serenely and repeatedly from the grave to mock those who would reduce him to a formula. His unholy ghost will not be pigeon-holed.

It is one of the marks of those who dislike him that they evince a lust for simple and final pronouncements—a lust as notable as their disparagement of anything in the nature of high praise. Not long ago a young critic who endeavoured, without a single reference to *The Way of All Flesh*, to sum up the Facts of English Fiction, was commended by his middle-aged confrères for disposing of Lawrence as a man of 'abnormal psychology' who 'was never greater than any situation in which he found himself' and whose books were 'essentially the expression of the rat in the trap' (as if Shakespeare were greater than the situations outlined in the Sonnets, or civilisation not impounded in a most formidable trap!). And earlier the same critics greeted with every sign of relief the emotional and able but self-justifying and impromptu effort made by Mr. Middleton Murry in his *Son of Woman* to 'prove to the world that it takes a great man to be wrong as Lawrence was wrong.' 'That's that,' said they, knowing better than Mr. Murry seems to know that the great thing about a great man is always that he is right. Did they not admit from the first that Lawrence was 'a man of genius'? Their real point was that Lawrence was a man that was wrong. Now that they have the assurance from one who ought to know, they need bother no more about Lawrence or themselves.

Such, glancing at this preface, will regret that I should permit myself to be 'on the defensive' even for a moment. It is a familiar complaint, reminding one of that other complaint that Lawrence was 'no thinker,' which is made without any definition of what thinking is taken to be. I agree that the defensive tone, with regard to one who was himself the least self-defensive of men, is regrettable. But the situation has been of a kind which renders it unnatural to avoid it altogether. Lawrence will presently stand in no need of defenders. But if present love hath present laughter, so too has it present wrath; and though wrath's a stuff will not endure, we have the Scriptural authority that we may at times 'do well to be angry.'

For final pronouncements the critics must abide the verdict of the future reader. Lawrence as a whole remains to be read and to be re-read. He has to create the taste for his work, and this takes time. But it is a taste that grows. Not only so: it is a taste that delicately transforms the palate and renews it for the re-trial of other tastes, ancient and modern. His books are easy to read but hard to understand. Therein lies part of their potency. 'A book,' said Lawrence, who had pondered deeply upon such matters, 'lives as long as it is unfathomed.' Or again, 'The mind understands; and there's an end of it.' Therein also lies their vital difference from the books of such writers as Joyce or Proust,

xl   THE SAVAGE PILGRIMAGE

which are hard at first to read, but comparatively easy to understand once the initial difficulty is overcome. These have evolved a new technique, but they belong themselves to an outworn way of life. What they do—and it is much— is to interpret and express the old in a fresh language. Lawrence, on the contrary, except that the drum-tap and emphasis of his style are as original to himself as they are at first irritating to many readers, has elected to speak in a familiar language. But his story-shapes, his incidents, his objects and his characters are chosen primarily as symbols in his endeavour to proffer a new way of life. That there can indeed be a new way of life—though possibly only by a recovery of values so remote in our past that they are fecund from long forgetting, and as far out of mind as they are near to our blind fingers—is the single admission he seeks from his readers, as it was the belief that governed his actions. Most, however, even of those who have vocally admired him, will make any admission except just this. It includes, they know, the admission that his prescience was unique in his generation. Here is much for one man to ask of his fellows. So they prefer to continue with simplifications that are away from the point, with 'patterns' and with set phrases, which serve at the best to show how evocative Lawrence is. If Lawrence invariably committed himself, his critics invariably give themselves away. Of all moralists he is the most demoralising.

I believe that there not only may, but must be, a new way of life, and that Lawrence was on the track of it. In his own words he wanted 'to put something through' by means of 'a long slow, dark, almost invisible fight,' with a victory that would come 'little by little' and that could be interrupted only by death. It was so interrupted, sadly, but not as will appear, fatally. Because of its undertaking, readers who find in themselves some answering spark and are content to wait without prejudice for fuller comprehension, will find nothing concerning Lawrence to be irrelevant. His immediate appeal is that of potent innocence which has met with a grave miscarriage of judgment. Here is a man who lived from a pure source and stedfastly refused to break faith with that source. And so we have another fountain for the heart, another proof that pure and living sources still exist and always will exist.

While my own memories are fresh, I have set myself to put down what I can recall about Lawrence. And interspersed with my own recollections are things credibly told me by other people who knew him, besides things I know about from letters. Without attempting to write anything like a biography I shall try to give a narrative—in his own words where possible—of this non-Christian saint, this hero who repudiated heroism. I shall show him as I see him—a man upon a dangerous but fascinating pilgrimage, who set forth from his City of Destruction in the English industrial Midlands, passed through the London and cosmopolitan Vanity Fair and traversed the physical and intellectual world, carrying a load of bitterness in his bowels and a talisman of purity in his hand, until such time as he died quietly and bravely with his work unfinished but with victory nearly enough in sight to place him as far beyond failure as he was beyond his fellows, because of the greater risks he ran. If I have not always been as simple as I should wish, at least I have tried to refrain from approaching the least solemn of men with graveyard graces.

In the assembling of material I gratefully acknowledge help given by several friends of Lawrence whose names appear in the text. Naturally I have not had access to the mass of Lawrence's letters. But with some two hundred of my own, and a fair number which have been shown to me by their possessors or have come upon the market, together with those that have already been published by Mr. Murry, Mrs. Clarke and Mrs. Sterne, I have been enabled to give a fairly detailed account of Lawrence's movements. This has been greatly aided by a scheme of dates and addresses kindly provided by Mr. and Mrs. Laurence Hilton from the collection of the letters with which they were entrusted for the formidable and confidential task of transcription.

I am deeply indebted to Messrs. Heinemann, by whose courtesy, and with the approval of Mrs. Lawrence, I have been permitted to quote from Lawrence's letters to me. I have further the generous consent of Mr. Martin Secker to quote a poem by Lawrence in full, as well as a synopsis written by Lawrence of a novel in which he wished to collaborate with me. From Messrs. Eric and Ralph Pinker I have had the substantial benefit of access to the letters from Lawrence to their father, the late J. B. Pinker. The frequent references to *Reminiscences* indicate the series of articles by Mr. Middleton Murry that appeared in *The Adelphi* in 1931.

To make clear the course of Lawrence's literary development I have prefaced each part of this book with a list of the works belonging to each period—not in order of publication (which in the case of Lawrence is most misleading) but in the approximate order of composition. I say approximate order of composition, because owing to Lawrence's habit of repeatedly recasting and re-writing, it is impossible to date any work with absolute precision.

Mistakes are inevitable, and I have noted several while this book has been going through the press. I think, for example, that on page 22, in regard to the first meeting of Mr. Koteliansky with the Murrys, I have telescoped events in time, though in substance the account is correct. In the middle paragraph of page 173 I have inadvertently described Lawrence's log-cabin at the ranch as 'two-storied', which was

true of his house at Taos.   I should further explain that the
Campbells mentioned on page 21 were the Hon. Gordon
Campbell and his wife (now Lord and Lady Glenavy),
who showed Lawrence much kindness in his early difficult
days.

HAMPSTEAD, *May* 1932.

CONTENTS

PART ONE

Aet. 21–29

Prose

The White Peacock
The Trespasser
Sons and Lovers
The Prussian Officer, etc. (short
    stories)
The Widowing of Mrs. Hol-
    royd (play in 3 acts)
Love among the Haystacks
The Rainbow

Verse

Love Poems and Others
Amores
Look! We have Come Through!
    (*in part*)

★

'There is nothing to do with life but to let it run, and
it's a very bitter thing, but it's also wonderful, for we
never know what'll happen next.'

PART ONE

I

In the spring of 1914 Henry James contributed to *The Times Literary Supplement* two long and characteristically sibylline articles on 'The Younger Generation.'[1] At that date it was still possible to include in the category of 'younger' Mr. Joseph Conrad, Mr. Maurice Hewlett, Mr. Galsworthy, Mr. H. G. Wells and Mr. Arnold Bennett, though, as the veteran admitted, these had 'not quite, perhaps, the early bloom of Mr. Hugh Walpole, Mr. Gilbert Cannan and Mr. D. H. Lawrence.'

Proceeding, by way of mixed metaphor, we learn that Mr. Wells and Mr. Bennett have 'practically launched the boat in which we admire the fresh play of oar of the author of *The Duchess of Wrexe* and the documented aspect exhibited successively by *Carnival* and *Sinister Street* and even by *Sons and Lovers* however much we may find Mr. Lawrence, we confess, hang in the dusty rear.'

That last phrase sounds ungracious, but was perhaps not so ungraciously meant. It was hardly in character for Henry James to back anybody as a winner, even while he might set himself to describe the field in its order as viewed through the prism of his Jamesian binoculars. Still less was it in character for him to back the dark horse of the field. But we may give him this credit at least. He perceived that there was a dark horse. The figure he employs would further lead us to conclude that by his admission he found it difficult to report on the contours of that entrant.

There were however some onlookers, younger, less cautious and not at all burdened with responsibility, who felt

[1] *T.L.S.*, March 19th and April 2nd, 1914.

that in this case there was a duty of more definite prophecy upon anyone professing to be a judge of form. In 1911 these had read *The White Peacock*,[1] in 1912 *The Trespasser*, and in 1913 *Love Poems and Others* and *Sons and Lovers*—especially *Sons and Lovers*. They had also read 'Goose Fair' and 'Odour of Chrysanthemums' in *The English Review*, and the poems under the same signature appearing from time to time there and in the *Saturday Westminster Gazette*. After *Sons and Lovers* it appeared to them—as indeed it had already appeared to several persons more powerfully placed —that no other writer was producing work of a like importance. Of a small group of these I was a comparatively passive member. One who was more impetuous, however, —Ivy Low (now the wife of Commissar Litvinoff)—was moved to repudiate the Jamesian pronouncement in the person of 'The Younger Generation.' She wrote to Lawrence through his publisher, and Lawrence answered. Lawrence always answered. His first letter, short but friendly, was triumphantly read aloud to me. I remember nothing about it now except that it was written from Fiascherino, near Lerici, upon coroneted notepaper, that the coronet had been crossed through with a pen stroke, and that beside it Lawrence had written the words 'My wife's father was a baron.' Even this I might not now remember were it not that precisely the same thing was repeated on the second letter—which made us smile. We wondered how large the store of notepaper might be and if Lawrence felt bound to repeat the formula every time he wrote a letter. This we were unable to test, however, as I don't think there was any third letter, but merely post cards, which confirmed the invitation extended to our representative in the second letter and gave travelling directions. Ivy

---

[1] I had reviewed it for the *Glasgow Herald*, and had been deeply impressed.

Low accepted the invitation at once. She spent what money remained from her own initial literary efforts (this being all she had) on a return ticket to Fiascherino, was rigged out for the journey in my only 'tailor made' ('so as to make a neat impression if possible') and seen off by me with best wishes. She returned after about a month, very full of her visit, which we gathered had been of memorable but mixed quality. Not long afterwards Lawrence and Frieda arrived in London and almost at once called on me in Hampstead. Ivy was there, and Viola Meynell, who was a friend of Ivy's and a warm admirer of *Sons and Lovers*, came to meet him.

By then I knew in outline what Lawrence's history had been. A miner's son, born on September 11th, 1885, in the village of Eastwood in Nottinghamshire, he had described his early life clearly enough in his three novels. And in the poems there had been the deeper, briefer expression of his youthful experience. More precisely, I knew that he had won a scholarship at Nottingham High School at twelve, at sixteen had worked for a short time as a clerk in a manufacturer's office at thirteen shillings a week, and after being seriously ill with pneumonia had become a pupil teacher at Eastwood. I did not know till recently that when he left the Eastwood school a year later and went to Nottingham University College, he had passed first in all England and Wales in the Uncertificated Teachers' Examination. He remained for two years at college, after which he went as a certificated master to the Davidsor Road Elementary School at Croydon.

He was still at Croydon when his mother died. That was at the end of 1910. *The White Peacock* appeared immediately after, in January, 1911. He had been able to place an advance copy in her hand, but she had not cared to read it. Off and on he had been engaged on it for over four years.

It was not Lawrence's mother, but the girl he was in

love with—the Miriam of *Sons and Lovers*—that had encouraged his writing. Over a year before, in the autumn of
1909, she had sent, on her own initiative, the poems 'A
Still Afternoon,' 'Dreams Old and Nascent,' 'Discipline,'
and the two 'Baby Movements' to the *English Review*. For
those who can see, all Lawrence's future is contained in
these five poems. Ford Madox Hueffer, who was then
editor, accepted them and got into correspondence with
Lawrence. It was to Hueffer that Lawrence sent the MS.
of *The White Peacock*, and Hueffer got it accepted by Heinemann. When the book appeared Violet Hunt wrote a
glowing review to the *Chronicle* and invited the author to her
literary club. It was a *succès d'estime*. To Lawrence's
amusement his work was taken for a woman's in several
quarters.

This interest, and the appearance at intervals of poems in
periodicals, had brought him the acquaintance of Edward
Garnett. Garnett's well-meaning hand was stretched out
with those of the Hueffers, and Lawrence grasped it gladly.
Here, without his seeking, was an opening from an existence
which had grown ever less tolerable. But he had none of
the conventional notions of a literary career. It signified
much to him that his dying mother had not cared to read
his book. Books to him would never mean what they do
to most writers. They would mean both much more and
much less. He never read one of his own published works.
'Books to me,' he wrote much later, 'are incorporate things,
voices in the air, that do not disturb the haze of autumn,
and visions that don't blot out the sunflowers.'[1]

After his mother's death he continued for another year
at Croydon, but after a second attack of pneumonia he
decided to leave schoolmastering for good. He had been at

[1] See 'The Bad Side of Books,' Lawrence's introduction to E. D.
M'Donald's *Bibliography* (Centaur Press, New York).

the Davidson Road School for five years and his work was
highly spoken of. After a visit to Garnett he spent three
months at home.

II

Eight years earlier, while at college in Nottingham, he
had become acquainted with Professor Ernest Weekley. The
Professor had helped him with the French necessary for his
certificate, and had noted his intelligence, but had not then
asked him to his house. Now, however, that he was spoken
of as a poet, Lawrence was bidden there. Upon his very
first meeting with the Professor's wife his course was determined. During the last year there had been a love affair
with a married woman older than himself in his home
district. But it was an affair in which the woman had set
the course and marked the end. When Lawrence met
Frieda Weekley he was free, and this time he would lead.
Never again would he be mothered by any woman. He
would even put behind him that first mothering that had
meant more than anything else to his youth.

After the provincial women he had known, this daughter
of a Continental aristocracy was a revelation to him. He
lost no time in committing himself. Early in May he and
Frieda Weekley were both in Germany, though not together.
She was with her people, he wandering and waiting about
with the unfinished manuscript of *Sons and Lovers*.

It was over a year since he had written *The Trespasser*,
and there had been a long-drawn debate about it between
him and his publisher, Heinemann. For the first and last
time in his career Lawrence was definitely unwilling, and
a publisher eager, to print. The book recorded an incident
of which he was ashamed. But suddenly in the spring of
1912 all this was in the past and did not matter—not at
least to Lawrence. Though he disliked the incident and did

not much like the book, the first was true and the second was his honest account at the time.—*Vogue la galère!* The wide and terrifying prospect which he now faced was everything. Courage to proceed entailed the courage that lets the dead past bury its dead. Some money too was absolutely necessary. At the end of twelve months there was nothing left of the £50 from *The White Peacock*, and he had no savings, for at Croydon he had earned but a bare living. This new book would not bring much, but it was honestly earned. Weighing the old importance against the new, Lawrence made his choice. He paid his fare to Germany in May, 1912, with money from *The Trespasser*.

Lawrence was sure of himself but not yet sure of Frieda. As for Frieda, she was sure neither of herself nor of Lawrence. How should she be? She was several years older than he, and vastly more 'experienced' in every worldly sense of the term. A daughter of Baron von Richthofen, who had been Governor of Alsace-Lorraine after the Franco-Prussian war, she was socially confident. In the midst of a gay and eventful girlhood she had married before she was twenty, and when Lawrence met her she had three children, a boy and two girls, the younger girl being only three years old. She was not unhappy, had never known unhappiness. Merely she lived in a placid dream, which was variegated at times by love affairs that were almost equally unreal. This made a rich tapestried background that satisfied her well enough so long as nobody woke her up and made her aware that it was no more. And until Lawrence came nobody had. Lawrence, incredibly raw and really innocent, felt the glamour deeply. But he refused to be intimidated. He held by his own experience, that was limited but intense. With Frieda added to him and dominated by him he could start in and live.

Frieda did not see it so. There were other things besides pure life for her to consider. And there were her children, who were certainly a large part of life to her. She was carelessly generous of herself, as no provincial woman could have been generous. There was nothing of bargaining here, nor of coquetry. This in itself was dazzlingly attractive to the many times wounded Lawrence. But all the more, and in its accompanying contempt for 'faithfulness,' it made him suffer. From first to last Lawrence was for fidelity in marriage. While he admired this woman's 'freedom' it was torture to him. At the same time he would hold his own and not be at her mercy. I have been allowed to see some of these early letters written by him from different parts of Germany. They are unlike any others I know in the range of poets' love letters. They rarely mention love, yet love letters they are, and they are exquisite as they are extraordinary.

He spent the early summer going from place to place alone, suffering intensely, seeing the Rhine, and little German places like Trier and Mayrhofen, with the clarity of suffering, getting on immediate human terms with the humble hosts and hostesses at his various lodgings, working on *Sons and Lovers* (which already belonged wholly to the past), and every day sending off letters of an explosive quality that was contained in quietness, to a wayward and uncertain and beautiful woman with features like those of a handsome creature of the wilds. It was as when a friend once introduced Lawrence to a tame fox that was his pet. Lawrence would not rest till he had found some touch that made the pet forget its tameness. Frieda has a nose like a puss fox, so fine and tremulous about the nostrils, and her eyes might be the eyes of a lioness into lady. It was not for nothing that Lawrence's mind often ran upon poachers,—and gamekeepers.

By midsummer Frieda had thrown in her lot with his. It would not be true to say that she had found her master.

Rather she expected to rule but could not resist this man who had discovered the secret of her wildness and was so insistent on his own power.   Or perhaps it was the challenge more than the man that she found irresistible.   Anyhow it was no conclusion, but only a beginning, when she and Lawrence set out one day in August on foot together to cross Tirol into Italy.   They had almost no money.   Frieda was entirely courageous.

That autumn, and winter and the following early spring they stayed at Lake Garda, moving only once from one place to another.   In February *Love Poems and Others* came out with Duckworth in London.   In the same year that publisher issued *Sons and Lovers*, which Heinemann had refused, giving as his verdict—or endorsing the verdict of his reader—that it was 'one of the dirtiest books he had ever read.'   The reviews were mostly favourable.   Some were enthusiastic.

In April, 1913, Lawrence and Frieda went to the Isarthal in Bavaria and stayed in a pleasant corner at Irschenhausen. The little wooden house with the fir and beech forest behind, the 'big open country' in front, and the mountains beyond, had been the scene of their setting forth together the summer before.   In the middle of June they returned to England, paid a visit to Edward Garnett in Hampshire and then went on to London.

It was in July[1] that Lawrence and Frieda first met Middleton Murry and Katherine Mansfield in the flat above the office of *Rhythm* in Chancery Lane.   Murry, as the editor of *Rhythm*, had accepted a short story by Lawrence from which the meeting naturally arose.

Lawrence once described to me his first sight of Katherine Mansfield.   She was sitting on the floor of a bare room, he

[1] Murry in his *Reminiscences* says 'early summer,' but the letters point to July.

said, beside a bowl of gold fish. When I asked him to describe her, Frieda, who was with us, took the words out of his mouth. '*So* pretty she is, such *lovely legs*!' she shouted. But Lawrence broke in violently, if not so loudly with, 'If you *like* the legs of the principal boy in the pantomime!' Here was a flick of a spinsterish tartness that he always had, but there was something more—an expression of his distaste for certain of the accepted forms of beauty, a distaste that later could alienate and puzzle a critic like Mr. Gerhardi.

But it had nothing to do with Katherine Mansfield, to whose great charm Lawrence made response as eagerly as to the emotional readiness of Middleton Murry. To them he had come from the circle of the Garnetts where, in spite of much kindness and appreciation, he had felt himself regarded as essentially 'a sort of queer fish that can write.' He foresaw too that neither the Garnetts nor the Hueffers would like his next novel. But with Murry and Katherine all was young, hopeful and untried. When Mr. 'Eddie' Marsh, always on the spot when fresh genius was about, introduced Lawrence and Frieda to Herbert and Cynthia Asquith, and the Asquiths invited the Lawrences to Broadstairs, where Mr. Marsh also was, Lawrence would have it that Murry and Katherine must come too. As they could not afford the journey, Murry has told how Lawrence insisted on paying for it, with solemn injunctions on the obtuseness of not letting others pay in such case. They went and they bathed, though Frieda insists that the Lawrence contingent did not bathe naked, as Murry professes to remember. Not that it matters.

When, after another week end with the Garnetts, they went back to the Isarthal at the beginning of August, they had Murry's light promise to join them in Italy with Katherine Mansfield—a promise that was not fulfilled. Lawrence, who would go anywhere if he wanted to go and felt it mattered, was disappointed, especially as Murry and

Katherine managed to get to Paris in May. But he built upon seeing much of them on his return to England the following summer. By the middle of September he and Frieda were at Lerici near Spezia, and after a fortnight, at Fiascherino, where they stayed till June, 1914.

After seven beginnings and many burnings the MS. of *The Rainbow* was complete before the middle of May. Lawrence sent it to J. B. Pinker, who was now to act as his literary agent. At Fiascherino too he wrote—or more probably re-wrote—*The Widowing of Mrs. Holroyd*, for a New York publisher not of the highest standing. He has recorded in print [1] how he re-wrote the play yet again almost completely over the proof, and how the enterprising Yankee bore with him, but—can it have been out of revenge?—how the same publisher also persuaded him to part with the American copyright of *Sons and Lovers* in return for a £20 cheque so drawn up that it could not be cashed. [2] Early in June Lawrence and Frieda were once more in England. By this time there was no barrier to their marriage. It was Lawrence, though he was far more terrified of the married state than was Frieda, who insisted upon regularising their union.

[1] Introduction to Edward D. M'Donald's *Bibliography* (Centaur Press, New York).

[2] Neither was it ever made good.

PART TWO

Aet. 29–34

Prose

TWILIGHT IN ITALY (essays)

REFLEXIONS ON THE DEATH OF A
PORCUPINE, ETC. (*in part*)

WOMEN IN LOVE

ENGLAND, MY ENGLAND, ETC.
(short stories)

STUDIES OF CLASSIC AMERICAN
LITERATURE

MOVEMENTS IN EUROPEAN HIS-
TORY

TOUCH AND GO (play in 3 acts)

PSYCHO-ANALYSIS AND THE UN-
CONSCIOUS

Verse

LOOK! WE HAVE COME THROUGH!
(*completed*)

NEW POEMS

BAY

★

*'I am tired of life being so ugly and cruel. How I long
for it to be pleasant. It makes my soul heave to see it
so harsh and brutal.'*

13

PART TWO

I

All this is to say that when I came to meet him Lawrence was at the end of that adventure which three years later he was to confide with some reluctance to the world in the cycle of poems called *Look! We have Come Through!* Besides *The Rainbow*, most of these astonishing, perfectly original poems were already in existence. Of course I did not know this. With Lawrence one was usually in the dusty rear in literary as well as other matters. His sister has told how in their youthful expeditions he always ranged ahead. He continued all his life to do so.

I have read that to Richard Aldington in those days Lawrence looked like a soldier and that to David Garnett he suggested a plumber's mate or the kind of workman that makes trouble with the boss. But to me, on that day in June, 1914, when I first set eyes on him, the immediately distinguishing thing was his swift and flamelike quality, which was quite unlike anything suggested by even the most fascinating type of British soldier or workman. I was sensible of a fine, rare beauty in Lawrence, with his deep-set jewel-like eyes,[1] thick dust-coloured hair, pointed underlip of notable sweetness, fine hands, and rapid but never restless movements. The stiff, the slow or the unreal had as little part in that frame as had any mechanically imposed control, but he was beautifully disciplined. In any kind of paid manual or even mechanical labour, if he had undertaken it,

---

[1] I always thought Lawrence's eyes were grey not blue, but I am assured on good authority that I was wrong, also that toward the end of his life they became intensely blue. In 1914 it was certainly not the colour of the eyes that was striking.

I should have said that Lawrence would have risen quickly
to a position of authority and would have been in favour
because of his good workmanship. This is not the kind that
'makes trouble' in the accepted sense of the phrase, anyhow
not so long as he is employed on a definite understanding. I
have seen Lawrence under many circumstances but I never
once saw him heavy or lounging, and he was never idle, just
as a bird is never idle. At the same time I never saw a trace
of strain or resentment in him when engaged in any of his
manifold activities. In these two ways—never being idle yet
never seeming to labour—he was unlike anybody else I ever
met. He was without human dreariness.

On this first meeting I was disappointed in Frieda, whose
beauty I had heard impressively described. I had lived in
Germany, and she struck me as being a typical German
Frau of the blonde, gushing type. She wore a tight coat and
skirt of horse-cloth check that positively obscured her finely
cut, rather angry Prussian features. To discover how magnificent she could look, I had to see her marching about a
cottage hatless and in an overall or, still better, in peasant
costume. After that her handsomeness never escaped me,
and I admired her greatly.

Nothing memorable was said over tea. But afterwards,
when we all walked down to the Finchley Road together to
see the Lawrences into their bus, he and I walked in front;
and as we passed the churchyard where my child was buried
and I had paid for a grave for myself, I found that I was
talking to him as if I had known him all my life. It was not
that Lawrence encouraged confidences. He had none of
the traits, still less the tricks of what is usually understood
to be the 'sympathetic' man. There were no 'intimacies,'
either physical or mental. But he gave an immediate
sense of freedom, and his responses were so perfectly
fresh, while they were puzzling, that it seemed a waste

of time to talk about anything with him except one's real
concerns.

I forget now how many times we had met before Lawrence
undertook to read the MS. of my first attempt at a novel,
but it was still June when I received his first letter, which
was all about it.

I must tell you I am in the middle of reading your novel. You
have very often a simply *beastly* style, indirect and roundabout and
stiff-kneed and stupid. And your stuff is abominably muddled—
you'll simply have to write it all again. But it is fascinatingly
interesting. Nearly all of it is *marvellously* good. It is only so
incoherent. But you can *easily* pull it together. It *must* be a long
novel—it is of the quality of a long novel. My stars, just you
work at it, and you'll have a piece of work you never need feel
ashamed of. All you need is to get the whole thing under your
control. You see it takes one so long to know what one is really
about. [Here follow some specific details.] When I've finished
it—to-morrow or Wednesday—we must have a great discussion
about it. My good heart, there's some honest work here, real.

And for a postscript,

You must be willing to put much real work, hard work into
this, and you'll have a genuine creative piece of work. It's like
Jane Austen at a deeper level.

Lawrence would always read anything that anybody tried
to write; but, though he was a valuable and astute literary
critic, his critical point of view was not 'literary,' as the word
is usually understood. He read that he might find out what
the writer would be at, and, having found out, that he might
expound it to the writer who, as often as not, is only half
conscious of the character of the impulses underlying all
literary effort.

It was this, with his astonishing patience, his delighted
recognition of any sign of vitality and his infectious insistence

upon the hardest work, that made him unique among critics. Even if you were incapable of carrying out in the work itself what you learned from his comments upon it, you could hardly refrain from coming, in some degree at least, to distinguish in yourself between what was native and impulsive and what was affected or imposed and in consequence confused. If the writing under consideration was by an acknowledged master it was just the same. Himself an accomplished artist, Lawrence never underrated accomplishment. But he was no more deterred by skilled than by unskilled expression from divining and revealing the underlying stream of life. He could neither be put off nor carried away by talent, a quality which, among others, makes his *Studies in Classic American Literature* a book of rare critical value.

His second letter followed next day—

I have just finished your novel. I think it's going to be something *amazingly* good. But it means work, I can tell you. I have put thousands of notes and comments and opinions in the margin, out of my troubled soul. I hope they'll help.

He wanted to 'settle it' with me immediately. I was to come the next day and have 'a real go at this MS.' with him from midday till four o'clock with a break for lunch.

The nature of the invitation overwhelmed me, but I went. Anything livelier than Lawrence in such a situation —anyone more emphatic or less portentous it is impossible to imagine. Though he sat quiet and teacher-like beside you at the table, you had the impression that he was darting about in the air like a humming bird—a humming bird with a very sharp beak. At the same time he was humanly charming. He made it seem natural that the author of any serious effort should be on his own footing, and soon one accepted it almost too easily. To encourage me he told me how many years and how despairingly he had worked over *The White Peacock* and how often rewritten *Sons and Lovers*.

At that moment he was very busy trying to get his own affairs into working order, and though I was not aware of it he had acute anxieties. Murry has said that Lawrence's agent had obtained an advance of £300 for the new novel on the strength of the notable reception of *Sons and Lovers*. It is true that such was the agreement. But Murry's assumption that in the summer of 1914 there was '£300, solid, all in the bank, and a brand-new banking account'[1] is unhappily not in accordance with the facts. The sum mentioned was to be paid on publication. What with discussions and drastic revisions the MS. was not ready for the printer until over a year later. Actually by October, 1915, when the book was out, Methuen was still owing £50, of which £17 would be retained for proof correction and £5 by the agent for his fee. In all, Lawrence could not count on receiving more than £253 over a period of nearly eighteen months after his first submission of the novel. And by July he was at the end of all other resources. He had not till then realised the discrepancy between a contract for '£300 in advance' and the slow, abbreviated payments of actuality. Pinker came to the rescue by advancing £45 out of his own pocket (*i.e.* £50 on the strength of the contract for *The Rainbow* less £5 commission) and a little later the Royal Literary Fund made a grant of £50. Otherwise Lawrence could hardly have carried on.

He never worried unduly, however, and prospects were not bad. He was seeing Lena Ashwell, who was hopeful of producing *Mrs. Holroyd*. A book of short stories was almost ready,[2] and he had been personally approached by another publisher who wanted from him 'an interpretative essay on Hardy.' It was to run to 15,000 words, and Lawrence would

---

[1] *Reminiscences.*
[2] *The Prussian Officer.*

receive £15 in advance on delivery, with royalties afterwards at 1½d. a copy in England and ¾d. in America. He thought he might throw this off without difficulty.

But Frieda and he got married without any of this new money, and when Pinker's £45 arrived a fortnight later, small accumulated debts asked to be settled and were settled. Lawrence never left loose ends.

His third letter to me, dated July 13th, told of the marriage.

I am awfully sorry we couldn't come to-night. I poor devil am seedy with neuralgia in my left eye and my heart is in my boots. *Domani sono i nostri matrimonii—alle* 10½. *Povero me mi sentio poco bene.*

And I was to see them within a day or two. That morning I left a bunch of anemones at Selwood Terrace. Long afterwards Frieda, laughing, told me how that day Lawrence's infectious insistence on the importance of fidelity, and so of marriage, had given Katherine Mansfield the desire to wear a wedding ring herself. But such trifles cost something, and money with the Murrys, too, was scarce. So Frieda lent Katherine her discarded ring to wear till Murry could give her one of her own. Frieda had looked to have it back. But Katherine misunderstood and nothing more was ever said.[1] On the 30th July, leaving Frieda in the South, Lawrence went for the week-end to his sisters in the Midlands. He then set off on a short walking tour in the Westmorland hills with three other men. Two of these were acquaintances to whom he had felt casually drawn. They were neither intimate nor literary friends. The fourth, who joined the party at the last moment, was S. S. Koteliansky. He knew nothing of Lawrence save what he had heard from one of the other two who had described him as a 'writer chap with

[1] Until Murry (*Reminiscences*) gave his version of the incident.

ideas about love,' with the usual implication that Lawrence
was an apostle of 'free love.' And though not particularly
attracted by the description, Koteliansky agreed to make a
fourth for the few days' tour.

Lawrence, slender, vivacious and friendly, in his corduroy
jacket, was entirely different from the companion he had
pictured. The second night of the walk they had to put up in
a cottage where there was only one bed, so that two of the
quartette had to lie on the floor. Lawrence, as the delicate
one, was made to sleep in the bed, and Koteliansky as the
visitor was urged to share it. He was very unwilling. Never
in his life had such a thing befallen him. But Lawrence was
so gay and easy that all shyness vanished. Above all, this
foreign stranger was captivated by a kind of sensitive innocence in Lawrence which he had never before seen in an
Englishman. It roused a jealously protective tenderness.
Lawrence spoke lightly, as was his way, and without being in
any degree confidential, of his recent marriage. He had a
wife, he said, who was a German lady of high degree. His
lack of sophistication made the boast somehow delightful.
Kot must visit them in the English countryside when they
had found a home there. Lawrence would have liked to
return immediately to Italy, but he did not see how he could
afford to do so.

Lawrence was still in Westmorland when war was declared. So far as I can discover, his first feeling about it,
which lasted for nearly six months, was not unmixed with
sober hopefulness. He did not think it would last long, and
it might 'shake people into a live seriousness' and 'set a
slump on trifling.'

After a few days back in London at the Campbells' flat,
he and Frieda went to a cottage near Chesham in Bucks.
Gilbert and Mary Cannan inhabited a windmill not far off,
full of the most wonderful nicknacks, and the Murrys took

a cottage two miles across the fields. There were ten days or so of picnicking together and the work of settling in, of which Lawrence always took both the direction and the lion's share. When they were settled, Koteliansky came down for a week-end, and before the evening of Saturday was come, had advised and rebuked Frieda for what he considered her too great self-importance by the side of her husband, with such effect that next day Katherine was called in to act as mediator. It was in this way that Koteliansky first became acquainted with the Murrys.

It fell also, I believe, to Katherine to put a laughing extinguisher on the great *Rananim* idea when that had run its course as a pleasant dream but was still harped upon by Lawrence as something he wished to realise.

Ranani zadikim l'Adonoi. Koteliansky had sung the Hebrew chant to them in Bucks as the war horror arose and increased, and it intensified the longing Lawrence had always felt to live remote with a group of kindred spirits. He and Frieda, Koteliansky and Katherine and Murry must get away to an island and be happy and busy. Others would follow. The Murrys took it up at first like a lovely game, but it was no game to Lawrence, and when Katherine, not without realistic mischief, went and obtained a mass of detailed, difficult information about suitable islands, Lawrence, says Koteliansky, fell sadly silent. He really cared. Though from that day *Rananim* was off, he still went on caring and hoping and planning.

The events of 1914–1919 all went to strengthen his strong and simple belief that the only thing to be done was for a few people to go together of their own desire to some distant refuge and breeding place of newness. Lawrence was not a 'conscientious objector.' He was not in principle opposed to war—far from it. But he quickly divined the dire significance of this war, which we now appreciate after

the event.   He could see no true way of ameliorating the
horror.   He believed that attempts at amelioration (such as
war work), like attempts at defiance (such as conscientious
objection) equally involved identification with the horror.
Springing from 'the nervous fire of opposition,' these were
secretly part of the evil and by opposing fomented it.   He
could but say that he would have no part in it, not even a pro-
testing part.   Nothing could have been harder for him than
the inaction thus imposed.   While he accorded a qualified
sympathy to the conscientious objector, his real sympathy was
for the soldier.   But the latter he could not and the former,
in the Quakerish sense, he would not be.   We must, he said,
'be done with half-truths.'   We must not 'adapt ourselves'
but rather go apart.

There are sane minds to-day inclined to the belief that
only by some such proceeding as Lawrence urged, mystical
in its import but active in its immediate bearing, can we save
ourselves and the world.   It is a proceeding as old as sin and
as simple as goodness.   There was Noah and there was Lot.
Civilisation itself was saved by the monastic retreat provided
by the Christian genius.   Lawrence felt the old need of
severance and departure, but he felt it in a new way, and he
would have nothing to do with catchwords or with the tricks
that accompany earthly leadership.   He had the genius of
direction enough to have exploited his 'personality' and
founded an order or an institute.   He knew, however, that
'personality,' orders and institutes could no longer be employed without the creeping in of bogus principles.   The
time had passed for any such attempt.   But the time could
never pass for obedience to a profound and simple impulse.
If several men and women felt the same impulse, even in
differing degrees, surely they should make the movement of
severance and departure in company?

In the War he came to believe fully in the putrescence—

worse because it was denied—of the Christian era. The only
thing to do was to get out and away, if possible to some
place where a newer growth or an older decay would save
us from using up our energies in protestation, reaction or
mere self-preservation.

In October I wrote telling Lawrence that I was going to
be married. He was surprised. He wrote from Bucks:

How exciting your letter is! We are glad to hear you are going
to marry Donald Carswell. Your life will run on a staple pivot
then, and you will be much happier. After all one has a complete
right to be happy. I only want to know people who have the
courage to live. The dying resigned sort only bore me now. We
are glad to have your news—soon we'll come and see you.

They were to come one day in the following week and
put up for the night at my house. Lawrence was in straits
for money, having nothing but the grant from the Royal
Literary Fund. (He and Frieda were actually trying to find
a market for their painted boxes and embroideries, and we
got as far as nervously taking some of these to a Hampstead
shop, that was dubiously interested.) I have another letter
of the same October in which he writes:

I have got about £70 in the world now. Of this I owe £145
to the divorce lawyers, for costs claimed against me. This I am
never going to pay. I also owe about £20 otherwise. So I have
got some £50. If you think the other fund would give me any
more—benissimo, I'll take it like a shot.

Oh, by the way [he adds in a postscript], I was seedy and have
grown a beard. I think I look hideous, but it is so warm and
complete, and such a clothing to one's nakedness, that I like it and
shall keep it. So when you see me don't laugh.

I never quite believed and do not now, that Lawrence
found his beard hideous. His saying so was one of the small
and transparent affectations which—in the absence of all

profounder deceits—made him so easy to approach and so impossible not to love. At the same time his warning was necessary, as it was something of a shock to see this new Lawrence with a beard quite different from the hair of his head, of a deep glowing red in the sun, and in the shade the colour of strong tea. And it marked a stage. The Lawrence with the moustache, the Lawrence of *Sons and Lovers* and tramps from Germany to Italy, had given place to the bearded, married Lawrence, the Lawrence of *The Rainbow*, and the War, and the long struggle with the woman and with the world that was begun and ended in solitude.

Donald was at this time on the staff of *The Times*, working in the same department with Mr. F. S. Lowndes, husband of Mrs. Belloc-Lowndes. Finding that Donald was acquainted with Lawrence, Mr. Lowndes, a kindly man, expressed great interest and, on learning also that Lawrence was very hard up, great sympathy. He hinted that something further might be done out of a fund in which his wife had some say, and added that Mrs. Belloc-Lowndes would be very glad to have an opportunity of meeting this remarkable young man. On hearing all this from Donald I at once invited Mrs. Belloc-Lowndes to come to my house and meet Mr. and Mrs. D. H. Lawrence.

Mrs. Belloc-Lowndes, whom none of us had ever set eyes on before, duly turned up. I remember how silent Lawrence sat as she told us (*a*) that she didn't know how on earth she was going to afford a necessary operation for one of her children, and (*b*) what splendid large sums she always got on account for her books, naming the amounts. Also, just as we were showing her out, we managed to disabuse her of her firm impression that Lawrence had eloped with the wife of the local butcher of his village, *i.e.* Frieda *geb.* von Richthofen, whom we had just left upstairs! But the literary fund which she was supposed to represent had melted in an explanatory haze. When we were left alone Lawrence indulged in some pithead language.

That night we talked—especially Lawrence. I was only beginning to know him. Often I disagreed with what he said or declared it to be exaggerated. But from the first I was sure that he was worth more than the lot of us. Also with Lawrence there was something that begot in the listener a kind of inward ear.

'Thank you so much for having us down. I like to stay with you—you are a perfect hostess. Please don't think me a fool or conceited for my tirade,' he wrote, enclosing a cheque for £1 which I must have lent him, with two shillings extra 'for the maid.' I was to go down soon to see them. He had pleased me very much by saying that mine was the only town house in which he had ever felt it might be possible for him to live. I think, however, that this was chiefly because, though it was old, there was an unpretentious air of impermanency about it, so that we always expected it to fall down when the anti-aircraft gun went off. Lawrence disliked an air of everlastingness about a home. For him it must have something of the tent about it, though he liked everything to be seemly and clean, and he approved of a few household gods.

II

I went once to Bucks but only, I think, for the day. There I met the Cannans, was taken over their Windmill, and went a hilly walk. For some reason it was also a gloomy walk. The grass of the hills looked black and I wished I were at home. I felt a great unhappiness in Gilbert Cannan which Mary's chirpiness did not dispel. And Lawrence seemed to be holding on to himself against depression. On the return to England the links between Frieda and her children had reasserted themselves, and he found the complication hard to endure.

Donald and I were married early in January, and Lawrence sent me a little blue plate 'as a love token from us. That it is a dragon is a fitting symbol, but I shall paint you a phœnix on a box.' The phœnix, as I knew, was his most fitting 'badge and sign.' Being married, I had now one of the chief qualifications for inclusion in the Lawrence exodus. There were to be, if possible, no single males or females in the party —as with the denizens of the Ark—and Lawrence caused much amusement by his suggestions for the mating of those among the probable starters who were still unattached. He thought, for instance, that Dorothy Warren might marry the writer who is now known as Michael Arlen.

Lawrence was not happy in Bucks, and I never heard him speak of his stay there with any pleasure. To him that countryside was dreary. Literary prospects too, instead of improving, looked blacker. The Hardy book was turning out as 'rum' unsaleable stuff that would not fetch even the promised £15. That good friend, Amy Lowell, who had met Lawrence in England and was now in New York, tried in vain to elicit the money owed by the New York publisher of *Mrs. Holroyd* and *Sons and Lovers*. The new novel, of which a contemplated title was then *The Wedding Ring*, was still undergoing final revision and wearisome typing by the author, with many of its pages queried by the publishers. *The Prussian Officer* came out, but Lawrence disliked the title, which had been chosen against his wish. 'What Prussian Officer?' he asked. When the money from the Royal Literary Fund came to an end, what next?

After a 'long, slow, pernicious cold' in January he accepted an invitation from the Meynells at Greatham in Sussex to occupy the barn which had been newly converted for Viola into a very attractive cottage. There were still finishing touches to be put to it—linoleums to be laid and so forth. Lawrence would undertake these and would give daily coaching to one of the Meynell grandchildren, who was kept from school owing to a serious accident. Viola, nobly if often disapprovingly, undertook to type the remainder of the novel.

Again I cannot recall any reference by Lawrence to his six months at Greatham which suggests enjoyment, as, for example, his references to Cornwall suggest enjoyment. But socially it was an eventful period—vide *Women in Love*. He met here for the first time people like Lady Ottoline Morrell and the Hon. Bertrand Russell (now Earl Russell), and he was at first deeply impressed by them besides being himself in his special way impressive.

The innocence of Lawrence has always to be kept in mind. It is this quality, with the force of his beliefs and the strength of his imaginative vision, that puts him humanly with Blake and with Shelley among the English poets. But because Lawrence was practical, with the realism of the English working man, his innocence is easily ignored. He had none of the charming foolishness in worldly affairs that distinguishes most of the poetic innocents. On the other hand circumstances had rendered him far less sophisticated in social matters. One result of this was that, upon finding himself mistaken about people, he would strike out with all his force.

Given any expression of natural sympathy Lawrence went forth at a first meeting blind to all discrepancies. It was only in the face of hostile assertiveness that he became either arrogant or reserved. He provided in general, as has been said, an immediate air of liberty, equality and fraternity such as I never breathed with any man of like gifts.

But though Lawrence practised the charity of culture and of his own nature—the charity that hopes all things, he definitely rejected the Christian petrifaction and prolongation of

this—the charity that endureth all things. For here he saw
a breeding-place of tyrants and of victims. He could hope a
long time. But when he judged the time for hope was past
he no longer endured.

In this, as in so much else, his moderation was marked.
He was always ready to revise a judgment and to start afresh
without rancour or a backward glance. But he affirmed the
right to judge, as he admitted the right of others to judge
him. 'Judge not that ye be not judged!' I once heard him
in conversation echo that sententiously uttered statement.
'But don't you see that if we live we *must* judge, for to live
is to judge—and to be judged too at every turn, even as you
are now judging me by bidding me not to judge!'

What Lawrence refused to do was to judge by any set
principle. He began by taking the life attainment of others
eagerly on trust. But he had no doubt as to the nature and
extent of his own. And when discrepancies appeared, he
measured the one against the other and lost no time in announcing the results. Being in the case of highly placed and
highly gifted persons more astonished by the discrepancy, he
was the more emphatic in underlining it.

Frieda apart, it was first and foremost on Murry that
Lawrence relied—Murry, young, gifted and sympathetic.
Before they had been three weeks at Greatham Murry had
come to stay with them. He was lonely (Katherine had gone
to Paris) and not well (after an attack of influenza) and just
nearing the end of his first novel. So he went to Lawrence
and Lawrence nursed him beautifully. An intimacy sprang
up, and Lawrence could not think or speak too highly of this
friend. The more that Frieda was increasingly fretting about
her children and fighting against Lawrence in the matter,
Murry seemed a man sent from God. Lawrence included
him in every plan, praised the MS. of his first novel and
expounded to him *The Rainbow*, which he counted upon

Murry to review in the face of a hostile, misunderstanding world when it should appear. He even saw in Murry a colleague and successor who would build up the temple when he, Lawrence, had cut out the ground.

To Murry also he poured forth the philosophy which he was then beginning to write down. This had become all-important to him, so that he saw himself as putting forth one novel after *The Rainbow* and no more. After that his 'approach to the revolution of the conditions of life'—a revolution profoundly opposed to socialism, with which he had merely a shallow intellectual and emotional sympathy[1]— was to take some more direct, active and human form. What form precisely he did not specify even to himself. But it involved a 'withdrawal from the world' and it called for support from at least a few people.

There was some talk of the Lawrences occupying a part of the ruins at Garsington Manor, the home of the Morrells. At the mere mention of monastic walls Lawrence saw himself building a new Jerusalem within convenient distance of Oxford and Cambridge. But this supposed monastery presently diminished itself to the offer of a gardener's cottage, which again diminished itself to nothing.

Lawrence was sharply ill at Greatham and very weak afterwards. But besides much philosophy he wrote some short stories and the sketches for *Twilight in Italy*. He wrestled hard too with his publisher for the totality of *The Rainbow* and, though he yielded in the matter of some words

[1] Lawrence had passionate feeling for 'the workers' and had nothing against the overthrow of society, in so far as that was necessary for the growth of a new way of life. But it was chiefly with the new way of life that he was concerned, and this was in opposition to the Marxist ideal. He disbelieved in working for a revolution on economic grounds as completely as in bolstering up the present system by reforms. In other words he was a religious teacher, and in some degree a mystic, though of a new sort.

and phrases, he refused to alter or omit any passage or paragraph. As well, he said, cut off your nose to make your face pleasant to people who say it is spoiled by that feature. He conjured his publisher, as he conjured Murry, to fight for the book, because it would both need and deserve fighting support. He knew it could not be popular, but he encouraged his publisher by the assurance that in years to come it would prove a sound financial speculation.

He also conjured for a further advance in money, his fear being that this, if delayed till the appearance of the book, would be claimed by the divorce lawyers before it reached him. Again J. B. Pinker rose to the occasion. Lawrence received £90. After this there would be only £33 to come.

The question was urgent—what was to be their next home? The way to the Continent was barred by the War—though Lawrence thought the War would be over by the autumn and that the appearance of his *Rainbow* would coincide with peace and new beginnings. In the interim it did not much matter where he lived so long as he and Frieda were independent. She wished to be near her children who were now in London. So, suddenly in July, they took the lower half of 2 Byron Villas in the Vale of Health at Hampstead. Having done this, he was for a time in a gay and careless mood. He asked us all for contributions—as small and cheap as possible—for the new home. I gave them an old-fashioned gilt mirror.

Lawrence loved making a home in a simple, transitory way; and though he looked upon this one as more than usually transitory, he threw himself into the setting of it up with ardour. Proudly he showed me the new pots and pans which were to be kept clean, not merely on the inside, as the Christians use, but on the outside, as the Pharisees use. In the process he sang all day long—as often as not the evangelical hymns of his youth. His next-door neighbours

wondered at the sound. Of all the stories told of Lawrence's
boyhood by his sister Ada (in her book *Young Lorenzo*) none
is more characteristic than that of the youthful company who,
under the threat of Lawrence's violence, stood up and sang
in the empty Easter-gay church at Alfreton, and this though
by then Lawrence had 'criticised and got over the Christian
dogma.' When I heard him lift up his voice in 'Sun of my
soul, thou Saviour dear,' I thought he would not be content
to die without having written hymns of his own. We have
his hymns in *The Plumed Serpent*.

One day I went with him and Frieda to hunt for second-
hand furniture in Praed Street. None of it was cheap enough,
and we trudged homeward through disagreeable weather late
in the afternoon. Frieda begged that we might stop somewhere for a cup of tea and I was all agreement. But
Lawrence turned on us with fury. We should *not* have any
tea! Were we not on the way home to our evening meal?
Money and time and stomachs might not be so wasted. I
was struck by Frieda's ungrumbling acceptance of this ruling
as we pushed wearily on. It now seems to me that we walked
home all the way from Camden Town. Even so, or rather
just so, life in Lawrence's company was so great an adventure that the utmost weariness or disappointment was
without boredom. He was *the* man in whose company to
miss a last train; and this not primarily because he was
sweet-tempered and entertaining. Frieda, though a rebellious
creature, submitted from the first to Lawrence's practical
direction, as she did at the last (after a long fight) to his
profounder guidance. For one thing she had what, to me at
least, is one of the most lovable qualities in a human being,
a simple animal stoicism in the face of pain or discomfort.
For another she recognised instinctively that in practical
matters Lawrence was well-nigh infallible. Besides, in
return for obedience of this kind, one got from Lawrence a

lovely assurance. I have a letter, written by Frieda nearly a year after his death, in which she refers to 'the glamour he gave to everything,' and says 'with Lawrence it was always worth while even at the worst.' There has not been a truer word spoken of him. Of how many can it be said?

III

They stayed at Byron Villas till Christmas (1915)—five important months to Lawrence as a writer. *The Rainbow* appeared on September 30th, and on November 13th was condemned at Bow Street as 'obscene' within the meaning of the statute of 1857 therein made and provided.

Work was being steadily turned out. Early in October the Italian sketches were complete, and the book was accepted by Duckworth. Soon afterwards the collection of poems to be called *Amores* was ready. All the while, short stories were written in rapid succession, and some of the philosophy saw print in the *Signature*.

Though I was asked both to go to the premises of the *Signature* (to which I contributed a rug for the floor), and to write for it, I did neither. I never believed in it, and Lawrence's own feeling, as conveyed to me at the time, tallies perfectly with his later account given in the preface to *Death of a Porcupine*. In that account no doubt, as Murry says,[1] the details of fact are inaccurate, but not, I think, the content of feeling. To me Lawrence appeared deprecating, almost apologetic at the outset, and he was clearly disappointed in the performance. That it contained nothing of importance except his own contribution, anybody may see who cares to look up the three issues. Lawrence said as much to me when he asked me, as a subscriber, if his essay on 'The Crown' conveyed anything to me. I had to admit, to his disappointment, that it didn't. One lives and learns.

[1] *Reminiscences.*

To-day 'The Crown' is the only thing in the *Signature* that has meaning for me; and it has so much meaning that I well understand how Lawrence was bound to take any chance to see it in print.

From all of this, however, there came scarcely any money. Lawrence was constrained to accept £30 from the Morrells, giving them in exchange the MS. of *The Rainbow*. (When was Lawrence ever known to receive without giving?) He had not been well, and dreading November in London, was still hoping to escape it by sailing away. He applied for passports to Spain. Then he had the offer of a cottage in Florida. Dr. Eder, who examined him, warned him against New York in the winter. But he would rush through New York to warmer climes beyond. Certainly he felt that London was dangerous to him. Those appalling 'colds' that laid him low! That he might be in readiness to go, the noble Pinker brought the Morrells' £30 up to £100. Immediately Lawrence delivered work to many times that value, though not immediately saleable. Bernard Shaw, too, being appealed to by the Morrells, sent £5 for Lawrence!

This was in October and November. Early in October I reviewed *The Rainbow* for the *Glasgow Herald*. I lacked Murry's advantages in that Lawrence had given me no exposition of the book beforehand. After *Sons and Lovers* it puzzled and disappointed me. I had been expecting a masterpiece of fiction, and this did not correspond to my notions of such a thing. Neither did I understand the book. But the processional beauty, the strangeness, the magnificence of the descriptive passages, which passed far beyond anything in the earlier novels, gave me enough to admire and praise whole-heartedly. No other writer could have risen to such heights or plumbed such depths, and I said so as well as I could at considerable length. But I had no grasp, and I found it a hard review to write.

Other critics praised in varying degrees; but many were offended, notably Mr. James Douglas, whose coarse and copious abuse was the efficient cause of the police proceedings. The review by Mr. De la Mare written for *The Times Literary Supplement* was, I believe, both long and largely favourable; but it was still in proof when the prosecution took place, and so was never published. Murry, when it came to the bit, shirked reviewing the book. His shirking was natural, even perhaps in its way, friendly. He 'simply,' as he would say—which means 'complicatedly'—disliked *The Rainbow*. But he ought not to give us to understand by implication that he wished to review it and was regretfully prevented by the prosecution.[1]

Lawrence was given no official notice of the prosecution, but he heard of it as early as November 5th through the late W. L. George. Noticing that the book was suddenly omitted from the publisher's advertisement, Mr. George had rung up Methuens, learned that legal action was being taken, and immediately informed Lawrence.

The affair kept Lawrence in London, hanging on to see if any remedy was to be found, till he was caught by December and really frightened by the severity of his colds. For his health, he knew he ought to have gone earlier. Now he was divided in mind whether to face it out in the hope of some concerted action in his favour, or to let the whole thing drop, and fly. Believing that ultimately his books must fight for themselves, he greatly preferred the latter course. The English did not like him. Why not stop writing for England and change his public? But from many quarters he was urged and encouraged to stay. He felt his publisher had behaved badly ('What a snake in his boiled shirt bosom!' exclaimed Lawrence), but the Society of Authors might help. Murry, perhaps forgetting what he later did when he was

[1] *Reminiscences.*

himself 'established,' has said accusingly that no established writer came forward in the matter.[1] Lawrence himself, however, has given some credit to Arnold Bennett, May Sinclair and others.[2] And he received many encouraging letters and calls. Sir Oliver Lodge came, and Mr. Drinkwater. The failure was in the matter of an organised protest. And this, no doubt, was because, like Murry, men such as Mr. Galsworthy and Mr. Wells *did not like 'The Rainbow.'* They were shocked by some of its details and, perhaps unconsciously, they felt its essential repudiation of all they stood for.

Lawrence, through Pinker, tried to sound his confrères — what did Henry James think of it, what Bennett, what E. M. Forster?—and the cautious or candid replies he received, alike convinced him of the deep contention between him and all the rest. They would allow that he had 'genius' but how they hated the manifestations of that genius! This was really what he had to accept. And he knew it. No protest would alter it. Besides he was incensed by literary strictures. 'When they have as good a work to show, they may make their pronouncements . . . till then let them learn decent respect.' So he wrote when he heard that a brother novelist[3] had criticised his 'construction.'

At the same time Philip Morrell asked questions in Parliament, the favourable reviews (mine among them) were collected as evidence, and several schemes—one of them by Prince Bibesco—were set afoot for publishing the book by private subscription. As Lawrence truly said, an energetic man could have done this and made it pay. But more than mere energy was needed. Even in those who would promote the scheme, there was scarcely any real enthusiasm for the book. Most people, like Murry, were paralysed by distaste.

[1] *Reminiscences.*   [2] See 'The Bad Side of Books.'
[3] Arnold Bennett.

The mere justice of a cause is seldom enough to carry it through. So it dragged. And Lawrence saw behind it well enough. He had to content himself with glowing praise in an American magazine (the *Metropolitan*) and with the prospect of the novel appearing shortly in U.S.A.

One way and another I saw a good deal of Lawrence when he was in Hampstead, but there was a thin veil between us and this, I think, he resented, though he was also grateful for it. It was of my making. Lawrence did not draw veils. He scoffed a little, though in the most friendly way, when he said that I made him think of that title of an old novel *The Guarded Flame* or reminded him of the bunched up, bell-clustered flower of the wild nettle. Himself he was a blown and dancing flame, and his flower emblem was the open-faced wild rose or the luminous outspread blossom of the campion, which he loved one of the best of wild flowers.

From beginning to end I had for Lawrence, as he well knew, a special kind of love and admiration which I never had for any other human being. It was impossible not to pay him the profoundest tribute and at the same time to rejoice in his companionship in ordinary ways. But I felt also the need to save myself, even to save myself up—for what I knew not, but for something that would come. For my age and experience I was still very immature. But there are wounds in life to which one does not twice expose oneself, and I had known such wounds. Yet again, where giving is demanded there must be the ability to take. Lawrence had the capacities of giving, taking and demanding in a marvellous if terrifying degree. But he was past the time of spending and being spent, and he had married a woman who would see to it that he did not return in his tracks. Lawrence was one thing, the combination of Lawrence and Frieda quite another. I have a cowardly dread of a mess. It was necessary, I believe, for Lawrence to create a great deal of mess in his human contacts—necessary to his work.   His marriage with Frieda was a step which inevitably created a morass about the paths of friendship.   I saw one person after another flounder in that morass.   For me, I preferred to signal across it.   My recent marriage was another barrier.   Lawrence knew perfectly what marriage meant to me.   And though there was an enduring respect between him and the man I had married there was no particular gush of sympathy.

I had not only a wholesome fear of Lawrence.   I was shy, and even suspicious of most of the friends by whom he was now surrounded.   I did not fit well with them, and there was something in their relation with him that saddened me. If he needed them, then he did, and it was his affair.   But I got the feeling that he did not think much of them, and was using them for what he needed, not so much willingly as *malgré lui.*

It was from his experience with these friends, and their interrelations through Frieda, that he wrote *Women in Love.* Later, when he gave me the MS. of that novel to read, I asked him why must he write of people who were so far removed from the general run, people so sophisticated and 'artistic' and spoiled, that it could hardly matter what they did or said?   To which he replied that it was only through such people that one could discover whither the general run of mankind, the great unconscious mass, was tending. There, at the uttermost tips of the flower of an epoch's achievement, one could already see the beginning of the flower of putrefaction which must take place before the seed of the new was ready to fall clear.   I gathered too that in the nature of the putrefaction the peculiar nature of an epoch was revealed.   And the more quickly we recognised and accepted the nature of the failure, the more speedily would the new unknown seed find a condition for its ger-

mination.   Achievement carried to its furthest limits co-
incided with putrefaction.   Those who sought the new must
take their stand right in the flux.

I am not now reporting Lawrence's actual words, which
I cannot remember, but I use remembered phrases to give
the impression he conveyed—an impression familiar to all his
readers.   I found his answer as I have described it, satisfactory from his point of view and illuminating to mine.   But
it left my practical position unchanged.   I gave it as my
opinion that whatever the value of the putrefying petals to
him as a writer, he would not find the human beings repre-
senting them much use either as friends or in the formation
of a group for the furthering of new life.

Even as I spoke, I felt that my obvious little truth did not
matter nearly so much as his difficult big one.   Yet beneath
what I said there was lurking a deeper truth—my still un-
formulated belief that Lawrence was meant to be under-
standed of the common people and that they would eventually
be the ones to profit by what he would bring forth.   I had
always noticed that he took for granted the common virtues,
and even many of what we call the Christian virtues.   He
built on a solid foundation.   So I persisted.

He was a little offended at my disparagement of his friends.
'Whom then would you suggest?   What kind of people?'
At his look, sadness overcame me.   It was something like
having to break the secret of suffering to a child, and in my
own helplessness in the face of this man's clear destiny I would
have been glad to eat my words.   But now it was started I had
to go on.   How stupid it was of me not to have seen from
the first that Lawrence must work for those who could not
understand him till long afterwards, and that those who could
give—or seem to give—immediate understanding, were absolutely needful to him, though they must soon prove to be
humanly detestable.   Failing to see this clearly at the time,

I could only blunder on with the thought that came nearest. 'You will have to be alone, I am afraid,' I said, 'all through and in the end, alone.' It was dragged out of me unwillingly, while I hoped with all my heart that I was talking bosh. Who was I that I should condemn a man like Lawrence to loneliness? But it sounded horribly like the truth.

Lawrence dropped his head. He admitted that it might perhaps be so. But I saw he could not quite accept it. Not yet. One thing was clear to me. The only way for me to help Lawrence in the slightest degree, or for Lawrence to help me, was for me to keep my hands off him. He knew this, with so much more besides. It couldn't be helped. The surprising thing was how much it meant just to have met and to know him.

He brought his sister Ada to see me one day. I had been baking oatcakes. We sat chatting and nibbling happily at the crisp warm oatmeal. He loved Ada. He told me afterwards that he and she had felt constrained together in all other London company except mine.

In small ways Lawrence could often be, as he has confessed in one of his 'Assorted Articles,' 'a bit false.' He could not bear being unpleasant to anybody's face. Once when I was at Byron Villas and he was in bed with a cold, a woman called. He heard her voice in the hall, grimaced viciously and in a whispered yell to Frieda said 'Don't let that woman come into my room!' But Frieda, not hearing or not caring or not contriving, ushered the visitor in. And Lawrence welcomed her quite charmingly. She could not possibly have guessed how he had looked and spoken a moment before.

IV

Till well on in December we were looking out ships for Lawrence to sail to Florida. But he was too ill, and the War made it all too difficult.　So he gave it up.　He spent Christmas week with his sisters at Ripley.

We got here with a struggle.　How terrible it is to return into the past like this—with the future quivering far off forsaken—to turn back to the past.

No wonder Lawrence hated Proust!　For a poet born in the mining Midlands there can be no *récherche du temps perdu*, behind sound-proof walls while the present goes by to muffled drums outside.　The mining Midlands see to that.　And I, from Glasgow, understood it, just as Katherine Mansfield from the sweeter home in New Zealand, could not.　Being herself able to be playful, affectionate, whimsical about 'home,' she felt a shade reproachful and superior towards those who could not.　For Lawrence, the more deeply touched he had been, the more he had suffered and been outraged.　The past had been no 'very perfect nest' for him.　But the scenes of childhood and youth, of course, have a clutching hold on the heart, and on Lawrence's more than on most.

Christmas over, he accepted most gratefully an invitation from the J. D. Beresfords to use their house at Padstow in Cornwall.　Never would he forget this kindness.　He began there by being two weeks in bed, but did not cease working.　In February *Amores* was returned by a publisher, together with 'instructions as to how to write poetry.'　Which elicited from Lawrence a letter calling his critic 'impertinent and foolish and presumptuous.'

My review of *The Rainbow* (to which the angry attention of my editor was drawn only after the prosecution) had lost me my reviewing of ten years' standing on the *Glasgow Herald*.　Lawrence did not hear of this till he was in Cornwall.　He wrote to me 'I am sorry about your reviewing because I believe you enjoyed the bit you had.　And one *does not* want to be martyred.' Somehow from this I understood that he thought it a good thing for me, if I could take it so, that I was cut off from that sort of newspaper work. I now think he was right in this.

Chiefly to keep in touch with him, and because I knew he liked it, I kept sending him poems of mine. There was only one—a Hardyesque poem about a graveyard—that he thought good. But he found fault with it for being 'verse which in spirit bursts all the old world, and yet goes corseted in rhymed scansion,' though immediately afterwards he apologised for his 'scribblings on it,' as 'only impertinent suggestions.' He need not have apologised. It was not a very good poem, though it had merit. The chief thing for me was that he recognised in it that bit of merit.

Of another he wrote:

There is a really good conception of a poem: but you have not given yourself with sufficient passion to the creating, to bring it forth. I'm not sure that I want you to—there is something tragic and displeasing about a woman who writes—but I suppose Sapho [*sic*] is as inevitable and as right as Shelley—but you must burn, to be a Sapho—burn at the stake. And Sapho is the only woman poet.

Or:

The essence of poetry with us in this age of stark and unlovely actualities is a stark directness, without a shadow of a lie, or a shadow of deflection anywhere. Everything can go, but this stark, bare, rocky directness of statement, this alone makes poetry, to-day.

Or he told how he liked Cornwall, which for him was a true land's end.

. . . It is not England. It is bare and dark and elemental, Tristan's land. I lie looking down at a cove where the waves come white under a low, black headland, which slopes up in bare green-brown, bare and sad under a level sky. It is old, Celtic, pre-Christian. Tristan and his boat, and his horn.

Again:

I love being here: such a calm, old, slightly deserted house—
a farmhouse; and the country remote and desolate and unconnected; it belongs to the days before Christianity, the days of the
Druids, or of desolate Celtic magic and conjuring and the sea is so
grey and shaggy, and the wind so restless, as if it had never found
a home since the days of Iseult. Here I think my life begins again
—one is free. Here the autumn is gone by, it is pure winter of
forgetfulness. I love it. Soon I shall begin to write a story—a
midwinter story of oblivion.

He was writing 'erratically,' being several times down
with his 'wintry inflammation' and 'so seedy he thought he
was dead'—'so ill that nearly everything has gone out of me
but a sort of abstract strength.' But he was hopeful—'this
is the last turn—I shall be solid again in a week.'

Philip Heseltine (the late 'Peter Warlock') had stayed
with them for eight weeks and—other plans for it having
fallen through—he and Heseltine had a scheme by which
The Rainbow would be published for subscribers at 7s. 6d.

I possess what may well be the only surviving copy of
the prospectus, a printed slip with a subscription form
attached. I reproduce the text here.

THE RAINBOW BOOKS AND MUSIC

Either there exists a sufficient number of people to buy books
because of their reverence for truth, or else books must die. In
its books lie a nation's vision; and where there is no vision the
people perish.

The present system of production depends entirely upon the
popular esteem: and this means gradual degradation. Inevitably,
more and more, the published books are dragged down to the level
of the lowest reader.

It is monstrous that the herd should lord it over the uttered word. The swine has only to grunt disapprobation, and the very angels of heaven will be compelled to silence.

It is time that enough people of courage and passionate soul should rise up to form a nucleus of the living truth; since there must be those among us who care more for the truth than for any advantage.

For this purpose it is proposed to attempt to issue privately such books and musical works as are found living and clear in truth; such books as would either be rejected by the publisher, or else overlooked when flung into the trough before the public.

This method of private printing and circulation would also unseal those sources of truth and beauty which are now sterile in the heart, and real works would again be produced.

It is proposed to print first *The Rainbow*, the novel by Mr. D. H. Lawrence, which has been so unjustly suppressed. If sufficient money is forthcoming, a second book will be announced; either Mr. Lawrence's philosophical work, *Goats and Compasses*, or a new book by some other writer.

All who wish to support the scheme should sign the accompanying form and send it at once to the Secretary, PHILIP HESELTINE, Cefn Bryntalch, Abermule, Montgomeryshire.

To justify himself and discredit Lawrence Murry has attributed the *Signature* and this second scheme to a single motive.[1] Did they not follow upon each other with an interval of only a few months? This is plausible at first sight. But it omits a major circumstance—namely that it was just within this interval that *The Rainbow* was prosecuted. At the date of the *Signature* such an event was not to be foreseen, and it made all the difference to Lawrence as a writer. It was one thing to know that editors could not be expected to accept difficult contributions like 'The Crown'; quite another thing to realise that publishers, hitherto amenable, would fight shy of future novels by the

---

[1] *Reminiscences.*

author of *The Rainbow*. One must recall that the now
familiar private presses did not then exist, anyhow not so far
as Lawrence's need was concerned. It was out of this
particular need that the second project arose. Though I
could not believe that it would come to anything more than
a possible reissue of *The Rainbow*, this was enough to make
me a hopeful subscriber. Support, however, was lacking. The
project fell through. That summer *Twilight in Italy* and
Amores would be 'flung into the trough' in the ordinary way.

At the beginning of March Lawrence and Frieda, finding
Cornwall congenial, went to Zennor thinking to look for a
furnished house:—'lovely pale hills, all gorse and heather,
and an immense peacock sea spreading all below.'

They stayed at the inn, the Tinners' Arms, for a fortnight,
then moved amid snow blizzards to an unfurnished cottage
not far off—at Higher Tregerthen on the St. Ives road.
Here 'under the moor and above the sea' they would 'live
in poverty and quiet.' They started collecting their scattered
bits of things from London. On leaving Byron Villas they
had distributed for storage, among their friends, anything
they wished to keep. One of these things was my mirror.

But the great attraction of the place to Lawrence was
that there were really two cottages, the one behind on the
seaward side being an annexe to the one fronting the road.
Both were the same size—'two *good* rooms and a scullery'—
and cost the same, £5 a year. Might not this be the nucleus
of that which had been Lawrence's dream? The thought
filled him with new health. And of course it was spring.
'I am beginning to feel strong again,' he wrote, 'life coming
in at the unseen sources,' though he was also 'so tired, so
tired, so tired of the world' that he could have died there
and then were it not that 'one must not die without having
known a real good life, and a fulfilment, a happiness that is
born of a new world from a new centre.'

I believe, if we cannot discover a terrestrial America there are new continents of the soul for us to land upon. Virgin soil. Only one must get away from this foul old world, one must have the strength to depart. . . .

In the same letter he speaks of the Murrys coming to live at Tregerthen. 'It is always my idea, that a few people by being together should bring to pass a new earth and a new heaven.'

But in the next letter, though still cheerfully engaged in furnishing—

I have made a dresser, which is painted royal blue, and the walls are pale pink! Also a biggish cupboard for the food, which looks like a rabbit hutch in the back place. Here, doing one's own things in this queer outlandish *Celtic* country I feel fundamentally happy and free, beyond.

—he already knows that there can be no abiding place for him in Cornwall:

It is queer, how almost everything has gone out of me, all the world I have known, and the people, gone out like candles. When I think of ——, or ——, even perhaps the Murrys who are here, it is with a kind of weariness, as of trying to remember a light which is blown out. Somehow it is all gone, both I and my friends have ceased to be, and there is another country, where there are no people, and even I myself am unknown, to myself as well.

He continued to take an interest in us, sending kindly messages to Donald, asking for our news and encouraging me to write. He thought me culpably lazy about writing and too strenuous in other ways. That spring he wrote:

I am very glad to hear of the novel. I firmly believe in it. I think you are the only woman I have met, who is so intrinsically unattached, so essentially separate and isolated, as to be a real writer or artist or recorder. Your relations with other people are only excursions from yourself. And to want children, and

common human fulfilments, is rather a falsity for you, I think.
You were never made to 'meet and mingle,' but to remain intact,
essentially, whatever your experiences may be. Therefore I believe
your book will be a real book, and a woman's book: one of the
very few.

He himself was busy helping to settle the Murrys in his
annexe.

Murry has told [1] how, in response to Lawrence's urgent
invitation, he and Katherine had left the French Riviera,
where they were snatching a brief, half-guilty happiness
under the nose of the War, and what a failure the Cornish
experiment was 'right from the beginning.' His account
shows how they each suffered in their different ways.

Lawrence, in his account to me, was brief and to the
point as usual.

The Murrys have gone over to the South side, about thirty
miles away. The North side was too rugged for them and Murry
and I are not really associates. How I deceive myself. I am a
liar to myself about people. I was angry when you ran over a list
of my 'friends'—whom you did *not* think much of. But it is true,
they are not much, any of them. I give up having intimate friends
at all. It is a self-deception. But I do wish somebody produced
some real work. I am very anxious to see your book.

If I am not conscripted, and Carswell isn't, I think we shall
furnish a *nice* room in the Murrys house, and if you would like to
come and stay in it, we should be glad. Barbara Low has an old
invitation for part of her summer holiday—she is our only prospect
in the visitor way. I like her enough.

It is very fine here, foxgloves now everywhere between the
rocks and ferns. There is some magic in the country. It gives me
a strange satisfaction.

Many greetings from us both to you and Carswell.

After a dose of Murry Lawrence was always well dis-

---

[1] *Reminiscences.*

posed toward Donald. He felt relief in thinking of someone who was unable to beat up emotions. 'I must say I quite frequently sympathise with his point of view,' he wrote to me much later. It was the same with the few men friends whom he met through us from time to time. These did not greatly interest him, and to some he was definitely hostile. But 'at least from Donald's friends one gets a *real* reaction, a true, human response,' he once said grimly. 'Better that than the Judas kiss of agreement which is no agreement.' It is significant that although Murry lived for weeks in the same house, he neither saw nor heard anything of the novel upon which Lawrence was working at the time.[1]

In the same letter he was anxious about my health. I had been overtired. Earlier he had written:

I think you have been exhausting yourself. . . . One has to withdraw into a very real solitude, and lie there, hidden, to recover. Then the world gradually ceases to exist, and a new world is discovered, where there are as yet no people. . . . I hope you will be better. Don't talk about me with those others.

Now in the later letter he went on:

. . . also you said how you alternate between a feeling of strength and productiveness, and a feeling of utter hopelessness and ash. I think that is fairly well bound to be, because I think your process of life is chiefly exhaustive, not accumulative at all. It is like a tree which, feeling the ivy tightening upon it, forces itself into bursts of utterance, bursts of flower and fruition, using up itself, not taking in any stores at all, till at last it is spent. I have seen elm trees do this—covered, covered with thick flowering, making scarcely any leaves, taking any food.

But one has to live according to one's own being, and if your method is productive and exhaustive, then it is so. Better that than mere mechanical activity, housework, etc. Tell me how the novel has got on. I think that is very important.

[1] *Reminiscences.*

V

This was in June, 1916. Though disappointed at his failure
to form a 'group' of the kind he desired—a kind different
in certain essentials from any of the groups imagined before
by men of prophetic genius—Lawrence did not strike me as
being unhappy. Rather he was angry, without depression.
He was annoyed by 'the idiotic and *false* review' of *Twilight
in Italy*, which appeared in *The Times Literary Supplement*
for 19th June, and told its readers that Lawrence 'might
have written a good book about Italy if he had been content
to take things simply, and to see no more than he really
saw'—which I take to mean no more than the reviewer
thought he would have seen himself! But he was nearing
the end of his novel, which he then thought to call *The
Sisters*. 'It has come rushing out, and I feel very triumphant in it,' he wrote to me. And to Pinker in May that
here was 'something quite new on the face of the earth,'
'a terrible and horrible and wonderful novel. You will
hate it and nobody will publish it. But there, these things
are beyond us.' The Murrys had served their turn in
Cornwall better than they knew; and because it was not
for this that Lawrence had asked them he must be absolved
from having 'used' them. Until he wrote *The Plumed Serpent*
he considered *Women in Love* his most important novel.

Ten days after his invitation to us he was going to
Penzance to be examined for military service. 'If I must be
a soldier, then I must—ta-rattatata! It's no use trying to
dodge one's fate. It doesn't trouble me any more. I'd
rather be a soldier than a school-teacher, anyhow.'

His next letter, which he wrote to me some days after he
had been examined and given exemption, is a useful commentary on the 'nightmare' passage in *Kangaroo*. It helps
to distinguish the 'voice' in Lawrence from the individual

man with his immediate reactions, both of which he fought
to maintain in their differing integrities.

'Something makes me state my position when I write to
you,' he says.

'. . . It was experience enough for me, of soldiering. I
am sure I should die in a week if they kept me. It is the
annulling of all one stands for, this militarism, the nipping of
the very germ of one's being.' He proceeds:—

Yet I liked the men. They all seemed so *decent*. And yet they all
seemed as if they had *chosen wrong*. It was the underlying sense of
disaster that overwhelmed me. They are all so brave, to suffer, but
none of them brave enough, to reject suffering. They are all so noble,
to accept sorrow and hurt, but they can none of them demand happiness.
Their manliness all lies in accepting calmly this death, this loss of their
integrity. They must stand by their fellow-man: that is the motto.

This is what Christ's weeping over Jerusalem has brought us
to, a whole Jerusalem offering itself to the Cross. To me, this is
infinitely more terrifying than Pharisees and Publicans and Sinners,
taking *their* way to death. This is what the love of our neighbour
has brought us to, that, because one man dies, we all die.

This is the most terrible madness. And the worst of it all is
that it is a madness of righteousness. These Cornish are most,
most unwarlike, soft, peaceable, ancient. No men could suffer
more than they at being conscripted—at any rate, those that were
with me. Yet they accepted it all: they accepted it, as one of them
said to me, with wonderful purity of spirit—I could howl my eyes
up over him—because 'they believed first of all in their duty to
their fellow-man.' There is no falsity about it: they believe in
their duty to their fellow-man. And what duty is this, which
makes us forfeit everything, because Germany invaded Belgium?
Is there nothing beyond my fellow-man? If not, then there is
nothing beyond myself, beyond my own throat, which may be cut,
and my own purse, which may be slit: because *I* am the fellow-man
of all the world, my neighbour is but myself in a mirror. So we
toil in a circle of pure egoism.

This is what 'love thy neighbour as thyself' comes to. It needs only a little convulsion, to break the mirror, to turn over the coin, and there I have myself, my own purse, I, I, I, we, we, we—like the newspapers to-day: 'Capture the trade—unite the Empire— *à bas les autres.*'

There needs something else besides the love of the neighbour. If all my neighbours chose to go down the slope to Hell, that is no reason why I should go with them. I know in my own soul a truth, a right, and no amount of neighbours can weight it out of the balance. I know that for me the war is wrong. I know that if the Germans wanted my little house, I would rather give it them than fight for it: because my little house is not important enough to me. If another man must fight for his house, the more's the pity. But it is his affair. To fight for possessions, goods, is what my soul *will not* do. Therefore it will not fight for the neighbour who fights for his own goods.

All this war, this talk of nationality, to me is false. I *feel* no nationality, not fundamentally. I feel no passion for my own land, nor my own house, nor my own furniture, nor my own money. Therefore I won't pretend any. Neither will I take part in the scrimmage, to help my neighbour. It is his affair to go in or to stay out, as he wishes.

If they had compelled me to go in, I should have died, I am sure. One is too raw, one fights too hard already, for the real integrity of one's being. That last straw of compulsion would have been too much, I think.

Christianity is based on the love of self, the love of property, one degree removed. Why should I care for my neighbour's property, or my neighbour's life, if I do not care for my own? If the truth of my spirit is all that matters to me, in the last issue, then on behalf of my neighbour, all I care for is the truth of *his* spirit. And if his truth is his love of property, I refuse to stand by him, whether he be a poor man robbed of his cottage, his wife and children, or a rich man robbed of his merchandise. I have nothing to do with him, in that wise, and I don't care whether he keep or lose his throat, on behalf of his property. Property, and power—

which is the same—is *not* the criterion.   The criterion is the truth
of my own intrinsic desire, clear of ulterior contamination.

Lawrence had now finished *Women in Love* all but the
title and epilogue chapter, and was starting to type it himself.
'It will be a labour—but we have no money.   But I am
asking Pinker for some.'   And he had bought about a pound's
worth of furniture (described in detail with prices) for the
two rooms of the annexe.

It is such a pleasure, buying this furniture—I remember my
sermon.   But one doesn't really care.   This cottage, that I like so
much—and the new table, and the chairs—I could leave them all
to-morrow, blithely.   Meanwhile they are very nice.

What I wrote in answer to this, the longest letter I had
yet had from Lawrence, I cannot wholly remember; but I
certainly told him that he seemed in his attitude to property
to admit something of the Christian spirit.   This brought
from him a letter twice as long as the last, and to me even
more interesting.   He began by saying I was right on 'nearly
all' my points and that he wanted people 'to be more Christian
rather than less: only for different reasons.'

Christianity is based on re-action, on negation really.   It says
'renounce all worldly desires, and live for heaven.'   Whereas I
think people ought to fulfil sacredly their desires.   And this means
fulfilling the deepest desire, which is a desire to live unhampered
by things which are extraneous, a desire for pure relationships and
living truth.   The Christian was hampered by property, because
he must renounce it.   And to renounce a thing is to be subject to
it.   Reaction against any force is the complement of that force.
So Christianity is based too much on reaction.

But Christianity is infinitely higher than the war, higher than
nationalism or even than family love.   I have been reading S.
Bernard's Letters, and I realise that the greatest thing the world
has seen is Christianity, and one must be endlessly thankful for it,
and weep that the world has learned the lesson so badly.

But I count Christianity as one of the great historical factors, the has-been. That is why I am not a conscientious objector: I am not a Christian. Christianity is insufficient in me. I too believe man must fight.

But because a thing *has been*, therefore I will not fight for it. Because, in the cruder stage, a man's property is symbol for his manhood, I will not fight for the symbol. Because this is a *falling back*. Don't you see, all your appeal is to the testimony of *the past*. And we must break through the film which encloses us one with the past, and come out into the new. All those who stand one with the past, with our past, as a nation and a Christian people even (though the Christian appeal IN THE WAR is based on property recognition—which was really the point of my last letter) must go to the war: but those who believe in a life better than *what has been*, they can view the war only with grief, as a great falling back.

I would say to my Cornishmen, 'Don't let your house and home be a symbol of your manhood.' Because it has been the symbol for so long, it has exhausted us, become a prison. So we fight, desperate and hopeless. 'Don't let your nation be a symbol of your manhood' —because a symbol is something static, petrified, turning towards what has been, and crystallised against that which shall be. Don't look to the past for justification. The Peloponnesian war was the death agony of Greece, really, not her life struggle. I am just reading Thucydides—when I can bear to—it is too horrible to see a people, adhering to traditions, fling itself down the abyss of the past, and disappear.

We must have the courage to cast off the old symbols, the old traditions: at least, put them aside, like a plant in growing surpasses its crowning leaves with higher leaves and buds. There is something beyond the past. The past is no justification. Unless from us the future takes place, we are death only. That is why I am not a conscientious objector. The great Christian tenet must be surpassed, there must be something new: neither the war, nor the turning the other cheek.

What we want is the fulfilment of our desires, down to the deepest and most spiritual desire. The body is immediate, the spirit is beyond: first the leaves and then the flower: but the plant is an integral whole: therefore *every* desire, to the very deepest. And I shall find my deepest desire to be a wish for pure, unadulterated relationship with the universe, for truth in being. My pure relationship with one woman is marriage, physical and spiritual: with another, is another form of happiness, according to our nature. And so on for ever.

It is this establishing of pure relationships which makes heaven, wherein we are immortal, like the angels, and mortal, like men, both. And the way to immortality is in the fulfilment of desire. I would never *forbid* any man to make war, or to go to war. Only I would say, 'Oh, if you don't spontaneously and perfectly *want* to go to war, then it is wrong to go—don't let *any* extraneous consideration influence you, nor any old tradition mechanically compel you. If you *want* to go to war, go, it is your righteousness.'

Because, you see, what intimation of immortality have we, save our spontaneous wishes? God works in me (if I use the term God) as my desire. He gives me the understanding to discriminate between my desires, to discern between greater and lesser desire: I can also frustrate or deny any desire: so much for me, I have a 'free will,' in so far as I am an entity. But God in me is my desire. Suddenly, God moves afresh in me, a new motion. It is a new desire. So a plant unfolds leaf after leaf, and then buds, till it blossoms. So do we, under the unknown impulse of desires, which arrive in us from the unknown.

But I have the power to choose between my desires. A man comes to me and says, 'Give me your house.' I ask myself, 'Which do I want more, my house, or to fight?' So I choose.

In nearly all men, now, the greater desire is *not* to fight for house and home. They will prove to themselves, by fighting, that their greater desire, on the whole, was *not* to fight for their nation, or sea-power, but to know a new value, to recognise a new, stronger desire in themselves, more spiritual and gladdening. Or else they will die. But many will die falsely. *All* Greece died. It must not be so again, we must have more sense. It is cruelly sad to see men caught in the clutches of the past, working automatically in the spell of an authorised desire that is a desire no longer. That *should not be*.

In the same letter he refers to his story *England, My England!* which he had written about a year before (though it had only recently appeared in the *English Review*) and had based so clearly as to give pain to kind friends. He had made the man in the story die in the War. Now, after his story was public property, he learned that the real man had since been killed in France.

It upsets me very much to hear of P—— L——. I did not know he was dead. I wish that story at the bottom of the sea, before ever it had been printed. Yet, it seems to me, man must find a new expression, give a new value to life, or his women will reject him, and he must die. I liked M—— L—— the best of the M——s really. She was the one who was capable of honest love: she and M——. L—— was, somehow, a spiritual coward. But who isn't? I ought never, never to have gone to live at ——. Perhaps M—— L—— won't be hurt by that wretched story—that is all that matters. If it was a true story, it shouldn't really damage.

But in a postscript he adds, 'No, I *don't* wish I had never written that story. It should do good, at the long run.'

Such quotations contain useful examples of the bewildering thoroughness with which Lawrence preferred life before logic. It must be faced that he was consistent only in the faithfulness of his aim and the unconstraint of his expression. He can rejoice in his possessions yet part with them to-morrow, exalt Christianity yet forsake it, regret his pain-giving story yet abide by it.

In another passage from the same letter he treats of the deception—as he considered it—which lay in the procreation of children by those who have in themselves no other hope than this, to bring forth.

There are plenty of children, and no hope. If women can bring forth hope, they are mothers indeed. Meanwhile even the mice increase—they cannot help it. What is this highest, this procreation? It is a lapsing back to the primal origins, the brink of oblivion. It is a tracing back, when there is no going forward, a throwing life on to the bonfire of death and oblivion, an autumnal act, a consuming down. This is a winter. Children and child-bearing do not make spring. · It is not in children the future lies. The Red Indian mothers bore many children, and yet there *are* no Red Indians. It is the truth, the new perceived hope, that makes spring. And let them bring forth that, who can: they are the creators of life. There are many enceinte widows, with a new crop of death in their wombs. What did the mothers of the dead soldiers bring forth, in childbed?—death or life? And of death you gather death: when you sow death, in this act of love which is pure reduction, you reap death, in a child born with an impulse towards the darkness, the origins, the oblivion of all.

Yet another passage speaks of that kind of 'disastrous act of love'

which is a pure thrill, is a kind of friction between opposites, interdestructive, an act of death. There is an extreme *self-realisation, self-sensation,* in this friction against the really hostile, opposite. But there must be an act of love which is a passing of the self into a pure relationship with the other, something new and creative in the coming together of the lovers, in their creative spirit, before a new child can be born: a new *flower* in us before there can be a new seed of a child.

Soon afterwards I was to have an argument with Lawrence about what then seemed to me his arbitrariness. He had said, I think, that he could foretell with absolute certainty from any given couple whether a child born of that couple would be in his sense of the word a 'living and life-giving child or a deathly and retrogressive one.' But I pleaded that there was always an unknown element, and that

this element had a way of upsetting the wisest calculations.
'The wind bloweth where it listeth' was my way of putting
it, and I held that God or nature had always an odd trick up
the sleeve. Lawrence, however, would have none of this;
anyhow, not then. Neither would he in such a case admit of
chance.

VI

Lack of money was again the difficulty: lack of money and
Frieda's insistence that she must see her children in London
when their autumn term began—for which again money
was needed. Her only way of seeing them was to wait outside of their schools as they came out, so to walk along,
have a word with them, give them some small gift, and keep
herself fresh in their memories. Lawrence hated and disapproved of this. But Frieda stayed firm.

By the middle of July they had exactly £6 left in the
world, and Lawrence had not been well. The *Smart Set*,
from which he had been able at times to get £10 for a poem,
had changed hands and did not want his work. There was
only a tentative offer from an American magazine, *The Seven
Arts*, for stories at a cent a word. He had poems for sale,
and stories, and four-fifths of *Women in Love* (which had
now acquired this title) in a pencil draft, which he jibbed at
typing himself and could not afford to send out. As soon as
it was finished, he would try to write *only* 'family' stories
that would be immediately saleable in some such magazine
as the *Strand*. He loathed alike debts or obligations. But
meanwhile what? Nothing for it but to apply once more to
Pinker.

Pinker, still hopeful of the financial future and always
kindly, sent along £50 on the strength of the unseen MS.
Then—lovely and unexpected—came a letter from Amy
Lowell in America enclosing a present of £60. Being her-

self a poet, she knew how to give in such a way that acceptance by another poet was as little painful as possible.   So
Lawrence thanked her warmly.   Prophets still are fed!

He foresaw, however, that *Women in Love* would be a
difficult piece of goods to sell.   And though he never once
failed to deliver solid commodities for every advance by his
agent, he chafed against this 'imminent dependence' on 'a
sort of charity.'   If only some publisher might see his way to
subsidise him.   Could not Pinker bring this about?   In
Cornwall he could live, he said, on £150 a year.   With £200
a year he 'could send everybody to the devil.'   Pinker said he
would try.   No doubt he did try.   But nothing came of it.

At this juncture a young and admiring American journalist, Robert Mountsier, had come to England largely that
he might make Lawrence's acquaintance.   With him came
a girl friend, Esther Andrews, who lived by drawings of a
frankly journalistic sort for the magazines.   These two went
down to stay for a time in the annexe in Cornwall.   Both
were immediately and violently attracted by Lawrence, and
Mountsier undertook to act, with Pinker's cognisance, as
Lawrence's short-story agent in U.S.A.

Though living with the Murrys had been a failure, and
they were away at Mylor near Falmouth, Lawrence kept in
communication with them and even visited them twice.   He
did not easily give people up.   Perhaps, he thought, it had
been a mistake living quite so close together.   People must
have room to be themselves without knocking against each
other at every turn.

In July he sent me *Amores*, which had found a home with
Duckworth and appeared that month with a dedication to
Ottoline Morrell.   Here were the last poems gathered from
his youth.   In August there was talk of his coming with
Frieda to London and using our house in September, but he
changed his mind and decided to let Frieda go by herself.—'I

can't come to London—spiritually *I cannot* . . . I am *much* too terrified and horrified by people—the world—nowadays. . . . I had much rather be Daniel in the lion's den, than myself in London. I am really terrified.' He was even terrified by the idea of 'getting into a big train.' It was decided in the same letter that I should pay my long-promised visit to them in Cornwall, arriving on September 3rd. Donald was asked too, but he could not get away. Other visitors by the middle of August had come and gone—

They make me feel how far off the world is—such stray, blown, sooty birds they seem. It is lovely to bathe and be alive now, in the strong remote days.

In the same letter he consults me about the title *Women in Love*. He does not feel at all sure of it. Lawrence often said he was 'no good at titles.' This did not prevent him from pouring forth suggestions for other people's books. Mine was to be '*The Wild Goose Chase*. It is so nice and gay.'

Or *The Rare Bird*, or *The Love Bird* (very nice that), or just *Cuckoo!* (splendid). Do call it *Cuckoo*, or even the double *Cuckoo! Cuckoo!* I'm sure something bird-like is right. *Cuckoo!* is so nice, that if you don't like it, I think I must have it instead of *Women in Love*. Then *Loose-strife* is a nice name. Then *Had* is a good one. *The Pelican in the Wilderness* is lovely, but perhaps inappropriate: I don't know. *The Lame Duck*—I'm sure there is a suggestion in the bird kingdom—*The Kingfisher*, which I am *sure* is appropriate, or *Ducks and Drakes*. Write me a postcard which one you choose: only *don't* be too seriously titled.

We shall be very glad to see you and the Hon. Bird on the 3rd September (historic day): The Hon. Bird is the book, which must be a bird: it isn't Carswell. I wish he were coming too.

In the letter of four days earlier:

I feel really eager about your novel. I feel it is coming under the same banner with mine. The 'us' will be books. There will be a fine wild little squadron soon, faring over the world. Nothing shall I welcome so much as books to ride with mine. Oh to see them go, a gallant little company, like ships over an unknown sea, and Pisarro and his people breaking upon a new world, the books, now.

This, after a letter in between, replying to my own suggestion of a title, *Bird of Paradise*, which referred to the legend that, being bereft of its feet, that bird can never alight:

We *love* the *Bird of Paradise* that is most beautiful and perfect a title—do not budge a hair's breadth further—the Hon. Bird is christened; we all dance his name-feast. Do, somewhere in the book, put the story of the Bird of Paradise—quite tiny.

I have thought that the plight of the heavenly but footless bird must have struck Lawrence as having a similarity with his own.

My visit to Cornwall was all happiness—of the quietest kind. It was my first stay with the Lawrences. I was their only visitor, sleeping in the other cottage, which I 'made' myself each day. Nothing particular happened. Chiefly we talked—though even that not so very much. We also walked, but not so very much either, as the weather was not of the best. One of the reasons I got on with Lawrence was that I enjoyed 'doing' ordinary things.

I seem to recall that Lawrence spoke a good deal of Dostoevsky. Murry had written a book about him and had sent a copy to Lawrence. Lawrence perfectly disagreed with Murry's findings, and was incisive as well as eloquent on the subject. It would appear that Murry stands by that book to-day,[1] although he finds it 'extravagant' as well as 'excessively intellectual'—two qualities that one might think hard to reconcile.

Lawrence's own view of Dostoevsky (by whom so many

[1] *Reminiscences*.

of us at the time were carried away) struck me then as difficult
to follow. It now appears as remarkably level-headed,
abounding in insight, and therefore surely, in the truest sense
of the word, intellectual. It is, indeed, very much the view
of the more advanced thinkers of to-day, with whom
Dostoevsky *as a thinker* has somewhat lost his place. According to Murry, 'Lawrence was willing to admit in theory
only,' 'that the "being" of man included his spiritual impulses also, and that these were just as profound and deep-
rooted as his sensual impulses'; but that when it came to
practice with Lawrence 'the spiritual and the sensual man
were implacably opposed. In practice, therefore, he could
only admit the one by denying the other. And it was the
spiritual man who had to be denied, and if possible anni-
hilated.' [1]

Now, as Murry writes this passage with reference to
Women in Love, I do not see how anything except theory—
i.e. thought—comes into question. In any case, one thing was
clear to me even then, when I understood so little what
Lawrence said or stood for, that alike in practice and in theory
Lawrence wanted nothing more than *equal power* for the
spiritual and the sensual. Were these implacably opposed in
life? Perhaps. But so were the two blood-streams within
the human body—the pure one coming from the heart implacably opposed to the charged one returning to the heart.
What Lawrence maintained was that now for too long the
spiritual had been given a spurious, an *ideal* lordship over
the sensual, as if the one blood-stream should be praised at
the expense of the other. He saw in himself, as in all his
generation, the disaster of a spiritual supremacy, which in the
end makes men first sensually and then spiritually impotent.
Because spiritual supremacy at the cost of sensual abnegation
was in his eyes inevitably followed by spiritual impotence.

[1] *Reminiscences.*

In restoring the just place and power of the sensual, the restorer must first *appear* to exalt it above the spiritual. But this is only in appearance and because the balance has been already destroyed. The theme of *Women in Love* is sensual impotence (not identical with sexual impotence) caused by the overweening lordly vanity of too long a reign of spiritual ideals. Hence it is intended to be what Murry was later to blame it for being, a 'deathly book'—deathly, but clearly displaying, for those who would see it, the hopeful seed of new human values. It was because Lawrence saw the restoration, the new adjustment, as so well worth fighting for, that he could neither enter into nor admire the point of view of Murry's soldier friend—that it was something fine 'to face death for a trick not worth an egg.' The trick for which Lawrence continually faced death and ultimately died was worth precisely an egg—the fertile egg of the future. And certainly the risking of death for anything worth less seemed to him either pose or folly. Still, Lawrence thought that Murry would perhaps come round. He was prepared to wait and to be friendly.

We carried on the daily work of the cottages without help from outside. With Lawrence one seemed, in such a case, to have enough time over for anything else one wanted. But the necessary daily jobs seemed so much a part of life that one did not fret to be done with them. Certain literary critics have found that in estimating Lawrence as a writer it is beside the point to note that even while washing up dishes he radiated life. But those who washed dishes with Lawrence know that it is not beside the point.

More than by his unceasing interest in my novel, which he had made me bring with me, I was pleased when he said that I 'fitted in' with their cottage life better than the Londoners did. Perhaps from his North Midland upbringing and origin, Lawrence had a warm feeling for Scotch

people. 'I don't care if every English person is my enemy,'
he wrote to me once later; 'if they wish it, so be it. I keep
a reserve for the Scotch.' He had not a good word to say
for the Irish character. He detested anything like professional 'charm.' There was prejudice here, of course, but
it could be tracked down to a radical feeling.[1] The inexpressiveness of the Northern temper, implying, as it does, a
distrust of easy verbal expression, was congenial to him just
as the so different Latin mentality with its subtle realism was
congenial. In the facile intellectualising of emotion he
found evidence of a certain poverty of nature. He saw this
at its worst in the Irish and the Americans. Here, however,
he was perhaps not more characteristic of the North than of
the English working class generally, whose experience it is
to associate true warmth with verbal inexpressiveness. 'I
think one understands best without explanations,' he said
often. Or of those who talked and talked—'they don't *want*
to understand.'

Another strongly 'working-class' trait in Lawrence was
his extreme distaste of anything that could be regarded as
indecent. It would indeed be easy to call him prudish. One
night in Cornwall, after having just begun to undress for
bed, I found I had left my book in the sitting-room where
Lawrence and Frieda still were, and I returned to fetch it.
I had brought no dressing-gown with me, but there seemed
to me no impropriety in my costume—an ankle-length
petticoat topped by a long-sleeved woollen vest! Lawrence,
however, rebuked me. He disapproved, he said, of people
appearing in their underclothes. No doubt, if I had not
privately believed my négligé to be attractive as well as decent,
I might neither have ventured to appear in it nor have felt

---

[1] Personal sympathies apart, Lawrence regarded 'Celtic' influences—
whether Welsh, Irish or Scottish—as essentially destructive of the English
genius and culture : this especially in politics.

so much abashed as I did by Lawrence's remark. So, essentially, Lawrence was right after all! How more than horrified he was—furious—when from his flat in Florence, looking across the Arno, he was compelled to overlook also a stretch of mud and shingle which the Florentine *gamins* found a convenient spot for the relief of nature. He hated the domestic dog on account of its too public habits. In such respects Lawrence was no advocate of what is often, but wrongly, called 'the natural.' Still less was he an apostle of the nude. I am sure that he put down all our civilised indecencies—our coquetries as well as our callousnesses, our sophisticated desire to shock as well as our prurience—to a departure from natural reticence. On first thoughts this may seem strange to those who have not considered the matter closely. On second thoughts it will be seen that such a man, and only such, could have become the author of *Lady Chatterley's Lover*.

All of Lawrence's critics and most of his friends were at this time united in wanting of him another *Sons and Lovers*. But with *The Rainbow* he had turned definitely away from any such easy end. How much strength was demanded in this turning away will not be fully known till his letters of the period are published.

Nobody who ever heard him describe the scenes and persons of his boyhood, or watched him recreate with uncanny mimicry the talk, the movements and the eccentricities of the men and women among whom he grew up, can doubt but that Lawrence, if he had liked, might have been a new kind of Dickens of the Midlands. Critics who contend that he was unable to create character or invent situations are confuted by the earlier scenes in *The Lost Girl* and by passage after passage from the short stories. We might have had from him a gallery of characters such as the housekeeper in *Lady Chatterley*, with all kinds of people—comic, touching or strange in their ordinary ways—if he had cared to try. Those who say, "What a pity he did not care!" have a point of view with which it is difficult not to sympathise at times. With Lawrence, and perhaps with Lawrence alone, the dumb cottagers and inexpressive 'workers' of industrial England might for the first time have found a voice. Even as it is, we now see them *because* of Lawrence, as they have not been seen before. We are pierced with a passional knowledge of them never even suggested by any other writer. But he has given us, practically speaking, no characters.

'Character' for Lawrence belonged to the dead past—to a way of life that he strove to transcend. Character, of course, was amusing and interesting, and would, of course, persist. But the interest in it was a literary interest, and so far as life goes, was static. Character—which Lawrence savoured as well as anybody—had been *used* as a demonstration of life until it had become stereotyped—a *made*, instead of a spontaneous thing. At the best it had now come to provide the merely sensational or merely intellectual excitement (and Lawrence found the modern division into sensationalism and intellectualism a division into two equal stalenesses) of working out a psychological problem. Given *a*, *b* and *c* acting upon each other and being acted upon by circumstances, what will be the result? All of which *seems* to have a lot to do with life, all of which is, indeed, so much the appearance of life that it is easy to mistake it for life itself. But it is not life.

The best writers have known by instinct that it is not. A writer like Hardy, as Lawrence well reveals in his exposition (everywhere rejected at the time and only recently published[1]), passes through the surface of human character to the deeper interest of life with its criss-cross currents beneath.

[1] *The Book-Collector's Quarterly*, Jan.-March, 1932. Also *John o' London's Weekly*, March 19th, 1932.

He shows his people in their relation to the moor and the sky. In our memory of their almost accidental conflicts with each other, we see rocks and trees and storms as equally, if not more truly, the protagonists.

One might continue showing at what points many of the most objective of our major novelists, including Dickens, make the necessary diving escape from character into the life flow. Lawrence went a stride further in consciousness and in practice than any before him. He repudiated 'character' entirely, and retained only the merest crust of outward form sufficient for the telling of a story. He knew so well how to tell a story, and his feeling for physical and outward appearances was so delicate and intense, that at first the repudiation is not noticed as such. It gives, however, the peculiar flavour to his books, which at first makes them so distasteful and so puzzling to many readers.

What is even more baffling than his repudiation of the old-fashioned, classic 'character,' is his refusal of the whole modern machinery of psychology. This, indeed, has been a greater stumbling-block than the other.

After *Sons and Lovers* he had been, naturally, pounced upon by the psycho-analysts; and for a short time he looked with interest, even fascination, into this new realm. But it was for a short time only. Quickly he saw in it merely another attempt at mechanisation which, by the time it was finished with us would have finished us as living beings. 'They can only help you more competently *to make your own feelings*. They can never let you *have* any real feelings,' as he said of one famous psychologist. And real feelings— a real self without any self-importance—was one of the things Lawrence thought worth fighting for.

So he turned not only from the old, but from the modern, the contemporaneous, the 'latest.' And he was lonely, which he found hard to bear.

Murry has made the frank confession that, much as he and Katherine Mansfield delighted in Lawrence as a man and a talent, they were 'against him' in his aims from as early as 1915.[1] But Murry goes on to say that all Lawrence's friends were against him. This is overstating the case. There was always a minority that believed enough in Lawrence throughout to believe also that his aim must be right.

I, for one, admitted that I did not comprehend his philosophy or see what he was driving at. But I knew that Lawrence was no madman and I was convinced that his combination of qualities was not to be found in association with a mistaken man. Besides this, though each new book, *as a book*, came to me as a disappointment, there was not only a curious cumulative effect, but there was in each book that which had the power to enter into the texture of one's life and to work there like a leaven. Who else was writing books which even partially possessed this power? So far as I could see, nobody. I was therefore prepared to take Lawrence on trust as somebody who must be essentially right or he would not possess either this power or this persistence. I began to understand how far from his aims was the production of 'masterpieces.'

Knowing this of me, Lawrence forgave my intellectual shortcomings. I would grow up, he said, and he was ready to love anybody who would grow up. 'But the hideous wasters who will only rot in the bud, how I hate them!' And again—'They don't *want* to understand, that's what is wrong.' So our friendship remained. But I was a very small drop of sweet water in his bucket. At times even Frieda feared that he was mad, declared that she would have to leave him, and shouted at him that she 'hated' all his writings now.

[1] *Reminiscences.*

This, of course, was said in anger, but it had enough in it to present itself as a ready weapon when there came the desire to wound. Lawrence knew how to take it. He was sure, as he had a right to be, of Frieda's fundamental sympathy, co-operation and courage. But he knew also, that being a woman and in untried circumstances, Frieda might at any time go back upon him momentarily. I, being a woman, should no doubt have done the same in her place, if in my different way. But I was not in her place and faith was easy for me. In Frieda Lawrence reckoned on such brief defections and, at the expense of a bit of rage, discounted them. They were not of the same order as the intellectual defections of those cleverer friends who were guilty of emotional stupidity.

VII

I was present at many 'rows' between Lawrence and Frieda, some of them violent and exhausting enough. But I never felt any one of them to be of that deadly 'painful' nature which is of frequent occurrence between many couples who all the while protest their love with endearments and never get within arm's length of violence. It was indeed the thing about Lawrence which I understood best at this time, and it made me see in him a courage that I never saw in any other man in the same degree. Nor had I read of it, for it was something utterly remote from what is usually understood as the subjection of a woman by a man, in that it was free from egoism on the man's part, free too from bullying or any reliance on tradition. Lawrence asserted himself on the strength of his power. And he asserted the male principle, which he believed was destined to lead. But there was no egoism in it, and it left Frieda the utmost liberty of her female assertion, so long as she did not try to 'put across' mere female egoism. On his male egoism, should it appear, she was welcome to jump with all her weight. She did. Since then I have come across a similar spirit in some of Gaudier-Brzeska's letters. Most other men—a notable instance occurs to me in Robert Louis Stevenson—seem always to have shirked the true marriage issue, and so played false with disastrous effect both to their women and to their own manhood. But Lawrence was no shirker, just as he was no seeker of conquest over another human being for the sake of conquest. '. . . if we break, or conquer anyone . . . it's like breaking the floor joists, you're sure to go through into the cellar, and cripple yourself.' He succeeded in making Frieda pay the required tribute and become, in doing so, the most triumphant woman in the world.

He had chosen (after shattering misadventures for which he largely laid the blame upon himself) a woman from whom he felt he could win the special submission he demanded without thereby defeating her in her womanhood. Sometimes it seemed to us that he had chosen rather a force of nature—a female force—than an individual woman. Frieda was to Lawrence by turns a buffeting and a laughing breeze, a healing rain or a maddening tempest of stupidity, a cheering sun or a stroke of indiscriminate lightning. She was mindless Womanhood, wilful, defiant, disrespectful, argumentative, assertive, vengeful, sly, illogical, treacherous, unscrupulous and self-seeking. At times she hated Lawrence and he her. There were things she jeered at in him and things in her that maddened him—things that neither would consent to subdue. But partly for that very reason—how he *admired* her! And to be ardently admired by Lawrence was something of a rarity and it meant that the admired one was somebody rare. In Frieda Lawrence found a magnificent female probity of being, as well as of physical well-being. She could bear the pressure of his male probity—his 'demon'—as no

other woman could have borne it.   Sure in herself she could
accept anything and recover from anything.   She was the
'freest' woman he had ever met, and if not mild she was by
Lawrence teachable.   She had this rare virtue—teachable-
ness without mildness.   Much will be written—something
has already been written about Frieda!   For myself, I find
that in her own very different way Frieda is a person as remarkable as Lawrence, and that Lawrence knew it.   Two
things are certain: that in all his journeyings he never saw
another woman whom he would or could have put in her
place: also, that Lawrence cannot be accepted without
acceptation of his wife.   Recently, in a popular daily newspaper as a result of an English home-to-home domestic inquiry,
I saw some such heading as this: 'The Old Loyalties Gone,
Husband and Wife now Simply Good Pals.'   Lawrence
and Frieda had dispensed with most of the 'old loyalties.'
Each was capable of bitter complaints against the other uttered
behind the other's back to a third party.   But they kept the
most ancient loyalty of all, and they never descended into
being good pals.   Lawrence with Frieda was the man who
does not shirk woman in any of her aspects.   In return for
her profound submission as wife to husband, he offered her
fidelity and richness of life.   She was a long time in coming
to it.   But the exchange, as I believe, was made.   In passing
it may be said—or rather circumstances compel that it should
be said—that if Lawrence had not been potent in body as well
as in spirit he would never have had Frieda to wife, or having
her would not have kept her.   The suggestion has been made,
though vaguely, that because the marriage was without issue
Lawrence was impotent.   To accept that would be to make
both Lawrence and Frieda and all the circumstances of their
life together a lie.   But the untruth lies elsewhere.   This is
not the place in which to discuss or expose it.   It must however be mentioned and denied.

I have said I was present at many rows between these two extraordinary people, the one so richly endowed with physical life, the other subtly and magnificently endowed with mind, responding with natural delight to the minds of others, yet bending all the force of his own to break the dominance of mind in our modern ways, and to destroy 'ideal' reactions in favour of true reactions out of which life would come trembling and renewed.

When I first arrived in Cornwall they told me in concert of a quarrel that had taken place shortly before. I don't remember what it was about—probably Frieda's children— but it had been fought out to what Lawrence took to be a finish, and he had gone into the scullery at the back to wash up. While he was thus engaged, with his back to the living-room door, singing quietly to himself (Lawrence was slightly deaf) and working with a bit of a clatter at the enamel wash bowl, Frieda came in from the living-room carrying one of the stone dinner plates. His unconcerned roundelay after what had just passed (I only wish I knew which song, sacred or profane, Lawrence chose on this occasion) so wrought upon her that her wrath boiled up afresh. Down on the singer's head she brought the dinner plate.

It hurt him very much and might, of course, have injured him seriously. But he was as far from bearing Frieda a grudge as from turning the other cheek. 'That was like a woman!' said he turning on her viciously, but on this occasion too much astonished to strike back. ' No man could have done such a thing when the quarrel was over, and from behind too! But as you *are* a woman,' he added ruefully, 'you were right to do as you felt. It was only lucky you didn't kill me. You might have. These plates are hard and heavy.'

No, Lawrence was no pacifist, though he could make peace; and he was far from believing that emotional differences could be settled by arbitration.   Rather, he would say, the more we recognise essential differences the nearer we are to true peace.   Also, the more we deny or elude that physical violence which is inherent in life, the more we deny to one another and ourselves those precious renewals of the vital flow which are to be had in no other way.   By our denial of them we are driven to indulge in the perverse or apologetic violence of sensationalism in its many forms.   Week-days and Sundays we cannot have too many murders to read about, and the slow ideal deaths we undergo are in the end worse than those of either the real murderer or his victim.   Being ourselves poverty-stricken in fear, in rage, in magic, in physical response, we crave for these things more than for bread.   Go into the first cinema theatre and see how we devour the husks that swine would refuse.   We do not even know in what our need consists.   It is our illusion, the great illusion of civilisation, that we have outgrown the simple magic of touch and of wonder, which is a kind of touch.   Just as we have put the moon into our pocket encyclopedias, and when we weep with boredom do not realise that we are crying for the moon in our blood: so, poor in the magic of naturally enlivening reactions of the blood from which fresh life can issue constantly, we are driven to that false, mechanical, organised reaction which is modern warfare.   The Great War came, Lawrence would have it, when we were individually too frightened to fight, too Christian to smite, too meek or indifferent to respond to insult with swift violence.

Danger apart, there was nothing terrible about Frieda's rages, though Lawrence's did make you sit up and look out. Even so, I never felt any sense of shame or of lasting misery as with so many human rages.   True, Lawrence never really raged at me.   Frieda, baffled and afraid of his intensity, felt more than once that he was mad and that she would have to leave him.   But the feeling soon passed.   She knew well

enough that even beyond his own conscious knowledge he
was fighting her for something worth while in which she
could share.

That I knew it too, was one of the reasons Lawrence
put up with me. On this same visit Frieda appealed to me—
not so much asking counsel as relieving herself by declama-
tion to another woman in Lawrence's presence—'What
would you do, Catherine, if you had a man like that to deal
with?' And I recall how deeply pleased they both seemed
when I said I would thank my stars that a man like Lawrence should think it worth while to fight things out with
me and bear no grudge that I fought with him.

This may not be missed in speaking of Lawrence. What
here and there a pure artist like Gaudier will half-practise
for a time by instinct, and perhaps before long throw up in
despair, Lawrence felt it his business to maintain as the first
urgent condition for everybody's health and happiness. A
revised relation between the man and the woman was
needed, and that not chiefly for the artist's sake, as in Gaudier's
case, but for the sake of any man and woman who would be
really alive.

'It needs a man and a woman to create anything,' he
wrote to me that autumn, '. . . there is nothing can be
created save of two, a two-fold spirit.' He put from him as
a devilish temptation the idea that in singleness there was
strength. In singleness of aim, certainly; in severance
from the world of conformity; even in renunciation of
adherents—alas! this also, as it must be! But never in the
sexual pride of singleness which he took to be a denial of
life at its source.

It is those who are married who should live the life of con-
templation together. In the world, there is the long day of destruction to go by. But let those who are single, man torn from
woman, woman from man, men all together, women all together,

separate violent and deathly fragments, each returning and adhering to its own kind, the body of life torn in two, let these finish the day of destruction, and those who have united go into the wilderness to know a new heaven and a new earth.

I hope I have made it clear that a miserable account of Lawrence at this time, or any other, would be a false and misleading account. He had far too magnificent a talent for enjoyment, far too fine a capacity for work, to be miserable in the true sense of misery, which is dreariness, regret, sterility and doubt. He had an aim worth struggling for to the utmost, and he felt himself growing strong in and for the struggle. One day you might hear him say he felt like never writing another line. And this he said, not so much in despair, as in the furious determination that life held better things than books. But within a week or so he would be sending you a volume of new poems in MS., or one of a series of essays that nobody would publish, or telling you that he was triumphantly typing the last chapter of a novel. At intervals he burned piles of MSS. Once he almost set the chimney on fire and revelled in its roaring. He enjoyed warming his hands at such fires of outgrown life. All along, when no entirely new thing was clamouring to be written for the first time, there would be something lying by, which waited upon his mood for its last revision. I came to take it as a sign, when Lawrence wrote to say he was writing nothing, that even as I read his letter he would be deep in some new undertaking.

When not engaged on a book or a story, Lawrence would be working at something else with precisely the same ardour and economy and dislike of outgrown accumulations. Once he bought a gauze shawl of Paisley pattern for Frieda—cheaply, because it had the moth in it—and set himself to make it whole without delay by mending it himself. It took him two entire days, working well into the night and allow-

ing only the shortest intervals for his meals. When I say I
never saw Lawrence idle, I do not mean that he was that
wretched thing, a time-haunted man. He was that as little
as he was the Shavian 'writing machine.' He did not seem
to be 'driven,' either by clocks or by conscience. He worked
more as a bird works, eagerly and unceasingly till the job
on hand was finished. But he certainly valued time as any
good worker must, and he was shocked in a light passing
way when he noticed other people dilly-dallying or spending
their hours on trivialities or lying unduly long in bed of a
morning. I have heard him say that he needed nine hours'
sleep out of the twenty-four, and he observed this as a rule,
being neither a late sitter-up nor an unduly early riser.
But throughout his fifteen-hour day he was 'doing things'
all the time.

Besides, Lawrence was happy in that he had no struggle
to create. The 'frail, precious buds of the unknown life,'
which for him were the only possessions worth fighting for,
came into being without his groaning or travailing. He had
to struggle only for the condition—the 'small, subtle air of
life'—in which alone these 'unborn children of one's hope
and living happiness' could appear, and he had to shelter
them in their growth from meddling or destructive hands.
The happy demon of creation was his. All that was demanded of him was the courage to see that the demon's
mouth was stopped neither by the world's disapproval nor by
his personal fears.

So there was always happiness for Lawrence. He was
always engaged upon something supremely worth while,
with no less in constant view than a new heaven and a new
earth.

'I feel pretty happy inside too,' he wrote during that
same 'bitter winter,' when telling me he had finished *Women
in Love*. '. . . I have knocked the first loop-hole in the

prison where we are all shut up. . . . I feel a bubbling of gladness inside. Frieda and I are in accord.' The same letter ends with a fancy of characteristic humour. 'It is wildly blowy here lately. I always expect to read in the papers in the morning that all England is blown clean and bare, and only a few people are hovering winged in the air.'

I have always greatly liked that picture of Lawrence reading a morning newspaper damp from the press which informs him that morning newspapers are a thing of the past! A man like this will, indeed must, suffer. But he is not subject to any pitiable misery.

The suffering was there all right. Not only in writing but in living, Lawrence had now discarded all the accepted 'ideal reactions' of his age in favour of those pristine, lost reactions from which, as we recovered them, he believed that life would come to us refreshed. And that he might the better do this he had made in sheer faith and hope the 'bitter act of rejection'—repudiation of his 'oneness' with the human world in which he found himself, and he had entered into a special kind of 'singleness' of which he was the initiator. With Christian idealism he repudiated also the ascetic ideal. While he accepted Milton's dictum—'he for God only,' he conceived that no man could be truly 'for God' who did not provide his woman with the full satisfaction of being the 'she for God in him.' For Milton it worked only in one direction; for Lawrence in two. And where for a Milton it was easy, because backed by the conventions, for a Lawrence it entailed misunderstanding, strife, and what appeared like a grave discrepancy in his being. But he saw this kind of singleness with its dual duty as the crucial need of humanity of to-day. If it entailed initial discrepancies largely because it must dislocate long habit, that must be faced and borne, with the blame for it.

Murry, perceiving the discrepancy, has based upon it his theory of Lawrence's failure.[1] Till we understand Lawrence's active recognition of this duality with all that it involves, we shall fail to understand the peculiar heroism of his achievement. This was further bound up with his recognition that his life would not be a long one. He had that hard 'something to say' which it takes a man twenty years to enunciate, if only because before enunciation is possible he must have stripped himself of fear while retaining the most sensitive and scrupulous responses to life at every point. One day I bewailed to Lawrence how unproductive my life appeared by the side of his. 'Ah, but you will have so much longer than I to do things in!' he answered quickly and lightly. Though we saw he was delicate, this certainty of his was so shocking that we did our best, with remarkable success, to believe him wrong. There was no mistaking his own certainty that time for him might not be lost.

In the preface to *Collected Poems* (the publication of which was first suggested by Secker that summer of 1916, though it did not in fact take place till the spring of 1928, when also the preface was written) Lawrence speaks of 'the bitter winter of 1916–1917' and 'the cruel spring of 1917.' He speaks too of the young man who 'is afraid of his demon,' and remarks upon having struggled 'to say something which it takes a man twenty years to be able to say.' In 1916 Lawrence knew that about his undertaking which we others are only now beginning to see clearly. There is illumination in one of his poems which in 1916 must, I think, have already existed.

> Something in me remembers
> And will not forget,
> The stream of my life in the darkness
> Deathward set!

[1] *Son of Woman.*

And something in me has forgotten,
Has ceased to care.
Desire comes up, and contentment
Is debonair.

I, who am worn and careful,
How much do I care?
How is it I grin then, and chuckle
Over despair?

Grief, grief, I suppose and sufficient
Grief makes us free
To be faithless and faithful together
As we have to be.

What Murry is too logical and too custom-bound to guess, is that Lawrence's paramount value lies precisely in the discrepancy he bewails.

VIII

My stay at Tregerthen was short—inside of a week—shorter than I had intended or than Lawrence wished. Donald, lonely at home, sent a telegram that fetched me back. Lawrence mocked at it all a little, but he had a way, not hurtful at all, of mocking gently at one. I remember our driving to the station at St. Ives and saying good-bye with the sense that my visit had been broken in half. Better that, anyhow, than to have overstayed my welcome.

Lawrence, though his eyes were troubling him and he wanted to see an oculist, shook his head over any suggestion that he might run up to London. He remained, in fact, at Tregerthen till the following April; and then again, after a short break till October, 1917.

It was to be a harsh fourteen months for him and Frieda. *Women in Love* was not to see print until November, 1920, and then only by private subscription in New York. It really looked as if no further book of his would ever see the light, with the possible exception of books of poems.

Lawrence, however, went on producing with unshaken faith. He was angry but dauntless. He was practical also, setting himself to get his poems, at least, printed in book form, and writing essays and stories for the few magazines (none of them able to pay well) which were interested. He kept his name before the public. Single correspondents were easily led to believe that he had ceased producing. In fact, however, a couple of weeks was a long enough cessation to make him declare that he was doing nothing. He would tell this when he would not tell that he was at work. As a rule his first mention of a book was when he had written a substantial part or was revising the whole.

At the same time there the War was. And so long as it was, Lawrence might as well stop writing novels. The novel needs for its creation an atmosphere and for its reception a public. So Thomas Hardy found even in peace time and ceased to write novels after *Jude the Obscure*. But poems and essays are made of sterner stuff; and short stories can slip by. Lawrence fell back upon these. Novels could wait. He must not.

But the existence of *Women in Love*, even in unpublished MS., was a fermenting element in the life of those remaining months at Cornwall. It went the round and evoked the most violent feelings. If Lawrence was the Eager Heart of our day he was also the *enfant terrible*. His innocence was not less disturbing than his insight. And he was far too completely dedicated to have much compunction in the matter of material for the expression of his vision.

In November he sent me a copy of the typescript to read—complete but for the epilogue. It made a painful but powerful impression on me. I did not know what to think of it, and, in fact, said little. Except for the interest which is maintained

throughout, the great descriptive passages, and the queer sense
of Lawrence's voice talking all the time; except too for a few
details, chiefly in the matter of women's wear, which struck
me as unnecessary and a little ridiculous, I found mainly
suffering in the perusal.   And I resented the infliction of an
almost physical suffering and malaise by what purported to be
a novel. ,All the same here was something. It made one
pause. The usual critical outfit had to be discarded. Wait a
bit! I must think about this! Anyhow, what a strange, new,
daring kind of richness of apprehension! '*Touché!*' cries the
heart of the reader at every turn.

It was first rejected by Duckworth. I think it must have
lain on the table at one time or another of every leading
publisher in London. As Lawrence touchingly remarked to
his agent, 'I *do* admire it, but I am not everybody.'

In December there was some word of Koteliansky placing
the book in Russia (translated of course).[1] But private as well
as public readers in England were mostly united in hatred.

An exception among the public readers was Mr. Cecil
Palmer, who, though he returned the novel, expressed a wish
that he were rich enough to publish it privately at his own
expense for his own pleasure.

The notable exception among the private readers was Mr.
George Moore. He was to 'praise it highly.' But this was
not yet, and anyhow it was praise of a nature only too strictly

[1] So, at least, Lawrence heard from Koteliansky. In fact, however,
this good friend, knowing how much in need of money Lawrence was at
the time, had made of the Russian idea an excuse for sending him £10.
He knew that only so, regarding this as money on account from Russia,
would Lawrence feel able to accept it from one who was himself not well
off. Koteliansky had certainly hoped that something would come of it,
but though *Women in Love*, with other novels by Lawrence, now exist
in Russian translations, the hope was then very premature. After some
months, upon inquiry by Lawrence, the failure had to be revealed, whereupon Lawrence insisted on repaying the £10.

private. Lawrence's fellow-writers, even when they admired him, fought very shy of saying so except in the most general terms. It became the fashion to remark of him, 'Of course he has genius, but . . .' Among those who saw the MS. was Mr. Galsworthy, and Lawrence wrote to Pinker asking to be told 'what dear old out-of-date Galsworthy had said.' One imagines Lawrence's face if he ever read the reply. But it would appear that Pinker had the discretion to draw a veil.

Private as well as professional barriers were set up by the as yet unprinted novel. By February, 1917, it had turned the author's most powerful and enthusiastic patroness— Lady Ottoline Morrell—into a fury against him. Taking the character of Hermione as a picture of herself she felt outraged. Poor Pinker, who by this time must have wished he had never heard of *Women in Love*, was invited to Garsington Manor just that he might see how unlike the lady of the Manor was to the lady in the book. But Pinker sagaciously stayed at home.

Lawrence sat perfectly tight. This, he declared, was a book 'that would laugh last.' It was 'true and unlying and will last out all the other stuff.' Again he inveighed against the world. It 'has got such a violent rabies that makes it turn on anything true with frenzy.' But he remained entirely confident, and not at all repentant.

Though he continued to produce, however, (his *Studies of Classic American Literature* had their beginnings early in 1917) he felt more and more hopeless of selling any kind of work in England to the extent of making a living. Could he even go on much longer producing in England? No, he would suffocate if he had to stay.

I wanted him to write to Thomas Hardy. And it seemed that the idea had also occurred to him. Hardy, especially in *Jude the Obscure*, had meant much to Lawrence. And it was to be thought that the reception accorded to *Jude* would ensure sympathy for the author of *The Rainbow*. But after a moment's thought he shook his head. 'No,' he said, 'old age is a queer thing. It would be no use. There's something gone dead, I feel, in Hardy these days. He's given way somewhere—gone. Nothing there you can appeal to any more.'

As things were, it could not be denied that the only active encouragement to Lawrence as a writer came from America. In that direction was the only chance of escape. He felt himself 'awfully like a fox that is cornered by a pack of hounds and boors who don't perhaps know he's there, but are closing in unconsciously.' Increasingly he believed that his country was 'capable of not seeing anything but badness in him for ever and ever' and that its 'vital atmosphere was poisonous to him to an incredible degree.' Even in Cornwall he had begun to feel 'smothered and weary' and 'buried alive.' Early in the year he applied for passports to America. He must transfer both himself and his public. If England would not have him, he would seek his 'virgin soil' elsewhere. And where else was there but America?

Not that Lawrence had any such pleasant, puerile illusions about America as Murry would attribute to him. 'The people and the life are monstrous.' He felt sure of this beforehand. But he felt that America 'being so much worse, *falser*, further gone than England,' was 'nearer to freedom.' England in his view had 'a long and awful process of corruption and death to go through,' whereas America had 'dry-rotted to a point where the final seed of the new' was 'almost left ready to sprout.'

'The Americans are *not* younger than we, but older; a second childhood. But being so old in senile decay and second childishness, perhaps they are nearer to the end, and the new beginning.'

At the same time, in America 'the skies are not so old,

the air is newer, the earth is not so tired.'   And, of course, to see how life was in other countries was necessary to Lawrence—part of his destiny, as he later recognised.   As he lost hope after hope of making a real life for himself in England, he became ever surer that his early Florida idea had been right in its essence—right, he admitted, 'all save the people.   It is wrong to seek adherents.   One must be single.'

But Lawrence had grown up in a tough school, and was a sage believer in 'waiting for circumstance.'   'There is a difference,' he warned me once, 'between "you never can tell what will happen," and "you never can tell *how* it will happen."   One can tell what will happen more or less.   Some things one knows inwardly and infallibly.   But the how and the why are left to the conjunction of circumstances.'

So he went on working, and all the while was 'hammering out' his philosophy.   During January he had re-composed the first part of *Women in Love*.   At the same time he was re-writing and putting into order the cycle of poems at first called *Man and Woman* which 'might as well,' he said, 'have been called *And Now Farewell*,' as it marked 'a sort of conclusion of the old life' in him.

Just because of this, the severance with his old life being still fresh, he felt 'most passionately and bitterly tender' about these poems—so much so that he could not bear either to keep them longer in the house or to send them to Pinker. 'It has meant a great deal to me and I feel more inclined to burst into tears than anything.'   On February 18th, the day he completed them, he posted them to me to read and hand on to Hilda Aldington.   He would see what she and I felt. '*Essentially*,' he had said in an earlier letter, 'I don't want to see a soul in London except you two, and perhaps Hilda Aldington and Robert Mountsier, who has gone back.' Thus Lawrence kept handing his past to us.   And even as one sat trying to catch up with his past, one had the certainty, not without a kind of sadness, that already he was making a new flight into the unknown.

Over every one of his books and every period of his life Lawrence would thus read the funeral service. He was a great discarder of the burden of living death which most of us drag about with us to the impediment of each new vital effort, even while we label them stepping-stones of our dead selves. But he never omitted from his funeral oration the passage about a glorious resurrection. In all Lawrence's graves—and he had many—there was a phœnix.

I shall never forget reading those poems in the author's neat handwriting in the tiny room over a garage to which we had moved upon Donald's being called up. We had let our house, had found these two rooms farther up the Grove at six shillings a week, and ourselves carried along enough of our furniture after nightfall to make them habitable. We should at least have this for a *pied à terre* so long as we could use it. My money was now greatly diminished, and Donald's, of course, was stopped, except for his allowance as a private when he went as a gunner to Woolwich.

By the light of a candle I read the poems through. I confess that no other poet except Hardy (and Shakespeare in his sonnets) has so deeply conveyed to me the wistfulness of humanity as distilled in a noble heart—a heart the nobler for its perfect admission of imperfections. It is as if the lost and naked but indomitable human heart has come to murmur its adventures in your ear. And what rare, what original adventures! With Lawrence, as with Hardy, the very imperfections in the telling are to me a beauty. They are of a piece with the nature of the adventure, giving a live pang of delight or sorrow, where 'the perfect poem,' because of its very crystalline perfection, will often divert the pang of feeling into one of sheer admiration of a miracle. Not but what this kind of imperfection may be a special, most difficult and conscious art.   I believe that it may, and that Lawrence's peculiar imperfections will prove to be preservatives of his thought.   He will remain, as he meant to do, a man, as well as a voice speaking.   In the case of *Man and Woman* I advised him to expunge a love letter—beautiful and interesting, but a real, sent letter, in prose, which he had included with the poems.   He did not at first agree about this, but came round later.

The title of *Man and Woman* was changed to *Poems of a Married Man*, and then again to *Look! We have Come Through!*   But as usual, and in this case more than usually, Lawrence shrank from the idea of public print.   Already there was a small book of poems[1] travelling round and meeting with rebuffs.   The more important book could wait.   Actually he did not bring himself to release this dove out of his ark to a world that 'was not ready' until April.   After some rejections the book was accepted in August, with a brace of reservations, by Messrs. Chatto & Windus.   Lawrence was puzzled by the reservations.[2]   They included the omission of a poem which had already appeared in an anthology.   But he submitted with a curse.   No use in making a fuss!   And he found in this publishing firm such 'nice old flavoured people.'   He was pleased with the format of the book when it appeared.   He asked for twelve instead of six author's copies, and got them.

He had been busy throughout the spring with essays begun some time earlier on 'The Reality of Peace.'   These he hoped to publish quickly—as applicable to the moment—in the magazines, and without too much delay in a little book to be called *At The Gates*.   Some, at least, of the essays appeared in the *English Review* throughout the summer of

---

[1] *New Poems*, published by Secker in October, 1918.

[2] 'Song of a Man Who is Loved' and 'Meeting among the Mountains.'

1917.   But neither in that form, nor re-written into something more metaphysical, did they find a publisher for their more permanent collection during his lifetime.

IX

That April, on his return from a visit to the Midlands (his first excursion from Cornwall) he was seized with illness while in London.   I had only a single glimpse of him, and did not know till after two weeks that he had been taken ill later that same day, had been nursed by Koteliansky at Acacia Road for five days, had then 'scrambled out to Hermitage' in Berkshire to the Radfords' cottage, and after a short time there, returned to Cornwall.   He wrote to me from Tregerthen on April 28th, explaining why he had not seen me again, and adding,

You were very sad when I saw you: and there seemed nothing that could be said.   Things must work themselves out.   It is a great weariness.   I felt, that as far as peace work, or *any* work for betterment goes, it is useless.   One can only gather the single flower of one's own intrinsic happiness, apart and separate.   It is the only faithful fulfilment.   I feel that people *choose* the war, somehow, even those who hate it, *choose* it, choose the state of war and in their souls provoke more war, even in hating war.   So the only thing that can be done is to leave them to it, and to bring forth the flower of one's own happiness, single and apart.

It is so lovely here, now, my seeds have come up, there is a strange joyfulness in the air.   For those of us who can become single and alone, all will become perfectly right.

You were queer and sad as the train went off at Leicester Square Station.   But don't be sad.   In the innermost soul there is happiness, apart from everything.

Come and stay here if ever you can, and if you feel like it.

Esther Andrews was then staying with them.   She was very unhappy, and in the strength of her unhappiness could not resist attaching herself to Lawrence and trying to match her strength against Frieda's—disastrously to herself. Yet she took away with her, when she left later that summer, an enduring admiration. And I daresay she would now assert that her visit to Cornwall was the least disastrous episode in her life.[1] Where Lawrence and Frieda were, mishaps would occur. But Lawrence had a way of communicating something that flourished in separation, and so was lastingly precious.

That spring Frieda was ill. She had a week or two of internal trouble that made Lawrence anxious. And again at the beginning of August she was crippled with neuritis in the leg, which gave great pain and kept her in and out of bed for almost a month. Lawrence nursed her with devoted skill.

Not that either Lawrence or Frieda made much of illness. Lawrence, if one may so apply the expression, had a talent of his own for it. If others were ill he was a marvellous nurse. For himself, while hating to be treated in any professional way as an invalid, he was patient and skilful with a kind of innate philosophy that worked remarkably well. It was the only matter in which he was 'adaptable.'

Though the enemy seizes my body for a time, I shall subtly adjust myself so that he pinches me nowhere vitally, and when he is forced to release me again I am the stronger.

In one of my letters I had mentioned a neuralgia which had cursed me for some time, and he replied:

I have a great horror of pain, acute pain, where one keeps one's consciousness. I always thank my stars that I don't have those

[1] In her book, *Lorenzo in Taos*, Mabel Dodge Sterne has a reference to this incident. It is both misleading and incorrect. At the time I heard the particulars from both Lawrence and Frieda.

pains that scintillate in full consciousness. I am only half there when I am ill, and so there is only half a man to suffer. To suffer in one's whole self is so great a violation, that it is not to be endured.

At the same time Frieda was ill I was laid up at Bournemouth, where Donald and I had now gone while he was at a cadet school. On the top of that I met with a slight motoring accident which kept me a fortnight in bed, and Lawrence wrote scolding and giving me good advice. Again he was full of suggestions for titles for my novel, which was only now nearing an end of its re-writing.

But his real news was that he had been refused a passport for America 'in the interests of national service.' It was a blow, and he felt that he would die with this the one loophole closed. He saw himself as one condemned to 'die of foul inward poison,' and England as emitting a stench that was fatal to him. England was his 'City of Destruction.' At all costs he must get out.

Again, though he was full of heartfelt curses for the country that could neither use him nor let him go, curses the more heartfelt in that he so loved his country, Lawrence behaved with remarkable commonsense. That late summer, as he has recounted in the 'Nightmare' chapter of *Kangaroo*, he occupied himself as a farm labourer, working as constantly and hard as any of the country labourers at harvesting. At the same time he made his own three gardens bloom. In addition to the tiny walled one which he had rented at a shilling a year with the cottage, he had acquired two more from the Hockings of Lower Tregerthen, the neighbouring farm where the Higher Tregerthen folk bought their milk and sometimes got their pies and puddings baked. And he combined the successful production of flowers and vegetables with the writing of 'philosophy.'

The two combined well, and this was by no means a time without happiness for Lawrence, though for Frieda it

was probably the most trying period of their life together.
Lawrence was a fine and rejoicing gardener. Wherever he
went he planted, and his plants came up. To work peace-
fully with the earth was the best antidote to the War and the
next best thing to migration. 'I sit,' he wrote to me that
summer, 'a very tender nursling on the knees of the gods.'
Till he could leave England, Cornwall was the best place to
be in. He loved it. It had a drugging effect on the hard
mentality that he felt was a modern evil. Also working in
the fields day after day with the dark-eyed young people of
Lower Tregerthen, he believed for a time that he had found
in one of the young men the 'blood brothership' which was
as needful as a refreshed relationship between man and
woman for the rich and complete life he sought. Murry
had rejected the idea—so ancient that it shocked his modern
mind—of a sacrament between men who would commit
themselves in friendship. Any formal 'laying on of hands'
outside of the Church had seemed to him puerile and even
revolting in its primitiveness. But a working man and a
Celt, a man with a subtly pagan face, born in the shadow of
these Druidical stones, yet English too, might, surely must,
have some wordless understanding of one of the oldest of all
human rites. I have heard Lawrence say that sexual per-
version was for him 'the sin against the Holy Ghost,' the
hopeless sin. But he cherished the deep longing to see
revived a communion between man and man which should
not lack its physical symbols. He even held that our modern
denial of this communion in all but idea was largely the cause
of our modern perversions. To recover true potency, and
before there could be health and happiness between man and
woman, he believed that there must be a renewal of the
sacredness between man and man.

But what he was to find later to his deep delight existing
among the Mexican Indians—that occasional religious segre-

gation of the male for the communal worship of something
greater than himself, and so for the increase of his male power
—he was excluded from by the barrier of race.   Race was a
barrier he admitted.   And among his own, he was to seek in
vain for what he wanted and believed to be of fundamental
importance.   It is doubtful if the subtle, uncultured Cornish-
man understood much better than the subtle, cultured
Londoner, or indeed than the simple German wife, who regarded any relegation of her man's emotion as a species of
'unfaithfulness.'   It is even fairly certain that the Cornish-
man's mystification—as he was also given to talking—added
to the cloud of suspicion that was now gathering over the
cottage at Higher Tregerthen.   It surely added greatly to the
loneliness of Lawrence.   Here was one of the closed doors of
the hated modern System, which he must hereafter refrain
from trying to shatter except with words.   If he hurled at it
his heart, that heart would be not merely bruised but branded.
Lawrence, for all his innocence, was no fool.   Loneliness was
preferable to certain kinds of misunderstanding.

The cloud of war suspicion, which had begun to gather
even before Christmas, was pretty thoroughly formed by
August.   Frieda was not only German but loudly provocative
and indiscreet.   In the spring Lawrence had committed the
extravagance of buying for five guineas a worn cottage piano
'with an old red silk front and a nice old musty twang': and
with its help he had set himself to increase his already considerable repertoire of songs.   Some of these—especially as
rendered in Frieda's loud, fresh voice—could not have been
mistaken for anything but German.   Others must have
sounded equally blood-curdling to the curious or the hostile,
who took to lying beneath the garden wall to listen.   Through
Cecil Gray, Lawrence had recently become acquainted with
the researches of Mrs. Kennedy Fraser.   And he had some
Hebridean numbers which he howled in what he ingenuously

supposed to be the Gaelic, at the same time endeavouring to imitate the noise made by a seal!

It was unfortunate that there was a flat-roofed turret to the annexe commanding a seaward view, that submarines were busy in the Channel, and that a foreign coal-boat chose to be wrecked on the rocks below Tregerthen. We, who lived through the War, know how favourable such a combination could be for the development of war spite against any individual who not only was not doing what the crowd was doing but openly condemned such doings. In Lawrence's case, though he himself was never to discover it, I am credibly informed that a half-demented woman, not belonging to the neighbourhood, had set herself deliberately to spy within the cottage on the pretext of doing an occasional day's charing there. It was a time at which such a being could win a hearing of those who lacked her excuse for such behaviour. By August Lawrence's letters were being held back and examined. I posted him one from Bournemouth on the 9th which did not reach him till the 13th. Nor was this a single occurrence.

Murry [1] has suggested that the Lawrences could have moved inland. In practice such a move was not so easy as it may now sound. The annexe was furnished and painted, the year's rent had been paid in advance, and Lawrence's gardens substantially helped their living. They rarely possessed so much money as would pay for a move. Besides they loved their cottage. It suited them, and Lawrence, true born Englishman that he was, would never consent to being shifted from his home by mere bullying. As for ceasing to sing what songs he pleased and when he pleased, by his own fireside, that would have been an unthinkable submission.

One day when he was with the Hockings at market in Penzance, and Frieda was across the fields calling upon Cecil Gray (who was now their nearest cultured neighbour

[1] *Reminiscences.*

and almost equally under suspicion with themselves), their cottage was searched by the military. Frieda, returning alone, was frightened; Lawrence, arriving later, was shocked and furious. Henceforward he would be on his guard, trust nobody, be intimate with nobody. Though there had been nothing to betray, somebody had undoubtedly acted as an informer. Any specified suspicions he may have had were groundless, though natural and indeed inevitable. Other facts besides the searching of the cottage had made him aware that there was considerable and disseminated spite against him, largely on Frieda's account. But now some individual had taken the definite step of going to the authorities. He was not to know who had done this. He knew, however, that for him and Frieda it was a matter of waiting for further developments. On Friday morning, October 12th, a young officer with a search warrant arrived with two plain-clothes detectives and a local police sergeant. The Lawrences were ordered to clear out of Cornwall within three days. No charges were made or explanations given. None, of course, were needed. Simply the Lawrences were undesirables. Lawrence was horror-stricken but composed. Frieda was voluble, argumentative and defiant to rudeness. In being her champion, Lawrence had to undertake the championship of her nation. This, without doubt, was unfortunate for Lawrence. It was also, without doubt, necessary. Frieda's insistence, combined with the ineptitude of the authorities, made it so.

They were at 'the fag end of poverty.' £13 : 10s. for several contributions in the *English Review* had come in belatedly in September. I doubt if Lawrence possessed £5 in the world when he reached London the following Monday and took a taxi with his luggage to Hampstead to find refuge with his staunch little friend, Mrs. Ernest Radford at Well Walk. That day or the next, he called round hoping to find

me. But I had gone to Edinburgh where Donald was ill
in a military hospital. It was some days later before I heard
from him what had happened.

When they had been a week at Well Walk, Hilda Aldington insisted upon their using her rooms in Mecklenburgh
Square, or rather her one huge room that had some kind of
appendix by way of a scullery. They accepted with gratitude,
remained there about a month—of necessity and her kindness largely as her guests—and then went to a flat in Earl's
Court Square offered by Cecil Gray's Scottish mother, whom
I had seen on Lawrence's account when in Edinburgh.

Mrs. Sterne is very far out when she asserts,[1] on the
alleged authority of Frieda, that Lawrence's English friends
deserted him at this or any juncture. They were as shocked
as Lawrence himself over the eviction, and as helpless. But,
with a few notable exceptions, they quietly did what they
could, distressed that it was so little, and the Lawrences were
enabled to live without running into debt. Lawrence himself was the last man to forget any kindness. Frieda, no
doubt unwittingly, gave Mrs. Sterne the kind of impression
that laid itself open to jealous misconstruction, causing the
kind of mistake that made Lawrence rage. Among his
friends at this time were Dr. and Mrs. Eder, and with them
Lawrence evolved a plan for migrating in spring to 'the
eastern slopes of the Andes.' Actually the Eders seem
to have produced somebody who was going to produce a
thousand pounds for the expedition.

x

While the Lawrences were still at Mecklenburgh Square,
we returned from Edinburgh and took two furnished rooms
in Hampstead. Our own house was let until Easter, as also

[1] In her book, *Lorenzo in Taos*.

now the tiny rooms over the garage. (So we eked out our living.) Upon being discharged from hospital Donald was also discharged from the army. I was expecting a baby in the spring. Lawrence came by himself to see us. Unfortunately that same afternoon we had another visitor, a young man who was anxious to meet Lawrence, but still more anxious to convince us that he had produced a literary masterpiece. Lawrence, therefore, sat silent, leaning his head on his hand and looking as if affected with sea-sickness. The last thing he was interested in was literary masterpieces as such, and anyhow he did not believe that this was one. When the young man had left, he uttered some expletives and became apparently cheerful. True, he hardly knew which way to turn next, or how to get the money to turn at all. But as usual he was full of plans and did not give the effect of being distressed. Would we join the party in the spring and go to the eastern slopes of the Andes? He liked the idea of taking a baby along, but as this baby was not to arrive till the end of May, we did not see ourselves as possible starters. It was decided that he would let us know what the eastern slopes were like, and that we should follow if we could. Meanwhile he rather surprised us by wanting to return to the Cornish cottage for Christmas. His idea was apparently to face the thing out, and he was trying to get the Asquiths to help him with the authorities. But sympathetic as the Asquiths were, they were powerless in this and told him so. Were they not themselves the object of active popular suspicion? One just had to grin and bear it. Everybody declared that the War would end that winter.

It was about this time that George Moore read the MS. of *Women in Love*, and 'says it is a great book and that I am a better writer than himself,' as Lawrence wrote to me later, admitting that it was 'really astounding.' Who sent George Moore the MS. I do not know. I am sure it was not Lawrence, though it was possibly Pinker at Lawrence's instigation. Nor do I know how the pleasing verdict was conveyed. It was certainly received and must, one thinks, have been given. But that it came direct from Ebury Street seems unlikely. Almost at the same time there was a suggestion that Bertrand Russell 'who used to be a fairly intimate friend of mine, but whom I don't agree with,' might be asked to write a letter recommending the novel to an Irish publisher.

Nothing came of either of these things, and the immediate situation remained very difficult. How was Lawrence to be helped? The only way we could think of was that he might write for *The Times Educational Supplement.* Donald knew the editor, Mr. G. S. Freeman, to whom he made the most urgent representations, with the result that an interview took place, and Lawrence promised that he would do his best to turn out articles such as were wanted. Having heard his account of what *was* wanted, I had my doubts, but held my peace. He set to work, however, willingly and without delay.

Of one thing Lawrence was sure, he could not remain longer in London. Shortly before Christmas he arranged to pay Dolly Radford a small rent for her cottage at Hermitage in Berkshire. It was bitterly cold with a half-thaw. 'God knows,' he wrote me, 'I am not in a good mood in any way whatsoever.' From there he went for New Year to the Midlands. To his sisters, at least, the War had brought added material prosperity.

It was not Lawrence's private friends, nearly all of them poor people, and like himself, harried by the War, who failed him in practical matters. (That they failed in understanding was less to be wondered at.) To-day, however, when one can view the question dispassionately, it is hard to forgive the literary leaders for their determined aloofness. Admitted that he was a difficult man to help, he was eminently eligible, and one thinks that with goodwill some way might have been found to tide over a rough passage that was largely due to the exigencies of the War. One is forced to the conclusion that the goodwill was lacking. He himself felt that he was deserving of the temporary financial support he so greatly needed. Though Murry [1] would make it appear that his demand was merely for intellectual support by way of 'recognition,' Lawrence's own letters show that he made a frank appeal for funds. He understood perfectly the futility of requiring understanding. But he felt justified on the strength of his known achievement in asking his fellow-writers to take his honesty and potency as an artist on trust. Early that February (1918) when he was ill with a severe sore throat which knocked him out for three weeks, he urged Pinker to tempt some money for him out of 'some rich good-natured author.' And he suggested that Arnold Bennett might give him some 'to get along with' till his day came, as he was certain it would.

Could anything be simpler or more direct? Lawrence drew the line only at going himself hat in hand. He would make the demand through his agent as his due. There was no use, he pointed out, in deluding himself that he could make a living under present conditions in England. But engaged as he was at that very moment on the final revision of his *Studies in Classic American Literature*, he was confident both in his future and in his immediate worth, *as a financial investment*. This, of course, in addition to his belief that what he was writing was of prime importance.

In an article written shortly after Lawrence's death Arnold Bennett has given his own account of this appeal. As Bennett was a very exact man there is no reason to doubt that his account, in its reserved way, is substantially correct.

[1] *Reminiscences.*

He saw the sense of the appeal.   He was ready to contribute if others would join.   But all the others refused.   They asked themselves and each other why they need give a hand to Lawrence and they found no answer; which most certainly was what Lawrence expected and even, I surmise, desired to elicit.

Bennett, I have no doubt, saw through the whole thing more clearly than would appear on the surface, and made a like surmise.   Of all the outstanding writers of the time, he, one fancies, had the most lively appreciation of Lawrence both as man and as writer.   Lawrence himself, never mistaken in such things, had an inkling of it, and more than once through Pinker he suggested that a personal meeting might be brought about.   Yet Bennett, for some deeply felt reason, shrank from this.   Evidently he could not believe that good would come of it.   What he does not tell in his brief narrative is that he himself sent £25 to Pinker for Lawrence.   It would seem that he sent it in such a way as to have it conveyed merely as a business advance by Pinker for work in hand.   We must give Bennett the credit for perceiving that, in sharp contrast to the typical beggar or borrower, the author of *The Rainbow* would find it far harder to accept than to demand money: that indeed the demand was for Lawrence a proud and permissible gesture, but the acceptance, should occasion arise, very difficult.

Though Lawrence remained in ignorance of this £25, he seems throughout the summer of 1918 to have felt friendly towards Bennett, while he was frankly scornful of the other literary leaders.   Something truly human, as well as sweetly reasonable, emanated from Bennett.   And to this Lawrence responded.   But he would push the affair to the utmost.   Bennett should not so easily escape.   That autumn, in yet more desperate need, he asked Bennett to find him a suitable London job.   'Bennett has publicly said that I have genius,' was the substance of his message.   'Then let me tell him that though men of talent are flourishing, this particular possessor of genius is forced to contemplate the fact that in a fortnight's time he will not have enough money to buy "bread and marge"—and this in spite of a pile of MS. that will certainly be saleable at a day not far distant. Till that day comes, will Bennett use his influence to supply the said man of genius with a suitable means of livelihood other than the risky one of literature?'

Bennett, as is well known, was at the time in control of an important department created by the War. But he refused point-blank to find Lawrence a place in it. The fact that Lawrence had genius, he replied only too truly, was no recommendation that he would be useful in any job he might have at his disposal. Rather the reverse!

Though it is easy to guess the anger with which Lawrence, and more especially Lawrence's wife, would receive such a message, Lawrence must have realised its truth. It is even presumable that in it he had obtained the answer he sought, and that Bennett understood this quite as clearly as he did. Because, though Lawrence might ask for, and might even see himself in some imaginary job, what discoverable one in England at this time would he have taken, or having taken would he have kept? The most suitable post for him, as being unconnected with War propaganda yet having the benefit of his experience, was indubitably school-mastering. And what school would open its doors to a man whose book had suffered public prosecution for obscenity? Not Bennett himself could have got Lawrence installed as a teacher, nor do I see Lawrence returning to the dominie's desk. Lawrence has illumined for me many dark Biblical sayings and incidents. This was a case of 'it must needs be that offences come.' But, now as always, there is 'woe to him by whom the offence cometh.' Little more need be said. Lawrence, in asking for money or for work, fulfilled his

destiny by acting as a touchstone. The condemnation for
his failure falls on the world he was there to indict. Also,
I think, in the painful necessary task of cutting himself
loose from that world he needed all the outside drive he
could come by. The utmost he was to get from *official*
England was a second grant from the Royal Literary Fund.
This was applied for and granted during that summer.
Pinker was one of the two signatories of the application. It
would be interesting to know who was the other.

The months between February and the Armistice in
November were spent by the Lawrences chiefly between the
cottage in Berkshire and Mountain Cottage at Middleton-by-
Wirksworth in Derbyshire, which his sisters, in great anxiety,
took for him at Easter. The Radfords needed their own
small retreat for the Easter and summer holidays.

In Derbyshire he much enjoyed a longish visit from his
sisters' children—a nephew aged three and a niece aged
seven—and he enjoyed the flowers which were unusually
rich that spring. But he was 'sick and surfeited,' he suffered
from the recurrent horror of the Midlands, and laboured
under 'poverty and incertitude.'

'I know exactly how it feels,' he wrote to me, sym-
pathising with my different state of waiting.

I feel as if I had a child of black fury curled up inside my bowels.
I am sure I can feel exactly what it is to be pregnant, because of
the weary burden of a kind of contained murder which I can't
bring forth. We will both pray to be safely delivered.

When, so far as I was concerned, his prayer was answered
—in London just a week after the last of the air raids [1]—he
sent me the very exquisite present of a shoe-box containing

---

[1] On that last raid a bomb fell in a back garden at Mecklenburgh
Square, smashing all the windows of the house which the Lawrences had
occupied.

perhaps twenty different kinds of wild flowers carefully
packed in damp moss, many of them having their roots
attached.   Here were yellow rock-roses—'pure flowers of
light,' milkworts, wood-avens, mountain violets, aconites,
woodruff and forget-me-nots.   Lawrence knew all about
wild flowers and could name most of them.   His friend
Millicent Beveridge, whom he met later when in Sicily,
has told me how she went walking with him once in the hills
near Florence at the height of the Tuscan spring, and how
as they went he named and discoursed upon at least thirty
varieties.   It was out of that walk that he wrote the three
fragrant, categorical and joyous essays on 'Flowers in
Tuscany' which appeared in the *Criterion*.

With my box of Derbyshire flowers there was a small
floral guide, tinily written by Lawrence, describing each
plant and making me see how they had been before he picked
them for me, in what sorts of places and manner and pro-
fusion they had grown, and even how they varied in the
different countrysides.

We were all three invited to come immediately to
Mountain Cottage, but instead we asked them to visit us
later in the summer when we were to have, of all unlikely
things, a whole vicarage to ourselves in the Forest of Dean.
My monthly nurse, a splendid woman of the old English
type, was sister to the vicar who wanted his house and garden
inhabited for a nominal rent during the latter part of August.
So it was arranged.   By August, Lawrence would have his
grant from the Royal Literary Fund.   At the moment he
was counting chiefly on £50 from the Oxford University
Press so soon as his *Movements in European History* should
be finished.[1]   He was also getting £10 from a small publisher

[1] This, the one acceptable piece of work he ever wrote to order, was
not completed till spring 1919. It came out later that year under the
disguised name of 'Lawrence H. Davison.'

for the little book of poems called *Bay* (selling it outright for this amount) and there was hope of placing *Look! We have Come Through!* in America. Things were hard, and money continually threatened to 'come to a dead end,' but Lawrence would never let himself run absolutely dry. His might be a bourgeois boast (as Norman Douglas has said) when he announced his determination always to keep a few pounds between himself and the world. It was at least never an idle boast. It was one of Lawrence's austerities that luck, and therefore anything founded on luck, was a vulgarity. Spiritually he would take all risks adventuring into the unknown. But to leave material things to chance was culpable folly. In all practical matters he looked and planned ahead. And he never became either penniless or gravely in debt.

To celebrate the birth of our boy, he not only wrote 'War Baby,' but embroidered a little cotton frock in red and black-cross stitch, while Frieda crocheted a cot cover of the gayest rainbow-coloured stripes in wool. It became known as 'Frieda's Rainbow,' and went everywhere with us, until with rough outdoor usage it fell to pieces.

Shortly before they came to us Lawrence was re-examined for the second time that year on account of the new Military Service Act. He was then definitely put in Grade 3.[1] There can be no doubt that his horror at the mere possibility of being called up for some kind of distasteful work under military orders was the chief cause of his last appeal to Arnold Bennett. Yet I do not believe he seriously thought he would be called up. It was rather that he would take no more chances than he could possibly help. Immediately after the examination he wrote me the following letter.

---

[1] It is this examination which is described in *Kangaroo*. He puts it, however, in September, that being the next and last date on which he was served with papers for re-examination.

Though it is easily subject to misconstruction, it voices something which needs to be understood in Lawrence, something upon which Murry's misunderstanding in *Son of Woman* is largely based.   I therefore quote the relevant passages here:

My dear Catherine,—I have been examined—am put in Grade III.—and from this day I take a new line.   I've done with society and humanity—Labour and Military can alike go to hell. Henceforth it is for myself, my own life, I live: a good jolly personal life, with a few people who are friends, and the rest can do what they like.   I am going to try to get a job: quick, before the military attempt to paw me again—for they shall *never* touch me again.   I shall go to London next week.   We shall meet again soon.   Then we can talk.

About the essays, I crossed out the 'Children' passages.   Who am I to dictate when hope lies or doesn't lie?   Let it lie when it likes.

Tell Don I shall see him again soon.   No more of the social passion and social insistence from me.   I can understand I've been a nuisance and a fool.

Love from both to you all.

He was coming to London alone, he said, with Frieda following in a week or so.

XI

We were happy in the Forest of Dean, though it was a strange, frightening place.   Lawrence told me afterwards that it scared him so that at first he felt like running away.   The dark and ancient steepness of those woods, with the mines inconspicuously burrowing everywhere, is unlike anything else in England.   But we had fine weather, and peaches were ripening on the walls of the old south-sloping garden, and we had the roomy stone house to ourselves.

Lawrence had looked forward to the visit with 'peculiar anticipation,' and when we met him on the platform of

Upper Lydbrook station we were struck by his high spirits. Frieda was beaming and ejaculatory as usual—perhaps even more than usual—but Lawrence was like a schoolboy home for the holidays. His festive array—a green-and-red striped blazer and grey flannel trousers—and the fact that both garments were so shrunken as to show stretches of wrist and ankle, added to this impression. One felt the boy had grown since we last saw him. In a gay aside he informed me that these were now his *only* trousers—and that he had to wash them himself of a night-time after undressing so that they might be ready for wear again by the morning. Owing to the fact that he wore *espadrilles* and no socks, his thin ankles were especially in evidence. I rather think his toilet was completed by an old panama hat. With this strange attire and his beard he attracted some local notice.

The holiday dwells in my memory, for, although he had his variations, his prevailing mood was of extraordinary gaiety, serenity, and youthfulness, such as we never saw again in him.

Having heard beforehand of the impossible Forest roads, we had brought no sort of baby carriage, and, as I was nursing the child, we had to carry him about with us, which meant taking turn and turn about. Frieda, that summer, vied with her husband in the inexpensive gaiety of her dress. She wore the largest and brightest of cotton checks, and when out together we attracted, to Lawrence's displeased surprise, something of the attention that might have been accorded to a travelling circus. Sometimes we took with us a home-made carrier for the baby, consisting of string bags strung upon two broomsticks to form a sort of hammock, which was decked with Frieda's rainbow. But though this was a real convenience Lawrence preferred to travel without it.

When Lawrence said he found the place 'scaring,' this must be understood, like so much else, according to his own idiom. In the ordinary way of speaking he certainly found it interesting, even fascinating. It was a coal-mining district—the oldest in these islands—and therefore he felt at home in it. It was different from any mining district he had known, and therefore it engaged his attention. Although he avoided contact with the natives he cast a professional eye over them and their place, and commented with brisk amusement on the tininess of the workings—*e.g.* the cages so small that only two or three men could be wound down at a time. Once in a walk through the forest he stopped suddenly to examine a half-derelict working that was not a perpendicular shaft but a low tunnel driven into a hillside, from which the coal was drawn up on a trolley worked by a hand-winch and cable. That was the 'gin-pit,' he said—an old sort of thing that was becoming a rarity.

Lydbrook lies in a pleasant fold in the hills, but it is a grey, squalid village—just one long shabby street of a mile or more. Lawrence expressed himself as puzzled why mining villages should be so *needlessly* ugly. He suggested the reason might be that miners through having to work underground had become blind to form values. They craved for 'a bit of colour,' and so loved and cultivated flowers with passion. But, though sensitive to natural beauty, they had a merely utilitarian regard for man-made surroundings.

Often we went far afield. One day we went by train to Monmouth and bought lard cakes there and picnicked by the river. Lawrence wrote of this to Donald when he had gone back to Mountain Cottage, saying how he had enjoyed it:

. . . the bright sunny town, and the tears in one's inside because there isn't *real* peace; and—*very nice*, the meal in the green riding: also our evenings. They are good memories—worth a lot really. And it pleases me that we carried the child about. One has the future in one's arms so to speak: and one *is* the present. . . . I

imagine you in that vicarage room this evening—no more 'What
are the Wild Waves Saying?' for a bit.

Not liking the vicarage drawing-room with its china
cabinets we always sat in the pleasant kitchen, which had an
outlook on the walled fruit garden; and of a night we used
to sing. Hence the reference to 'What are the Wild Waves
Saying?' which was a great success given as a duet by
Lawrence and Donald, with Lawrence in the male part.

Lawrence had brought with him a little manual of French
songs which he carried about everywhere like a Bible, and
even the hated china cabinets did not keep him away from the
drawing-room piano at which he was often to be found
seated, picking out melodies from his manual with one finger.
His expression at such times was one of intense and concentrated earnestness, as he hummed the tune over and over and
learned every verse of the longest ballad by heart. Though
he had an odd sort of a singing voice he knew supremely well
how to sing any kind of folk-song. But I liked best of all to
hear him in English ones, like 'A Cottage Well Thatched
with Straw' or 'Twanky-dillo,' which he wrote out for me,
music and all, and he rendered deliciously the prim absurd
charm of Offenbach in English:

> Evoë! Wonderful ways
> Have the goddesses now and then
> For beguiling the hearts of men!

One evening we tried charades, in which Lawrence excelled, having invented a special kind of his own. But I am
the worst of performers and Donald is not much better, so
that we failed in playing up while we could not be spared to
act as audience.

It was here that Lawrence first thought of his story called
The Blind Man. We had an old and lovable, but almost half-
witted servant, a woman like a squirrel, with squirrel-coloured

hair piled high over a pad on top of her head in a fashion so elaborate that she used to rise at five in the morning to complete her toilet by seven. I can still see her face of bewilderment as Lawrence, seated one day at the kitchen table, tried to include her with me in his outline of the story. Stupid as Letty was, and far as this was from any tale she was accustomed to, she seemed, as well as myself, to breathe the dark air of the stable, to see the blind man delicately groping about it, and to feel the sad, enclosed, yet natural atmosphere in which these people moved. Friends have assured me that the woman in *The Blind Man* was suggested by me, and it may be so. There was nothing superficially like me in her, and nothing that could not be easily refuted. Yet somewhere the truth smote me, just as I doubt not that the truth smote Katherine Mansfield when she read about Gudrun in *Women in Love*, or Ottoline Morrell when she read about Hermione, or Dorothy Brett when she read *The Princess*. Here was little of portraiture, still less of summing up. But what an inescapable reading of the pulse of a life!

That September we were to have gone to Mountain Cottage, but could not. Lawrence wrote on his thirty-third birthday to say that he had received papers calling him up for medical re-examination, but that he was determined not to go. I never heard what happened. Possibly the authorities accepted a doctor's certificate.

That autumn and winter—the autumn of the Armistice—things were as hard as ever for Lawrence, and more upsetting as he had no place of his own. The money situation would have been desperate but for hopeful news from America where there seemed to be a growing market for his stories and Huelsch was negotiating for *Look! We have Come Through!* Still almost nothing was coming in, and in England he could not command more than £5 for one of his *Studies in Classical American Literature*, while the indigent *English Review* seemed the only magazine that would print his short stories. The four little essays on 'The Education of the People'[1] ('Good,' wrote Lawrence, 'but most revolutionary') did not meet with the approval of *The Times Educational Supplement*, and were returned with the request for something 'more suitable.'

We had been obliged to go to Scotland. It was the winter of the great influenza epidemic, and Donald went down with it badly in Edinburgh. The next we heard—at the turn of the year—was that Lawrence, in the Midlands for the holiday, had been at death's door with the same epidemic, 'with complications.'

During an alarmingly slow recovery he went on as well as he could with his plans for leaving England at the first opportunity, which would not be, he was told, till peace was ratified. The idea of going with the Eders to the eastern slopes of the Andes had since been modified into a visit to Palestine. But both had fallen through. Lawrence had a great longing at this time for the sea. This too turned out to be impracticable, and there was nothing for it but to re-occupy the cottage at Hermitage so long as the Radfords were not there. It was less cold and bleak than Derbyshire, and further from the deathly reminders of home. Also it was nearer to London. On the revival of the *Athenaeum* under the editorship of Middleton Murry, the suggestion had been made that Lawrence should become a regular contributor. 'I am to contribute,' he wrote me of this piece of news— 'good thing if I could earn a little weekly money. But,' he added, 'I don't trust Murry.'

In spite of this addition he was very anxious to try what

---

[1] The following January, through the influence of Barbara Low, Stanley Unwin offered £15 on account of royalties for a book which should consist of the four essays 'and as much again.' But this was not carried out.

could be done. He was longing to 'meet and have a little happy time together.' So he came south in March.

Upon the joyous news of Murry's editorship Koteliansky had immediately seen the chance for helping Lawrence. He therefore lost little time in speaking to Katherine about it, and she, seeming as eager as himself, agreed that of course Murry would want Lawrence as a contributor and would give him a free hand. She authorised him to write to Lawrence in that sense, which he did. It was, as Lawrence told me himself, his first news of Murry's connection with the *Athenaeum*.

Murry has given us his own story.[1] But as it is much abridged and has gaps in it, possibly owing to limited space; as moreover it contains an element of self-defence, it may be as well to set another by the side of it. He has told us that he welcomed, though with some natural trepidation, the idea of contributions from Lawrence. He became editor in January, 1919. On April 11th, under the pseudonym of 'Grantorto,' Lawrence's beautiful and suitable essay, 'The Whistling of Birds' appeared. But the next essay, says Murry, was unsuitable and was returned as such, whereupon 'Lawrence was annoyed, and sent us nothing more.'

By this it would seem that these two efforts covered the extent of contributions tendered by Lawrence. Both Koteliansky and Frieda, however, have informed me positively that Lawrence sent in considerably more than would thus appear. Koteliansky speaks of 'a sheaf' of articles; Frieda of 'several.' Both are equally positive that some, at least, of the submitted articles were perfectly suitable. To my own knowledge there were then in existence some of the essays which later appeared in the collection, 'Assorted Articles,' none of which could have given serious

[1] *Reminiscences.*

offence to readers of the *Athenaeum* even in 1919. Or so
one thinks, given the smallest amount of courage or goodwill in the editor. After telling us that Lawrence sent nothing more, but without connecting the two events, Murry
admits that he went himself in May by Lawrence's request
to stay a few days at Hermitage and 'talk things over.' He
admits too that he then found Lawrence 'ill and weary,'
as well as poor and depressed, and despairing of his life in
England. Clearly Lawrence was making an appeal for help
in a most reasonable way; equally clearly Murry refused
that help. We visited Lawrence at Hermitage the same
month, and this was undoubtedly his own impression.
'Murry does not *want* to help me, and he won't.' This is
borne out by all the other recollections. These suggest that
Katherine Mansfield wished to have more from Lawrence,
but that Murry would not have it and would not risk it—
that profoundly he did not *want* it. It was the period of
Lawrence's greatest need of English literary support. Murry
has denounced with eloquence[1] the English literary men who
earlier withheld this. We have already seen that as a comparatively unimportant reviewer he avoided doing what he
could for *The Rainbow*. Now that he had some standing,[2] we
find not only that he could risk nothing to give Lawrence a
hand, but that as time went on he lost no opportunity of dis-
paraging Lawrence in public. He believed that Lawrence
was finished, and he had his own growing reputation as a
critic to safeguard. So every book by Lawrence that appeared
was persistently slighted or attacked in the *Athenaeum*. Thus
Murry, unable to enter on a new relation of the kind Lawrence

---

[1] *Reminiscences.*

[2] Although he has said that his position was 'precarious,' he remained
there until the amalgamation of the *Athenaeum* with the *Nation* in
December 1921, after which he continued upon the staff as an important
reviewer.

longed for between men, was able to forsake the traditional
decencies of friendship.   When he was at his most 'sincere,' it
was only with regard to an abstraction—to an ideal or a new
notion.   His was the 'white, egoistic and benevolent
volition,' that Lawrence saw as the vampire of warm life.
Of heart loyalty he never showed a trace.   No wonder that
Lawrence, who had a heart, moaned in his sleep over such
a one.   It was not until 1922, when Lawrence was well
enough established neither to need a hand nor to involve
any risk for those who gave it, that Murry deliriously discovered a masterpiece in a book of far less significance than
either *The Rainbow* or *Women in Love*, a book that is certainly not superior as a novel to *The Lost Girl*—namely
Aaron's Rod. With that and the *Fantasia of the Unconscious*,
he would have us believe, Lawrence reached the 'pinnacle
of his achievement,' before wallowing once more in the
disintegration—this time a final one—of his later work.   As
belonging to the later work *The Plumed Serpent*, *The Man
Who Died* or *Apocalypse* are not mentioned, as these would
derange the invalid chart with its ascents and descents which
Murry's case has obliged him to make out.   To describe
that case, *Fantasia of the Unconscious* would seem the most
charitable of labels.

XII

It was at Whitsun, falling in the latter part of May, that we
three went down to Hermitage for a few days to stay at the
local midwife's cottage which was quite close to Chapel
Farm Cottage where the Lawrences were.   Lawrence had
taken the rooms for us there, and we had goat's milk for the
child, who was now weaned, from a white nanny that was
tethered in the back garden.

Again it seems to have been mostly good weather that
summer, though I remember some slashing showers one day

when Lawrence and Donald and I went to Silchester (*Calleva Atrebatum*) in high hopes of seeing something spectacular by way of Roman remains. We missed the last train back, and had to walk a long way home, without having set eyes on anything more exciting than some grass-covered mounds.

Usually Lawrence was to be found sitting on a kitchen chair, under the apple tree, in the garden that was open to the road, writing steadily and rapidly on his knee.[1] (He had asked us to sell his typewriter for him, and my brother bought it for £4, which seemed a lot to all of us.) He was putting the finishing touches to the history book and writing short stories. That spring too, after 'gnashing his teeth in vain' over something more acceptable upon the controversial subject of education for *The Times Educational Supplement* ('I couldn't write the educational stuff,' he said in a letter to me, 'I tried so hard—it wouldn't work in me—no go.') he wrote the play *Touch and Go*.

Between-whiles at Hermitage we went wooding with a ricketty push-chair among the sheets of bluebells, which were just past their best, and so were outshone by the suits of bright blue coarse linen worn by the Lawrences. Frieda and Lawrence were justly proud of these suits, which they had themselves cut out and made. As a woodman Lawrence excelled, collecting twice as much as anybody else and constantly rejecting our faggots as worthless. With all he had to do, in and out of the house, he found time to help the midwife's little daughter every day with her lessons, and he was ready at any time to take a turn in minding John Patrick, our boy, who was now of an age to walk round the kitchen

---

[1] The short story, 'The Fox,' belongs to the Hermitage. Also, I believe, the rabbit story, 'Adolf,' which Lawrence thought highly of himself, but could not place in England. It appeared in the *Dial* in Sept. 1920.

table by clutching its edge.   For the first time I had the
chance to see how good Lawrence was with children.   He
made no special business of them, but knew how to include
them warmly and naturally in his life.   He was devoid of
tricks with them, either old-fashioned or modern, and I was
struck by the children's response to a certain light astringency
in his treatment of them.   It was either here or at the
Forest of Dean that seeing me bathe John Patrick, he remarked with a sigh, '*He* won't be having any chest trouble!'
And again with a little grin, 'I suppose he'll grow up into
what they call a virile man!'

   Lawrence himself was looking delicate, and as if still waiting to be delivered of that 'contained fury' of his.   His chief
hope now lay in the expected visit of Huebsch, his American
publisher, who would, he said, make arrangements for an
early visit to America.   His failure with the *Athenaeum* had
given him an additional shove towards the wilderness.
England was become more than ever distasteful.   As late as
the July of that year, Lawrence's letters to Pinker and others
showed signs of having been tampered with.   Frieda was 'in
accord' with him that go they must.   Of their plans he wrote
to me, 'Don't tell *anybody* what I say here.   I don't tell
anybody but you.'   And his parting advice to me was, 'Don't
be cast down, don't get used up.   Above all conserve yourself,
and live only in marriage, not elsewhere.'

   There had been talk of them coming to us in August—
this time to the New Forest, where we were friendly with
one of the agisters, lived in a rough farm, and got any amount
of riding on the forest ponies.   But we had no more than a
glimpse of them in town in the early summer, when they
were on their way to the Midlands.   After that, being offered
a cottage at Pangbourne by Rosalind Baynes, they went there,
and Lawrence's sisters came to stay alternately till the middle
of September.   We then saw them again in London, when

they stayed with Koteliansky. As Ada, since getting home, had been very ill, Lawrence made yet another trip to the Midlands. But it was his farewell. Now he was really on the wing. Somebody had told him of a farm at Caserta, near Naples, and this made a good enough objective. The passports were ready at last. Lawrence has somewhere described vividly how he saw Frieda off, with a malicious grin on her face, to see her mother in Germany. Attached as he was to the old Baroness,[1] he shrank just then from visiting Germany. He would go later. For the present he asked us to find through friends in Rome a 'very simple room' there. He would wait for Frieda in Florence, and they would go south together to prospect, staying in Rome on their way. Except by introduction he knew nobody in Italy.

Now he ran down alone to Berkshire to sell at Reading what books he had in the cottage. Lawrence never collected much of a library, as he was obliged so often to disperse his belongings. And, anyhow, he never wanted a library. On this occasion he gave us his tattered but complete set of De Quincey's works, with the hope that some day we might be rich enough to have them rebound. He wrote: 'He is a very nice man. I can go on reading and reading him. I laughed over "Goethe" yesterday. I like him, De Quincey, because he also dislikes such people as Plato and Goethe, whom I dislike.' We too find that we can go on reading and re-reading De Quincey. He still remains in his original state on our shelves.

[1] When she was in London before the War, Lawrence had brought his mother-in-law to see me, and I well understood his affection for her. She, for her part, from first to last, regarded Lawrence as a most satisfactory son-in-law. There was real peace and steady devotion between them. How he managed it I can't think, but he was able to give regular and practical help to her when she was in grave need of the necessaries of life during the worst time of post-War hardship in Germany.

For the understanding of Lawrence it is needful to remember how completely he disliked and wished to transcend that classic ideal of human balance which was initiated by Plato, and of which Goethe was the great modern embodiment. The whole current of Lawrence's life and work represents a movement towards a new and different kind of balance that would be consistent with all human imperfections.

We, on our side, gave as a parting present a somewhat worn coat-lining of natural camel's hair, which we afterwards learned was 'a godsend' in Sicily in winter. And he accepted with protest, but obvious pleasure, a voluminous black and white shepherd's plaid which had been my mother's and grandmother's! This was destined to figure in *Sea and Sardinia*, but ultimately to fall into the hands of an Italian robber.

We both went to see the solitary pilgrim off. So far as I remember, nobody else was at the station except Koteliansky. Lawrence felt the wrench of the departure, but he was glad, very glad, to be going.

PART THREE
Aet. 34–36

Prose

AARON'S ROD
THE LOST GIRL
INTRODUCTION TO MEMOIR OF
    THE FOREIGN LEGION
SEA AND SARDINIA (travel essays)
THE MAN WHO DIED
THE LADYBIRD, ETC. (3 novelettes)
FANTASIA OF THE UNCONSCIOUS

Verse

BIRDS, BEASTS AND FLOWERS (*in part*)
TORTOISES

Translations

MASTRO DON GESUALDO (Verga)
LITTLE NOVELS OF SICILY (Verga)

★

'It is hard to hear a new voice.'

PART THREE

I

SOME friend, beforehand, had made known the date of his coming to Norman Douglas, who had taken a room for him at 10 lire a day at the Pension Balestri (called the 'Cavalotti' in the introduction to Magnus's *Memoir of the Foreign Legion*). Douglas and Magnus were themselves living at the Balestri. In that same introduction we read how on the dark, wet, wintry evening, after his through journey from London, Lawrence found the kindly and practical note of directions waiting for him at Cook's, and how on his way to the Piazza Mentana he was overtaken at the Ponte Vecchió by Douglas with Magnus in tow. No account of the days that followed could hope to rival that given by Lawrence in the Magnus introduction. He said to me once that he considered this the best single piece of writing, *as writing*, that he had ever done.

On the evidence contained therein, it seems to me that Lawrence's activity with the typewriter, which, on a third visit eighteen months later, was to cause so much amusement —of the friendliest sort—in both Douglas and Rebecca West when they welcomed him again to Florence, was not of the precipitate order they fancied.[1] It was more probably an endeavour, with Magnus's *Memoir* in mind, to provide his 1919 impressions with the refreshed significance furnished by his 1921 arrival. The sordid tragedy of poor Magnus had been played to a finish during the period between the two visits.

I had two postcards from the Balestri, the first beginning : 'Am here in the rain, waiting for Frieda, of whom I hear nothing yet. Italy is rather spoiled by the War—a different

[1] *D. H. Lawrence,* by Rebecca West, p. 22.

temper—not so nice a humour by far.' In the second he said he had a really sunny room over the Arno, with good wine, an easy going *padrone* and altogether such 'a nice carelessness' that he felt he would 'loaf away all his substance.'

Lawrence had from first to last a great liking for Florence, which he felt was a man's town. He loved to move among the throng of men in the great Piazza on a market day, and, though I believe somebody has announced the contrary, I have heard him refuse to have a word said against the rich and dominating maleness of Michael Angelo's 'David.'

When Frieda joined him, he waited on there with her yet a while before they went on together to Rome, where my friend had found what she thought was a suitable pension. In Rome during a short stay they met with two calamities. They were turned out of the first pension (whether English or Italian I am not sure, though I think it was Italian) on the discovery that Frieda was German. Given eager hospitality then by my friend, who, as it happened, was the heroic support of a strangely mingled household, they were robbed of the greater part of their ready money. The position was painful in more ways than one. Lawrence had at once conceived a real liking for his hostess, who, moreover, though by no means wealthy, had refused to consider payment from him. He knew not only that she was herself above suspicion, but that, whether the thief were discovered or not, she would insist upon refunding the lost money (something like £10, which had just been changed into Italian notes). What was even worse was that, rightly or wrongly, Lawrence had come to his own conclusions as to the nature of the theft and the identity of the thieves, and he reckoned that if the crime were brought home, it would cause a lasting wound which would injure the innocent more than the guilty. He decided accordingly to say nothing about it. As the household is now broken up by death and other causes, I feel at liberty to narrate the incident

which the Lawrences told me in confidence years after it
happened.

In Florence too, either on this or some later visit, Lawrence was robbed of his much-needed cash. He was getting
on to the crowded train at Fiesole when his wallet was taken
from his pocket. He described to me his feelings when he
made the discovery—first the sensation as if his heart had
dropped from his breast through the soles of his feet, then
the mounting fury that flushed him to the roots of his hair.
But yet more characteristic of him was his philosophical
summing up of the mishap. 'It is a good lesson,' he announced with crisp emphasis. 'One gets into a silly soft
way of trusting one's fellows. One *must not* trust them, for
they are not trustworthy. One must live as the wild animals
live, always wary, always on one's guard against enemies.
It makes one more alive, anyway, and not really more suspicious. It is best to recognise the truth that most people
will do you if they can.'

Such a determination in Lawrence was compatible with
an enviable lightness over losses. He never made moan and
never wasted time over them, blaming his own softness as
much or more than the cupidity or dishonesty of the other
fellow. The swindle, already referred to, over the American
rights of *Sons and Lovers* was another case in point.

When asked why he did not make such a matter public
and fight for his legal rights, Lawrence only shrugged his
shoulders. It was not that he claimed or possessed the
orthodox Christian emotion or that he was non-resistant on
principle. He resented such injuries, and made no pretence
of forgetting or forgiving them. But neither would he let
them prey upon him. In this, as in so much else, he evinced
a sense of life which might be called transcendentally practical. He never forgot the limits of a man's time and strength,
especially when that man is handicapped by poverty and

'unhappy bronchials.' To the loss of money—always partly
due to one's own fault—he would not add the expenditure
of more precious forms of energy.   He was profoundly
philosophic, and had he been both stronger and richer, I am
sure his view would have remained unchanged.   For him
the law, though admittedly necessary, was always 'a hass.'
He would not even allow, what I was at times inclined to
urge, that one must on occasion fight for one's clear rights,
if only to discourage villains and encourage the other victims
of villainy. He admitted the need of courts of justice; but,
'No,' he would say, 'let others do as they like or as they
must.   For me it is nothing but waste to invoke justice or to
inflict punishment.'   After all, such an episode as that concerning *Sons and Lovers* could be 'counted off,' said he, with
a light arrogance, as 'the price of fame.'   So, perhaps, could
the later striking depletion of his profits by the folly and
failure of an American publisher, who meant no ill, but
reckoned on a better turn of fortune for himself and a longer
life for Lawrence than was decreed.

Lawrence's point of view was vitally aristocratic.   That
is to say it was the point of view of the man so assured of his
rights that he feels no obligation to fight for them.   He
allowed himself immediate fury in plenty and a warning
memory of the chicaneries, slights and breaches of faith
which it was his lot to suffer.   But they were permitted no
abiding place in his life save by that heightened awareness
which he took to be an element in vital being.   This, I
take it, though he framed it courteously, was what he meant
when, long after the event, he told Murry that he bore no
grudge for the review of *Women in Love*.   To bear a grudge
was a sin against life.   But he felt no call to 'forgive' Murry's
sin against the heart.   Once more, as it seems to me, Lawrence, by repudiating the Christian doctrine, discoverd its
soul afresh, and that in a way which would have been im-

possible without initial repudiation. For him the emotional
tenet of Christian forgiveness was closely connected with
that organised revenge from which came the Great War.

Almost certainly the theme of *Aaron's Rod*, as well as
its charming and unusual opening, belonged to the period
before Lawrence left England. Both theme and opening
must have suggested themselves during his visit to the Midlands for the Christmas of 1918. In a letter written in
February, 1920, he speaks of a half-finished novel in MS.
being held up with Frieda's luggage in Germany owing to a
railway strike, and a fortnight later tells of having just
'started a novel.' The first-mentioned, I take it, was
Aaron's Rod, and the second, *The Lost Girl*.

The failure to find a resting-place in the neighbourhood
of Caserta was certainly productive of the memorable Italian
section of *The Lost Girl*, which Lawrence completed in May,
1920. Such a dove-tailing of literary circumstance works
havoc with the psychic pattern, or clinical picture designed
for us by Murry in *Son of Woman*. As a picture it is both
plausible and impassioned. But it fades away in the hard
light of chronology.

After some wandering from place to place during the
early part of December 'in a state of restlessness,' the
Lawrences were at Picinisco. But they found that it was
impossible. 'Beautiful beyond words but *so* primitive, and
so cold.' Almost they thought they would have died.
'Mountains stood round in a ring, glittering like devils,'
and on the Saturday before Christmas it snowed all day long.
So, as he wrote me early in January from Capri, they
extricated themselves on the Monday, by getting up at 5.30,
walking five miles to Atina, catching the post omnibus there
which carried them ten miles to Cassino, which was the
only station, and reaching Naples by train in time to catch
the 3 P.M. boat to Capri. As they left the bay the sea rose,

and by 7.30, when they came into the shallow port of Capri, it ran so high that the boats could not put out to land them. There was nothing for it but to go back and seek the semi-shelter of Sorrento, there to roll horribly all night with a ship-load of moaning Italians. Luckily neither Frieda nor Lawrence was sick.

At Capri for 160 francs a month they took the top floor of the old and 'extremely beautiful' Palazzo Ferraro which had 'a staircase like a prison, not a palace,' and was 'on the very neck of the little town, on the very neck of the island,' so that they felt they could almost touch 'the queer bubbling Duomo' from their balcony, and they overlooked all the island life as well as the bay of Naples and Ischia on their right, and on their left 'the wide open Mediterranean.' They had two large rooms to themselves and shared a kitchen with a young Roumanian Socialist who lost no opportunity of pouring his Socialism into Lawrence's ear. Down to the sea was only a short, steep mile, and though they sometimes felt the need of a fire in the evenings, the days were warm and stormy. 'The narcissus flowers still are many in the rocks, but passing: sweet they are, Greece. A few pink cactus flowers too.'

It was now that Lawrence severed his connection with the firm of J. B. Pinker. As early as November, 1918, there had been a threatened break. At that date, it will be re-called, Lawrence, hard-driven, had appealed through Pinker to Arnold Bennett for a job—unsuccessfully. He had suffered from a resultant nausea, which was not helped by the per-sistently miserable sums offered for his work in England, nor by his constant need to approach his agent for advances. It had even been a nice question as to whether it was worth while having a story like 'The Fox' typed, acceptance being so unlikely. But the situation had been tided over, partly perhaps by the client's inability to meet a settlement of the account. It had not grown more tolerable, however. Increasingly Lawrence had felt unhappy in the connection, conscious that he was a 'bother' and an 'unsatisfactory person' from Pinker's point of view, and that Pinker's faith in him as a business proposition had been over-tried. The strain had become so great that Lawrence dreaded either the writing or the receipt of a letter bearing the Arundel Street address. So, in 1920, being at last enabled to square up by the receipt of Huebsch's cheque for the American *Look! We have Come Through!* he seized the chance and made an end. By March everything was settled, even to the repayment of Bennett's £25 ('Who *is* E. A. Bennett?' inquired Lawrence in some irritation!); and with full acknowledgments of all that Pinker had done for him throughout the past five years, this 'unpleasant handful' received his small parcel of agreements and his large parcel of unpublished MSS. into his own keeping. After all, he hoped soon to go to America where Pinker had not then, as he has now, an extensive connection, and Mountsier was already selling short stories by Lawrence at 250 dollars apiece. To-day one wonders if Lawrence's business affairs might not have prospered better had he been able to round his Cape Horn without a change of ships. Humanly speaking, too, when Pinker had done so much and had faced so many unprecedented difficulties, it was hard that his firm should not have reaped the benefit. Frieda especially regretted the termination. But it could not be helped, and no blame attaches to either party, whereas the credit of the one and the honesty of the other stand high in any perusal of the correspondence. The determining factor was that, with all his kindness and generosity, Pinker had not much hope of Lawrence left. So Lawrence had to cut loose. Murry has said that the only way he can make up his mind about anybody is to write a book about them, which means they must be dead first. Lawrence greatly needed a few people who could make their minds up while he was still alive.

II

The cosmopolitan island life was amusing for a time—
'pleasant and bohemian. I wish you were both here'—and
before he tired of its scandalous unreality he wrote home about
it entertainingly, and not without malice. Of this order was
his account of a New Year's Eve celebration in Morgano's
Café. Primarily an Italian affair—given over to the barbaric
performances in song, dance and recitation, of bands of young
men—it became towards midnight, according to Lawrence, a
mere background for the decorative figure of Mr. Compton
Mackenzie flanked by rich Americans and issuing com-
mands for champagne. ' "Head of the realistic school of
England, isn't he?" ' asks the Roumanian with whom, in
company with an aged Dutchman, Lawrence and Frieda were
sipping a humble punch. Later, Lawrence was to become
friendly with Mackenzie. For the present, though he has
already lunched and dined sometimes with his *confrère*, he
watches the rich English-American party with these shrewish,
almost old-maidenly eyes of his. 'He is nice,' he records.
'But one feels the generations of actors behind him, and can't
be quite serious. What a queer thing the theatre is, in its
influence. He seems quite rich and does himself well and
walks a sort of æsthetic figure . . . walking in a pale blue
suit to match his eyes, and a large woman's brown velour
hat to match his hair.' Of the Americans who with 'an
excruciating self-conscious effort' were trying 'to look
wine and womanish,' he says, 'Oh God, the wild rakish-
ness of these young heroes! How conscious they are of
the Italian crowd in the background. They never see
the faint smile of the same crowd—such a smile. A glass
of champagne is sent out to the old road-sweeper from
the bounteous English Signore. It is the right thing to
do. Meanwhile we sip our last drop of punch, and are the

Poor Relations at the other end of the table—ignored—to
our amusement.'

But in the same breath Lawrence finds that he is 'nearly
as spiteful as the rest of Capri' and 'The English-speaking
crowd are the uttermost uttermost limit for spiteful scandal.
My dear Catherine, London is a prayer-meeting in comparison. . . . We've got a long way to go, such mere people
as us. It would be an interesting document, to set down this
scandal verbatim. Suetonius would blush to his heels, and
Tiberius would feel he'd been a flea-bite.'

He finds too that commodities are beyond his purse—
'butter 20 francs, wine 3 francs a litre the cheapest,—sugar
8 francs a kilo, oil 7 or 8 francs a litre, carbone a franc for
two kilos—a porter expects ten francs for bringing one's
luggage from the sea—and so on. With the exchange at 50,
it is just possible and only just.'

There came, however, an unexpected present of £20 from
America. I do not know who sent this, but it must have been
one who could afford it or Lawrence would not have taken
it. As it was, he at once sent £5 of it unasked to Magnus,
guessing that he was hard pressed, and he was enabled toward
the end of that January to make the strange, much-desired
trip alone to the monastery of Monte Cassino. This meant
an exhausting day's journey each way for a visit of only three
nights. It was like Lawrence that he took with him only the
smallest surplus of money over and above what was required
for his bare necessities. The present had been for Frieda as
much as for him, and he foresaw that Magnus would victimise
him for all there might be of loose cash.

Again a peerless record is to be found in the introduction.
In it he combines the fullest admissions of a limited humanity
with the limitless desire to remain faithful to that which is
beyond humanity. It rises to its height in that part where
Lawrence, looking down from the mountain top where St.

Thomas Aquinas was educated, as if from 'the last foothold
of the old world,' finds himself racked, as no other man of
our time has been racked, between the 'bitter and barren'
present in the plain below, and 'the poignancy of the not-
quite-dead past' which lingered above in these old walls.
To those who would comprehend Lawrence, here is a passage
of the utmost significance.   On Monte Cassino, as on no
other single occasion, he saw his temptation and his destiny,
and he put the first from him and accepted the second open-
eyed.   To the lovely past, as worshipped by the monks
behind him, he would not bow down, though it might bring
peace. He must live in the hard and often loathsome present,
an individual man's life, with all its needs, contradictions and
errors proclaimed as it goes along: and at the same time he
must be an unswerving conduit from the very origins of life
—so far back that they were lost—to the undiscovered
future, in some way that transcended, while it never elimin-
ated or absolved the individual.   The conception, I believe, is
new and it is potent.   But a kind of sensitiveness akin to
the sensitiveness of Lawrence, which is a thing far removed
from emotionalism, has to be acquired before either the
novelty or the potency becomes apparent.   In Lawrence's
own perception of it he felt that his heart was 'once more
broken.'   But it is characteristic that, when questioned
by Magnus, he merely put it that he was 'too worldly' to
think of becoming a monk.   In conversation, at any rate,
Lawrence habitually refrained from casting his pearls
before swine. Neither did he ever wear his heart on his
sleeve.

At the moment literary affairs were by no means satisfactory. The appearance of his *History* was still deferred,
and he still awaited revised proofs for indexing. He had
refused a first offer to publish *The Rainbow* with certain
omissions and alterations on condition of the selling of all

rights for £200, and he was negotiating with another publisher for simple publication on the basis of 'a first royalty,
which is all I want.' He hoped, this once settled, that the
English publication of *Women in Love* might follow with the
same publisher.

Again, the tiny hand-printed and illustrated book of
poems called *Bay* had taken seventeen months in production,
and except for the beautiful paper and print it was all that
Lawrence wished it not to be. Poems and inscriptions which
he had intended for inclusion were left out. He was confident
that some, at least, of the poems were 'really beautiful and
rare.' Otherwise, in his judgment, this was 'a silly-looking
little book . . .' with 'silly little woodcuts, so out of keeping
with the poems.'

At about the same time there was printed the play *Touch
and Go*, which Katherine Mansfield had not liked—that
I well understood—but which she described as being 'black
with miners,' which I find hardly more enlightening as a
criticism of a play that concerns itself with miners, than was
Murry's criticism of a novel dealing with death, that its
message was 'deathly.' If it be true, as I believe, that Gudrun
in *Women in Love* was derived from Katherine Mansfield,
the same derivation must be found for Anabel in the play.
Lawrence had written the jarring but interesting seven-page
preface to this paper-covered book (issued by Daniel, Ltd.,
in 1920) while at Hermitage in June, 1919. It was the
second (and the second-last) of a series projected by Mr.
Douglas Goldring for a People's Theatre. The original
understanding was that performances were to be given either
at the Lyric, Hammersmith, or at the Court Theatre, with
Lawrence's play first in order, and afterwards plays of social
interest by any 'member' who had become so by paying a
guinea (or was it two?) to the projector. Desiring to see a
play by Lawrence put on, and having a possible one of my

own up my sleeve, I became a member. But I neither saw
nor heard of any performance in connection with the scheme.
The third play on the list—*The Kingdom, the Power, and
the Glory*, by Mr. Hamilton Fyfe, was given three performances at the Lyric by 'the Play-actors.' But this, I
understand, had nothing to do with the People's Theatre,
and was, no doubt, brought about by the author's own enterprise or influence. Like Lawrence (who did so with Pinker's
disapproval) Mr. Fyfe had given Goldring his play for nothing, so far as the book was concerned, on the understanding
that it would be seen in performance. Performance, however,
was never attempted. Lawrence wrote to me of it in
February, 1920:

. . . That will be another fiasco. Yesterday I got Douglas
Goldring's play—*Fight for Freedom*. It is the first of the series—
and is a pamphlet play with a detestable and inartistic motive.
Goldring got *Touch and Go* out of me, saying it, *Touch and Go*,
would be the first of the plays for a People's Theatre. Then the
sly journalist went and put this offensive *Fight for Freedom* as the
first play—and for sure has damned and doubly damned the lot.
I don't *want* to be associated with the *Fight for Freedom*. . . .
And there is *Touch and Go* with a preface written specially. Curse
the sly mongrel world. Fortunately the *Fight for Freedom* has
been utterly ignored—so that, publicly at least, *Touch and Go*
escapes much connection. I know you don't like the play—but
anyhow it's not *base*.

It was indeed far from base, this dramatic effort which
escaped publicity so completely that few readers of Lawrence
seem to know of its existence. And though at the time I
did not like it—shrinking from its frictional character and
the inconclusive painfulness of its final scene—I find, upon
re-reading it, many virtues, including an easy vivacity and a
clear and pregnant dramatic statement. The scenes between
the lovers, Gerald and Anabel, give one an odd foretaste of

Noel Coward at his best, while the speechifying of the miners is both vivid and true to life.   It was written while the successful 'theatre' of Galsworthy's *Strife* was fresh in mind ('Mr. Galsworthy had a peep at the Strike situation,' says the preface, 'and sank down towards bathos') and in it Lawrence draws firmly the distinction between non-tragic disaster and that fate, agonising but veritably tragic and therefore fruitful, which follows the working out of some immediate passional problems within the soul of a man.   In the true tragedy of 'creative crisis' Lawrence would say, the many 'still know some happiness, the very happiness of creative suffering.'   And we have, he would urge, at least 'the moment of pure choice,' in which each may decide whether he will 'go through with his fate, and not dodge it'; or by piling accident on accident, 'tear the fabric of our existence fibre by fibre.'   By the second—which is the method of 'a mechanico-material struggle,' even if it brings disaster and death to millions—we get no more than an accidental 'crawl from under one cart wheel straight under another.'   By the first, though the fighters themselves may die, death becomes only 'a climax in the progression towards new being.'   For 'the whole business of life, at the great critical periods of mankind, is that men should accept and be one with their tragedy.'   From this alone new life can come. And here, if nowhere else, we exercise free will in choosing or refusing.

Its intrinsic interest apart, *Touch and Go* is of use to readers of Lawrence in the elucidation of both *Women in Love* and *Lady Chatterley's Lover*.   In the character of Gerald, which is common to the first-named novel and the play, Lawrence records his sympathy with the gifted employer— the powerful and proud young man of aristocratic temper and keen intelligence, who has given of his disinterested best to an industry, and refuses to be bullied by hands who are no more than hands, however great may be their show of numbers. Gerald is essentially the man of organised achievement, to whom, as such, Lawrence pays hearty tribute.

'You meet a man,' he wrote to me in December, 1916, defending his deferment of information concerning Gerald in *Women in Love*. 'You get an impression of him. You find out *afterwards* what he has done. If "you" have, in your arrogance, writ him down a nobody then there is a slap in the eye for you when you find he has done more than you have done. Voilà!'

We get too, in this play, the scales held evenly between the genuine Christian sweetness (so unavailing) of Gerald's father, and the honesty and pride (made crazy and of no avail by our modern life) of Gerald's mother. These two horribly cancel each other out. And we get the voice of a miner who is a genuine man, as well as the voices of miners who beat an unmanly retreat behind the fiction of a merely economic struggle.

Later in the same month—February, 1920—I received from Lawrence the announcement of a forthcoming production at Altrincham near Manchester of his first play, *The Widowing of Mrs. Holroyd*. The performance was to be by a company of experienced amateurs, and Lawrence was anxious to know how it went. He wished me, if possible, to see it and to write a notice which would get into print. To this end he insisted upon sending me £5 for my journey to Cheshire and back. But this, happily, I did not need, as I managed to obtain a commission from *The Times*.

He was now sick of 'this cat Cranford of Capri,' this 'stewpot of semi-literary cats.' It was too much for his nerves, he said. He had come to like Compton Mackenzie, but 'not his island nor his influence.' When I asked why he did not write a satire on the Capri society, he said No, satire 'just dries up one's bowels—and that I don't like.'

The MS. of the half-written novel was stuck with the heavy luggage somewhere between Turin and Naples owing to a three weeks' railway strike. But with or without his possessions, Lawrence was determined to move to Sicily. To Sicily we too must come, travelling by sea and bringing John Patrick (now aged twenty months) for whom a Sicilian nurse would be found. This, before they were themselves assured of a foothold! But in the first week of March the invitation was renewed from Fontana Vecchia, Taormina. 'One should not take the world too seriously. I wish you could both come out here to Italy and vegetate—why should one always strive and struggle?' And then—'such a lovely house and garden here—taken it for a year.'

III

Lawrence had taken the house at Taormina for a year, at the rent of £25, or 2000 lire (the exchange being then at 80). 'Heaven knows which way we shall be moving next,' he wrote in May. 'Depends which way the wind blows us. But one's instinct is to go south, south—and away, away from Europe. Here we are almost on the last tip—and my face still looks south, as if one must step off into space somewhere.'

In April he had visited Syracuse with new friends he had made in Sicily (probably Mr. and Mrs. Brewster) and it was soon after his return that the fugitive and penniless Magnus descended upon him.

The pamphlet written by Norman Douglas as a counterblast to Lawrence's narrative of Magnus is well known and will always hold its place in the archives of literary dispute. It is brilliant and creditable—I mean that it does credit to the writer's heart and head. Some of Lawrence's best friends have agreed with its finding that a poor wretch who has been driven to take his own life, should not have been subjected, anyhow within the covers of his own book, to so searching an examination. While I respect and understand, I do not share this view. Having lately re-read both productions, it seems to me that Lawrence who, after all, was far less the friend than the victim of Magnus, has given his subject full human dues while nailing for good to the barn-door a particular kind of predatory fowl, which to have done is to have rendered a service to honest men in this naughty world. The man whom Douglas defends—naturally and properly as they were on a footing of tolerant affection—does not command the outside reader's sympathy in anything like the same degree as does the man whom Lawrence condemns. In the first case our tribute goes to Douglas; in the second it is compelled for Magnus. At the same time, the sentimentality of this age having run somewhat to the excusing of charming bullies and semi-artistic good-for-nothings, it is a relief to find the inherent nastiness of dishonesty made plain. This, quite apart from other values to be found in the Lawrence narrative. It is true, as Douglas says, that Lawrence gives himself away as much as he gives away Magnus. And that also is good. It contains one of the most vivid of his self-portraits and was never seriously regretted by him. In two words, the Lawrence production will stand as a creative, and the Douglas one as a pious effort.

That May, when Lawrence was bailing Magnus out, his own funds were low enough, and I wanted very much to give him fifty pounds. After long and vain travelling from one publisher to another (one firm would have accepted it if I would have cut it down by two-thirds) my novel had won a 'First novel' prize of £250. So I had this, and I thought it only fair that Lawrence should have a slice. From the first, however, he would consent only to 'hold it' for me in case I could come out there that summer. He had at last signed an agreement for *Women in Love* and *The Rainbow*

(£100 to be received on publication for the first, and later the same sum for *The Rainbow*, with the cautious proviso that this should not be paid until three months after publication, and even so, that it should be subject to deduction by any charges of legal proceedings that might arise). He expected 'pretty soon' to have the money for *Women in Love*. But the typing of *The Lost Girl* in Rome cost 1000 lire, and immediate supplies were short.

Unlike Murry Lawrence thought *The Lost Girl* 'quite amusing: and quite moral.' 'She's not morally lost, poor darling,' he added, '. . . marries an Italian.' He wished to serialise this book, but did not succeed in doing so. It brought him a good new friend, however, and a Scottish one—the painter Miss Millicent Beveridge. Reading this as the first of his novels, she became determined to meet the author. She has told me how that meeting took place, at a party in Sicily where she found Lawrence in a rage because, not made aware beforehand that it was a party and that he was to be lionised, he had turned up barefoot with sandals and in his 'pottering about' clothes. In this respect Lawrence was no bohemian. He believed in suiting the occasion. Miss Beveridge, amused and astonished as much as she was charmed, became sincerely attached to him, and the friendship remained firm till his death. Mrs. Sterne in her book has said that women meant more than men to Lawrence. This is not so. Apart from his mother and Frieda it was men that really counted. But though the last thing that can be said of him is that he was a lover of women, his liking was a very precious thing, lasting, and with depths of tenderness in it. Also it was reciprocated.

May was very hot in Sicily.

Do you know what it is to be in a *dry* southern country—dry, like Africa? I never knew before. But I like it. The sun is a bit overwhelming. Nearly all foreigners have left here already.

To-day we are going down to the sea to bathe. But it is a good ½ hour down, and 1 hour up. Mary Cannan has a studio here—nice— for 3 more months. She is dying to go to Malta—the boat runs from Syracuse. But she can't go alone. So she wants us to go if she pays our ship fare—it's only 8 hours crossing. It might be amusing, for 4 or 5 days. But Malta isn't wildly attractive, and I am doubtful if I want to spend the money.

But Mary Cannan had set her mind on it, and the Lawrences went with her. Norman Douglas has quoted an extract from a letter in which Magnus describes with malicious veracity the boredom of Lawrence in Malta. Back in Taormina on May 28th he wrote to me:

. . . we were to stay only two days—then a steam boat strike, and we only got back to-night, after some 11 days. Oh, and it was *so* expensive, and I feel so displeased. Malta is a strange place— a dry bath brick island that glares and sets your teeth on edge and is *so* dry that one expects oneself to begin to crackle. Valetta Harbour is wonderful: beautiful. But I get set on edge by the British regime. It is very decent, I believe, but it sort of stops life, it prevents the human reactions from taking full swing, there is always a kind of half measure, half-length, 'not quite' feeling about, which simply arrests my digestion.

Upon his return he had found my cheque waiting for him, and again he gave me to understand that he would not use it but would keep it for me in his bank. A day or so later, however, he suddenly decided otherwise. From America had come 2000 lire for stories. 'I have enough money. And why should I hold any of yours in fee. So I accept the gift all the same: and have burned your cheque.' Again, 'what you do want is money, so you must get it.' Once he started, he felt confident that *he* could make money. 'Then we'll share mine. It won't be long. You see if it is.' I had by then been to Altrincham to see *Mrs. Holroyd*

and I confess that on my way there the undertaking began
to assume the nature of a penance.   Lawrence had betrayed
that he was eager, even nervous as to the results.   'I have a
dreadful feeling that it may be a fiasco,' he had written.
So too had I.

The presentation, however, was creditable if no more.   It
compared favourably with the performance given in London
by the Stage Society in December, 1926, which also I saw.
To do justice to the Altrincham players and the Altrincham
audience, no sniggering was elicited by the scene where the
dead miner's body is washed by his women.   All the same,
I felt that in a play so realistically written and produced, a
body-washing scene was theatrically unacceptable.   Either it
must be done 'off' with only the voices and the footsteps
of the women to give it reality, or the stage must be darkened
to a firelight glow and the whole production lifted into a
plane beyond realism with movements that were classically
simplified.   To read, the scene is simple and tragic.   Outside
the Irish People's Plays I reckon we can hardly match it in
English with any other scene of dramatic dialogue having
working folk as the protagonists.   And the play holds its
own against the Irish plays.   Yet, as things are, it does not
quite 'do,' and I believe the reason lies in the fact that the
theatre itself was antipathetic to Lawrence, so much so that
even when writing for it he maintained his antipathy.
'Here is drama,' one imagines him to say—'here is prose
drama as authentic as any the English theatre can show.   It
is not "good theatre!"   Then the English theatre must
change itself to accommodate a living contemporary English
play.'   The first scenes of *Mrs. Holroyd*, like the first scenes
in *Touch and Go*, prove that Lawrence had the art of crisp
and pregnant stage dialogue.   The action besides, the exits
and the entrances are finely devised, and the conflict is real.
It is not surprising to find that in his youth Lawrence

contemplated the production of a volume of plays, nor that he could not resist occasional returns to the dramatic form. But the theatre is a task-mistress who demands not only obedience but enslavement. And Lawrence would not bow the head to such a muse. We find, accordingly, that though his plays are far from being mere literary dramatisations, and are most genuinely plays, they are not truly adapted to the mechanics of our stage.

Of contemporary productions, opera, with its light-hearted formality and transparent artifice, was probably most to his taste. He was not interested in 'problems,' effective situations, or any of the sophisticated trickery of the modern theatre. I question indeed if he ever found enjoyment in witnessing a play unless it might be one of the older classics. Once, and only once, I was so ill advised as to book seats for him and myself to see—what he thought might be interesting —the translation of Tolstoi's *Living Corpse* at the St. James's Theatre with Henry Ainley and my friend Athene Seyler in the leading parts. And *how* he hated it and everything about it, so far as the theatre was concerned! The more the germ of the thing appealed to him, the more he was appalled by what he considered to be the falsity and ineptitude of its stage appeal. It made him so unhappy, that before the performance was half through he found himself unable to endure it longer, even with his face buried in his hands. 'Do you mind, Catherine, I just can't bear it any longer!' he whispered. There was nothing for it but to squeeze our way out from our upper circle seats (particularly narrow in that theatre) earning, as we did so, black looks from a long row of earnest Russophil playgoers. Immediately afterwards he was apologetic and charming. "All that good money of yours!' he mourned. 'But no, it was *too* much to expect us to see it through!'

My only other theatrical experience in the Lawrence

connection was when, at a date I have forgotten, I took
Frieda to hear Marie Lloyd. It was, I think, Frieda's first
chance of listening to one of England's idols of the comic
sort. From her childish wonderment, not unmixed with a
delight that was a trifle timid of itself (as though Lawrence
might suddenly appear and wag his head reprovingly) I suspect that this was her first visit to a London music-hall.
Frieda would not have been Frieda had she been able to
resist Marie Lloyd. But when we got home and recounted
our enjoyment to Lawrence (who had been otherwise
engaged) she was cautious and—in her half-defensive, half-
belligerent way—non-committal. 'Yes, yes. I *do* think
she is a great artist! I *did* enjoy her, and I believe, *Lorenzo*,
that you would have liked her real vulgarr-ity.' But though
Lawrence was glad we had enjoyed ourselves, he shook his
head a little over Frieda, as some fond but austere Victorian
parent might shake his head upon catching his child poring
over the pages of *Ally Sloper*—without, however, reproving
the child or removing the periodical. Though he loved
abandon, and could be the gayest of the gay or the funniest
of the funny, it was not in Lawrence either to be frivolous
or to contemplate frivolity with pleasure. One felt that while
he would make the fullest admission of Marie Lloyd's artistry,
he would still feel that this was rather a silly way of spending
the evening.

Lawrence was disappointed by the general lack of notice
of *Mrs. Holroyd*, and I doubt not, though he never mentioned it, disappointed in particular by *The Times* notice.

In my anxiety I had made a bad mistake. Instead of
keeping myself within 500 words in which the praise would
not have been amenable to scissors, I had run to nearly a
thousand words. I was accordingly disgusted to find that in
the printed version all my warmest commendations were
omitted. What remained was not even good criticism.

'. . . am afraid *Mrs. Holroyd* was altogether a bit of a bore and that you were miserable. Am sorry.' Lawrence wrote. To-day, it is interesting to learn that after receiving accounts of the 1926 production, Lawrence said, 'I think, if it were being done again, I should alter the end, and make it more cheerful. Myself, I hate miserable endings now.'[1]

IV

That summer it was difficult, and therefore easily appeared impossible, for me to get to Italy either with my family or alone. Lawrence, finding Sicily too hot, went for a time with Frieda to Baden-Baden, to return alone to Florence. It was during his solitude of a fortnight there that he wrote *Tortoises*. He then went on to friends in Venice, where he was joined by Frieda, and together they went back in October to Taormina.

Till the end of the year he was writing hard—the introduction to Magnus's Memoir, most of the poems for *Birds, Beasts and Flowers* and the second half of *Aaron's Rod*. I had very few letters from him, only an occasional greeting, or a book, or the announcement that he was 'unbearably tired of Europe.'

America seems to you looney? Well, I don't care, perhaps there's more sense in lunacy than in our national mechanism. God knows what one will do. I am thinking of next spring. I shan't stay in Taormina, I think—perhaps go to Germany for the summer, perhaps to Sardinia,

he had written from Venice in October. And round about Christmas—when he was ill in bed with a cold—' We really want to sail away to New Mexico in January or February.'

---

[1] Letter to Miss Cooper. *Early Life of D. H. Lawrence,* by Ada Lawrence and Stuart Gelder, p. 148.

But in January, instead of going farther, he and Frieda made the trip to Sardinia, which he has described in *Sea and Sardinia*. He wrote that book rapidly in the early spring, when he worked further upon *Birds, Beasts and Flowers*, as well as upon a 'first vol. of a funny novel: but a *tiny* first vol. Quite a lot. Yet not much.' This probably refers to *The Man Who Died*.

At last that March the *History* had come out, and he sent me a copy—'Some of the chapters I think are good: first worst. Don't read it if it bores you.' After a year of managing his own affairs, Lawrence had now taken Curtis Brown as his agent. But as usual, after a hard working spell, books had become comparatively unimportant to him, and the need to live was everything. 'If only I had money I should buy a Mediterranean sailing ship that was offered me: *so* beautiful. Then you'd cruise with me.'

In the gloomy and tearful picture of Lawrence given us in *Son of Woman*, there is a singular omission. It is forgotten that after all Lawrence was an artist, and that he stood in need of the delight and the fresh interest, which it is the artist's nature to seek for his greater productiveness. Fury, as we know, was Lawrence's in plenty—that dark, coiled-up child in his 'bowels,' begotten of the Midlands, to whom he must give birth. But he needed also a careless *joie de vivre*, which was as native to him as his anger, and of which he was starved in England, though England found the means to feed his anger in abundance. The stimulus of anger, as Lawrence knew, can easily be overdone. It heads a man toward bitterness, and what is worse, solemnity. 'A man must keep his earnestness nimble, to escape ridicule,' as he said of Baron Corvo. England had seemed to him ' worn on the nerves.' And though 'Sicily indeed is cross and swindles one . . . somehow it doesn't affect one: annoys and amuses one: which is different.' Besides there was the loveliness—'the orange blossom is passing, northern trees, apple and pear and May blossom are out: the wood is tall and green, the mornings are fine. I feel I do not care a bit about the trials and troubles of the world. Suppose they'll be coming down on my head just now to make me care: but even so I cannot trouble before-hand.' This too was needed. And where another would have been held in one place by habit or fear or sloth, Lawrence followed his desire. In *Touch and Go* he makes the sculptress Anabel incapable of modelling more birds and animals, though she possesses genius, simply because she has lost that joy of life which had once enabled her to render in stone the thistledown lightness of a kitten. Until her joy returns, she will produce nothing lively. Lawrence knew so well what it was to feel inspired, that he could not fail to recognise the lack of inspiration in himself or in others. England had in-spired him, but England refused recognition of the fruits of her own inspiration; and though he had continued to produce under the hard pressure of poverty, neglect and obloquy, he was aware that pressure can be borne too long and all in vain. For the artist escape may become necessary for survival. Im-peratively he must seek both fresh inspiration and the support given by recognition in the most natural way open to him—by moving away from places where these things have failed him. It is easy to call this a morbid restlessness, or to describe it as a symptom of illness. But may it not with quite as much justice be called sanity and courage? Both are certainly needed for it, and no artist ever needed or evinced more of these virtues than Lawrence. If the stages of his pilgrimage may be put down to the restlessness of failure, we must bear in mind that the pilgrimage itself was undertaken by deliberate and difficult choice. Ultimately it must be judged by results. Belonging to this period in Italy—a period of little more than two years—we find *The Lost Girl, Aaron's Rod*, the introduction to Magnus's Memoir, *Sea and Sardinia, Birds*,

Beasts and Flowers, 'Tortoises,' and 'Evangelistic Beasts'—
besides which the new novel already mentioned began its
existence, and several long short stories or novelettes were
given their final form for publication in `America. Accom-
panying all this was continual letter-writing, always by hand,
and travelling of the most economical kind, which was exhausting when not actually adventurous. It is not a bad
record for an admittedly delicate man, of whom at home it
was busily alleged that he suffered from 'decaying' gifts, dis-
integrating spirit, and general decline in creative power!

These expressions are taken from Murry's long review
of *Women in Love* printed three months after the book's
appearance in the *Nation* that August—'The Nostalgia of
Mr. D. H. Lawrence'—'nostalgia,' be it understood, 'for
the slime.' After its five-year wait, the novel had appeared,
not, as Murry says, a year, but only six months after *The
Lost Girl.* This, if he had cared to look into the matter,
might have thrown light on the chronological order of the
two books upon which he partly based his attack. As things
are, he stretches, in reminiscence, the six months to a vague
twelve (even so trusting to his readers' ignorance of Lawrence's ways) and while refusing to regret the nature of the
attack, offers a partial excuse that it was 'by the irony of
fate' that he announced—with what unmistakeable relish!—
the end of Lawrence, just as Lawrence was engaged upon the
books which Murry was later to announce as his finest. We
all make mistakes, especially where Lawrence is concerned;
and this review—with that other, 'The Decay of Mr. D. H.
Lawrence'—might be allowed to blush unseen, were it not
that Murry has himself dragged it out to say that 'strangely
enough' there is little in it he would withdraw to-day. It
is, therefore, necessary to repeat his verdict therein, which is
that Lawrence is no longer an artist, that he has sacrificed
his art to a vain philosophy (*i.e.* not Murry's philosophy) and

that he is a 'writhing' and 'obscene' and ridiculous failure, with no command over himself or his characters. Murry ignores the wonderful, the touching, the interesting and the new things in the book, which one thinks that a friend might wish to bring into prominence even while failing to understand or agree with the book's intention; and he displays unconvincing hilarity over passages that he well knows are most easily liable to misunderstanding by the vulgar. It is of interest that Lawrence in the novel makes a thoroughly corrupt and heartless couple agree, with a like hilarity, concerning Birkin, that, 'a man who is always talking about corruption . . . must be corrupt himself to have it so much on his mind.' Certainly Murry allows that Lawrence believes in his own vision. But even Lockhart did not accuse Keats of dishonesty, merely of ineptitude. Nor had Lockhart ever been Keats's friend.

It would more truly seem to be 'by the irony of fate,' that Keats himself once had a friend named George Felton Mathew, and that it has been left to Murry to tell us of this friendship,[1] which in certain cardinal points is the parallel to his own friendship with Lawrence. Mathew had been one of the very first to praise the immature Keats. But Mathew disliked and misprised the mature Keats, finding him 'in danger of becoming "a proud egotist of diseased feelings and perverted principles,"' and after thirty years he still tried to justify a review in which he feared that the poet might contaminate purity, and innoculate degeneracy and corruption—a review which Murry recognises to have been actuated by 'ill-concealed antagonism.' It is difficult not to fancy that some Murry of the future—a critic of emotional gifts who can be trusted only in his dealings with writers who have been dead for fifty years or more—will discover and elucidate for us the Murry-Lawrence affair in a similar

[1] In *Studies in Keats*, by J. Middleton Murry.

manner.   Even to-day it is impossible to turn over the phrases
of Murry's *Lost Girl* review — 'sub-human,' 'esoteric
language,' 'quack terminology,' 'mysteriously degraded,'
'corrupt mysticism,' 'slime,' 'loss of creative vigour,'
'paralysis,' and 'decline,' without at least the suspicion
(shared by him in the similar case of Mathew) that the writer
of these 'simply insufferable terms' is 'resentful about
something,' and that this is the language of spite.   As for the
'this hurts me more than it hurts you' assurance, which
is provided as a sort of ground bass in *Son of Woman*, every
schoolboy knows the significance of that.   How much more
truly 'simple' had Murry summed up his 'great man' in
the classic manner—'I hate him, he's a liar, he can't dance,
his feet stink, and he doesn't love Jesus.'

To return to *Women in Love*, what foundation Murry
has for his up-to-date defence that Lawrence had 'abandoned
the ground he had taken up' in this novel, 'even before the
book was published,' he does not tell us and it is hard to guess.
Because quite certainly the novel remains a vital expression
of much that its author held to the end of his life, even while
it is not the novel he would have written at the end of his
life.   But nothing of this really matters.   Poor criticism is
merely poor criticism.   What does matter about Murry's
review is its heartlessness and vanity.   It was a knowing and
vindictive blow at a man who, not yet being dead, dared to
defy critical reduction to a formula.   It was a carefully
executed attempt of the very kind which best demonstrated
the horror Lawrence believed to be inveterate in 'Christian
love.'   Under the pretence of 'intellectual sincerity' it was
an effort to annihilate.   No different derivation can explain
its particular flavour.

That October of 1921 Murry further used his position
on the *Nation* to join the name of Lawrence with others of
whom nothing might now be expected.   In a long and

favourable review of a novel by Frank Swinnerton, called *Coquette*, he seized the slender, gratuitous chance to praise at Lawrence's expense.   And in passing his verdict upon a string of contemporaries, he refused to the author of *The Rainbow* a place anywhere on the same plane as the authors of *Kipps*, *The Old Wives' Tale*, and *Lord Jim*.   In his judgment Lawrence was no longer even 'in the dusty rear.' He had fallen out of the race.   Nothing was to be got out of either faith or friendship.   So both went by the board— for the time.

v

In March Frieda had been summoned to Baden-Baden by the serious illness of her mother.   Lawrence, left alone, went to Rome and Florence (this being the occasion described by Rebecca West) and in June he joined Frieda in Germany. The old Baroness was better, though still weak, he wrote, when sending us a box of the tiny Black Forest toys for the child.   They stayed for two months, living mostly at a place three miles from Baden, near the end of the Forest 'with the Rhine Valley and the Vosges beyond,' where they were 'very well done' for three shillings a day.   But though there was plenty of food and friendliness, and 'a great sense of magnificent, spacious country,' there was also a sense of depression—'sort of stupefied or numbed rather than any-thing else,' and Lawrence felt a stranger.   As he put it, 'I feel a stranger everywhere and nowhere.'

That summer we had arranged to leave the boy at home, and to meet the Lawrences either in Tirol or in Italy. At first it was to be the former.   By the middle of July they were at Constance on their way to Lake Zell, near Salzburg.   Frieda's younger sister Johanna (it was the older sister Else to whom Lawrence had dedicated *The Rainbow*) had taken a house at Tumersbach and was there with her

husband and children.   But lovely as this was, Lawrence soon
wearied to be gone.   'I have been waiting,' he wrote on
August 3rd, 'to see whether I could really stay on here . . .
the villa is on the edge of the lake, we bathe and boat and go
excursions into the mountains.   The snow isn't far.   And
the Schreibershofens are really *very* nice with us.   And yet,
I feel I can't breathe.   Everything is free and perfectly easy.
And still I feel I can't breathe.   Perhaps it is one can't live
with people anymore—*en ménage*.   Anyhow there it is.
Frieda loves it and is quite bitter that I say I want to go
away.   But there it is—I do.'   He did not want to live again
at Taormina, but Germany made him home-sick for Italy.
We were bringing him various things including signed passport forms, as their passports were almost expired and they
did not know how to have them renewed in either Germany
or Italy.   Though he sent us all the needful information and
was ready to engage a room in the neighbouring peasant
hotel, we could feel that he was restless.   Also the weather
broke at Tumersbach.   We therefore made our own plans
to walk from Innsbruck independently, and to reach Florence
when he should be there in September.

After crossing mainly on foot in hot but stormy weather
from Innsbruck to Meran we turned up the Brenner again
and wandered through the battle-area to Cortina d'Ampezzo,
where we got on the train for Venice.   We did not stay there
long.   What with bad weather and bugs—1921 was a great
bug year in Italy and Austria—after a day or two we were
glad to leave for Florence.

The Lawrences, whom we had advised of our train, were
to meet us.   But something not anybody's fault went wrong,
and Lawrence spent a large part of the morning meeting
trains in which we were not.   When we did arrive there was
nobody about for us, but just as we left the station we caught
sight of Frieda hastening away.   She had seen the train come

in, but somehow had missed us. Such missings are a fatality in my family. Our joyful greeting on the road outside has quite obliterated what followed immediately upon it. I know we appointed to meet later for lunch all four together.

Lawrence and Frieda were in a furnished upper flat on the other side of the Arno, 32, Via dei Bardi, the house that is traditionally pointed out as Romola's. Lawrence had recommended a pension on the other side of the river where he had lived himself, but we found it too grand for us, and going farther on took a room in the Rigatti, a pleasant bell-haunted remnant of the Palazzo Alberti, at which Donald had stayed on a former visit.

Of our daily meetings for the week we were there, our meals together, our walks and our talks, Lawrence wrote to me soon afterwards—'it seems only a moment we saw you—but the sympathy is there.' Both these remarks ring true to me to-day. Looking back now the week presents itself as rather less than a moment—a hazy moment at that, and we seem to have said and done nothing in particular, nor to have been particularly happy. Though I never felt more drawn to Lawrence, there was about him something restless, remote and even impatient, which blurred the approach and made me doubt sadly once or twice if my own sympathy found any response. I therefore did my best to conceal it. Sometimes I was glad to get out of his presence. Not that he engendered such a feeling by any word or action.

To use his own phrase, he was now 'done with Italy,' and with Europe. It might turn out to be only for the time—it did in fact so turn out—but that made it none the less urgent. Even Sicily, which he had so loved, had ceased to hold him and he was willing to return to it only that he might pack up and be off. He knew that we could not or would not go with him and he was bound to identify us in some degree with what he longed to leave. As companion adven-

turers we had failed him. But we were still acknowledged
friends, more deeply acknowledged perhaps than ever before,
as he needed friends, if only to leave behind. Even if we were
only pillars of salt we stood for something. Lawrence was
like the young son in the fairy tale who would one day come
and touch his stony brethren with the far-fetched herb, and
turn them once more into brethren of flesh. Meanwhile we
were safe in our surroundings and he was of that threatened
frailty of flesh that needs all its wits about it.

Lawrence had loved Italy as much as any English poet
ever did, and he got from it more than most. He was grateful
till the end of his life for that carelessness of the South which
dispelled like an unconscious benison the harsh and petty
carefulness of his Northern upbringing. Travelling north
would always make him feel ill and resentful. Turning south
would always offer ease and healing. 'It cures one of caring,
and a good thing too!' He felt this at the beginning and
returned to it at the end, but bask as he might now for a time
in the essential tolerance of southern Italy, with its classical
mentality and its good-humoured physicalness, it could not
assuage forever his northern thirst for 'something beyond.'
He must seek further for that *other* world that is within and
behind the real world. The easy and eminently workable
Latin compromise with life had gone a little stale, a little
rancid in his mouth. It, or something like it, might yet prove
to be a practical solution. But there was much to be looked
into before this could be accepted.

Lawrence's friends, the Brewsters, who were Buddhists
and were shortly leaving Sicily for the East, were urging him
to follow them to Ceylon where he could see the working
out of Buddhism. At the end of the week he was going to
see them off. He was in a restless state of waiting. He knew
that he must move soon himself, but was still undecided as to
whether the move should be East or West.

As always, there were several stray people who whirled for the time in Lawrence's orbit. I vaguely remember a large American woman who was studying singing, and who had brought with her a son of about fourteen who carried a cudgel in Fascist fashion, and Lawrence introduced us to at least one of the well-known residents among his acquaintance in Florence. I seem to remember a smallish clean-shaven face that managed to be at once red and dried up. Even this picture, as of something both parched and glowing, may be mistaken. A casual introduction will often thus afflict me with blindness and deafness as well as aphasia.

Again I remember a young woman whom I cannot place, and of whom I have only a single recollection. We were all on the roof of the Lawrences' house. A camera is a thing I scarcely ever use, but I had brought a Brownie with me for our walk across the Dolomites, and when I saw Lawrence standing laughing near the parapet I had the sudden desire to take a snapshot of him. I don't think he was more than faintly irritated. Anyhow he went on laughing and did not say anything to stop me. But the young woman thought she divined in Lawrence some serious distaste and tried to prevent the photograph from being taken. At any other time I believe I might have submitted. But feeling certain that Lawrence did not really mind, and longing to have a picture of him in his present light and gay mood, I persisted. I am very glad to have the picture now.[1] It is, I think, a misfortune that by far the most of the photographs and portraits of Lawrence show him as thoughtful—either fiercely or sufferingly so. His usual expression was a kind of sparkling awareness, almost an 'I am ready for anything' look which was invigorating to behold.

The Lawrences' flat was second from the top. In the small top floor was Mary Cannan. Once at least we all went

[1] See frontispiece.

to her room for a meal, which was more sumptuous and varied than the meals we shared with the Lawrences. White-haired and with exquisitely pretty features, Mary was always the elegant one of the company. One day when she was out, Frieda displayed to me a cupboard full of Mary's enviable clothes. While the rest of us were still content with knitted wool or silk of the common kind, Mary had several hand-knitted dresses of silk *bouclé*—then the very latest thing from Paris. Passing it appreciatively through her hands Frieda, who prided herself on a 'feeling for textures,' assured me with solemn emphasis that it was 'enormously expensive.' It was perhaps a certain lack of response in me on this occasion that led Frieda to the conclusion that 'Catherine had taste but no *feeling* for textures.' I admired the *bouclé* frigidly and without desiring to handle it.

I was jealous of Mary. That summer Donald and I had been roughing it—drenched by storms, devoured by bugs, several nights bedless in the mountains—which was all very well *in* the mountains, but now in civilised sur-roundings, tired out from over-walking, I was obliged to appear on every occasion in a faded garment of flowered cotton which had originally been intended as a garden overall. When it fell to me, as it often seemed to do, to walk behind Lawrence and Mary, Lawrence attired with impressive suitability in natural coloured silk (a sort of Palm Beach suit) and Mary all that was urbane and charming, I almost hated Mary. Frieda had advised me to apply to her for the secret of a particular face-bleaching lotion which she used and, I understood, had received directly from Sarah Bern-hardt. This I never did, but I have often wondered about it since. I saw that Lawrence liked to walk with a fashion-ably dressed woman, and though he could and did make fun of Mary behind her back (as indeed he could and did of any of us) and was sometimes clearly bored before her face, he was fond of her and took a lot of trouble over her, largely because she looked always so nice. She had written a book, still in MS., about all the dogs she had ever had as pets. Lawrence, at her request, went over it most carefully, suggesting alterations and improvements. Remembering my experience with my own novel, I found this distressing.

Though not in the least rich, Lawrence just then, owing to the placing of short stories in the United States through Mountsier, had become distinctly more prosperous than he had been when I last saw him. This was reflected in his and Frieda's clothes. He would never be a dandy, but he liked to appear in the unmistakeable rôle of *il signore*. I felt we Carswells were failing to keep pace. It was unfortunate too for me that I had Anglo-Italian cousins in Florence to whom I introduced Lawrence without good effect. My cousins had the right to consider themselves of the Italian aristocracy. But they showed themselves blind alike to Lawrence's genius and his charm and he disliked what he saw of them. Like so many well-bred Italians they knew nothing of English literature later than Oscar Wilde, except for modern rumours of Hall Caine, Marie Corelli, and possibly Mr. Galsworthy. As they had been associated with some of the romantic passages of my childhood, this state of matters made me feel absurdly jangled, especially in view of several unlucky contacts which I brought about. I suppose most lives contain similar 'pockets,' in which a fetish of youth has remained so long undisturbed that the turning out demands a certain resolution.

One specially unlucky incident distressed me out of measure. One of my cousins lived in an old villa, really a little castle some way out of Florence. This existed in its own world, with some hundreds of peasants living on the estate under the *mezzadria* system. Everything, from the wine and the bread to the restored panelling of the rooms,

was home-grown and home-made. Having boasted to
Lawrence and Frieda of the beauties of this place, at which
Donald and I were going to spend a week-end, I arranged
that an invitation should be given. The Lawrences—and,
I think, Mary Cannan—were to take the tram from
Florence to the nearest hamlet that was some two or three
miles from the villa, and a carriage ordered by my cousins
was to bring them out to spend the Sunday and meet Professor Guglielmo Ferrero.

Sunday came, but no Lawrence party arrived, and only
at the hour they were expected did I learn that my cousin
had forgotten, or had anyhow omitted, to order the carriage
which should have been done beforehand in the hamlet as
she had not one of her own. In desperation I set out to meet
them on foot, but when, after traversing about a mile, I saw
no signs of them, I knew it was useless to go on. By the
time I reached the village, if—as it appeared—they had
failed to find a carriage for themselves, they would have
gone home. It was a frightfully hot day.

On the Monday in Florence we found, as I had feared,
that they had come as far as the hamlet by a wearisome tram,
had found no further means of transport, and had gone back.
Lawrence treated the matter lightly and said it was of no
consequence. The worst thing was that my cousin didn't
think it of any consequence either. She regarded Lawrence
as nothing more than an obscure English bohemian friend
of ours. The lapse was a nightmare of abasement to me, all
the more that so little was said on either side. So I could
not help rejoicing in my cousin's humiliation when, to his un-
disguised and very vocal rage, she inadvertently introduced the
great Ferrero under the name of his father-in-law, Lombroso.

On Lawrence's thirty-seventh birthday, which fell during
our week, we supped alone with Frieda and him at his flat
and were gay in a quiet sort of way. I cannot remember

much that was said, except that we discussed the break with
Pinker, and I recall much praise of the Italian newspapers
at the expense of the English ones.   How much better than
The Times was the *Corriere della Sera*!   How much less
'base!'   When reading the English newspapers in Italy he
felt ashamed to be an Englishman, and that was a thing he
hated.   His John Bullishness was able to raise its head again,
however, and its voice, in acute disgust of the use to which
the shingle on the other side of the Arno was put by the
Florentine *giovinezza*.   If anybody should find an incon-
sistency or a discrepancy between this disgusted Lawrence
and the Lawrence who painted certain of his pictures,[1]
that person must think again and think hard.   Because the
very crux of Lawrence's intention lies just here, and the
discrepancy—such as it is—is a conscious one; also a fruitful
one, being of nature's making.

Another day the Lawrences ate with us at a little downstairs restaurant off the Via dei Calzaioli.   I remember
only one thing vividly.   Shortly before we met for our meal
I had been nagging at Donald for what I took to be some
small breach of manners on his part with regard to the same
cousin who failed to send the carriage for Lawrence.   In
certain ways, I had argued, the Italians are formal, and in
not observing their formalities we give them the opening to
despise us and our friends.   Smarting under her lack of
courtesy to Lawrence, I was annoyed by any possible lapse
on our part.   So I had been scolding, and Donald at dinner
had complained of this, good-naturedly, to Lawrence.   'You
ought to hit her!' said Lawrence fiercely—'Hit her hard.
Don't let her scold and nag.   You mustn't allow it, *whatever*
it is you have done!'   We all laughed and felt refreshed.
When, the other day, I recalled this to Donald he had no

[1] I refer especially to 'Dandelions'—a picture that was withheld from
the Lawrence exhibition lest it should give offence.

recollection of it. But I never forgot. Not that I have never nagged or scolded since, nor that I have been hit for it. But I admit I ought to have been, and admission makes a difference.

I have said that the young son of the American lady singer carried a cudgel in the Fascist fashion. During that summer of 1921 the Fascist order had not yet been established in Italy, but it was coming on fast and there were constant street fights in Florence. Though I witnessed several rushes of a street crowd I never saw any actual shooting. Lawrence, however, had, and his descriptions were so lively that I had to think twice before saying just now that I was not present myself. He told us how, on the sound of a shot, the crowded street was an empty one before you could wink. The people, he declared, ran up the fronts of the houses like flies and down into the earth like mice. One moment they were there strolling slowly and thickly after the manner of a Florentine crowd. The next moment not a soul in sight. When Lawrence had seen anything like this that excited him, he was able by word and voice and gesture to make you share perfectly in his bygone excitement. As in his description of the bullfight at the opening of *The Plumed Serpent*, he made a point of avoiding all the more familiar forms of exaggeration. But when, especially in talking, a single, carefully selected enlargement was necessary to convey the force of his own emotion to the listener, he chose his point infallibly. I never once heard him exaggerate the wrong point or fail to convey the strict emotional truth by means of the exaggeration he had chosen. He would have made a great descriptive reporter.

Our time of holiday was nearly done, and we wished to go on to Rome before returning to London. Lawrence had seen neither Perugia nor Siena. I had associations with both places and liked Perugia in particular. Lawrence specially wished to see Siena. So it was arranged that if possible we should meet him there on our way back. We talked about how much we should all enjoy ourselves. There would just be Frieda and Lawrence and Donald and I.

But somehow I did not believe it would happen, and it did not. We went by ourselves to Perugia, and we heard from Lawrence that on arriving in Siena he had hated it so much that he could not bear to stay on another day. What happened to make Siena so hateful to him I never learned. I agreed, however, with his finding that travelling was 'peculiarly disheartening' that year, when the debris of the War was still everywhere and one was depressed 'not so much with inconveniences as by the kind of slow poison one breathes in every new atmosphere.' His restlessness too, I guessed was at a height. He had felt that he must rush away to Capri to see the Brewsters off to Ceylon. This he wrote to us from Siena the day he was to leave, saying he was sorry to miss us but felt sure we should soon be coming to Italy to live. In case that note should not get us, he left another at the Bank in Florence with a parcel of six stone plates which he begged us to take to England for Ada. My heart felt a bit like this parcel, but we got it triumphantly home and eventually to the Midlands without one of the plates being cracked, which was something. In this puzzling world it is always a comfort to be of some small practical service to those whom one honours most.

It was nearly a week later, on the last day of September, that we, still in Florence, heard again—this time from Sicily. The Brewsters had been seen off, and the Lawrences had reached Taormina on the night of the 29th in a whirlpool of rain—'but so glad to come to rest, I can't tell you—still like this place best—the sea open to the east, to the heart of the east, away from Europe. I had your letter—it seemed only a moment we saw you—but the sympathy is there. You must come here. . . . Love.'

From then till after the middle of February 1922 Law-

rence stayed on at Taormina. He was still resolved to go to
America but shrank from the directly westward journey.
Neither did he see his way financially clear enough to
warrant it.

VI

Meanwhile several disagreeable things had happened in
England. The *John Bull* attack upon *Women in Love*,
headed 'A Book the Police Should Ban,' and with the sub-
title, 'Loathsome Study of Sex Depravity — Misleading
Youth to Unspeakable Disaster,' had appeared on September 17th. The calm and cultured easily make light of *John
Bull* attacks; yet we can understand—especially as in this
case most of the aforesaid elected to side with *John Bull*—
that Lawrence's publisher felt 'alarmed and upset,' and
wrote to say so. The assistant editor of *John Bull*, who in
manly fashion signed his article, did 'not claim to be a
literary critic,' but he 'knew dirt when he smelt it' and here
was dirt 'in heaps—festering, putrid heaps which smelt to
high Heaven.' And, in phrases not in substance very different
from those used a month earlier in the *Nation* by one who *did*
claim to be a literary critic, he had gone on to protect the
'unsuspecting public' by calling the book an 'obscene study,'
a 'neurotic production,' and a 'shameless study of sex depravity which in direct proportion to the skill of its literary
execution becomes unmentionably vile.' He might almost
have read Murry's article! He shares, it will be seen, with
Murry, the virtue (for which Murry lays some claim to a
monopoly of credit) of taking Lawrence seriously; but he
differs from Murry in that he grants art and power to the
book, and he refrains from the facetiousness which Murry
was to permit himself in the process of relegating Mr. Lawrence to the slime. It was left to a foreign critic ten years
later—Professor Paul de Reul of Brussels University—to say

of one such passage as Murry holds up to ridicule, 'Ne sourions pas de ce geste qui est pur et grave.' [1]

At almost the same time Secker had to inform Lawrence that Philip Heseltine, who was no longer friendly towards him, was threatening a libel action, alleging that the Halliday of the novel was a portrait of himself, which in fact it was, though Lawrence modified the character for the English edition and altered the colour of his hair. In law, I believe, Heseltine had not a leg to stand on; but there was already trouble enough about the book, and for peace' sake Secker paid him £50 as solatium for injury to feelings and reputation.

Towards the end of October Lawrence wrote from Taormina one of his long, characteristic letters in reply to one of mine in which I had said that my second novel had failed to please the publisher. He wrote affectionately, maliciously, lightly, damning his enemies—'snotty little lot of people' — heartening up his friends, and describing his mood of the moment as one of not really giving 'a damn for any blooming thing,' usually a preliminary mood with him to caring ardently for some one thing in particular. He still thought that Sicily was 'probably better than any other place,' and though he could not get a 'little taste of canker out of his mouth' he admitted that perhaps it was his mouth that was to blame. As usual it was only man that was vile, or rather, at the moment, ludicrous.

Here of course it is like a continental Mad Hatter's teaparty. If you'll let it be, it is all teaparty—and you wonder who on earth is going head over heels into the teapot next. On Saturday we were summoned to a gathering of Britons to discuss the erection of

[1] Prof. de Reul's article, 'D. H. Lawrence,' published in the *Revue de l'Université de Bruxelles*, 1930–31, and also in pamphlet form (Imprimerie Médicale et Scientifique (S.A.) 34, rue Botanique, Bruxelles), is probably the most discriminating literary survey of Lawrence that has as yet appeared.

an English church here, at the estimated cost of £25,000 sterling
— signed Bronte: which means of course Alec Nelson - Hood,
Duca di Bronte. I didn't go, fearing they might ask me for the
£25,000.

But he was not idle. In spite of the severe scirocco in
November—'hot billows of wet and clinging mist—and rain.
Damn scirocco'—he was 'pottering with short stories' for
a volume. One of these, which he had finished by November
15th, was 'The Captain's Doll.' Earlier, he had written to
Donald to ask 'which regiment of Scots wears the tight
tartan trews: the quite tight ones' and all about them. He
was also pondering, with some kind of a book in view, over
the fascinating lost Etruscans, and he was preparing to trans-
late Giovanni Verga's *Maestro Don Gesualdo* and some of his
shorter stories. This last, he thought, would be 'fun,' as
Verga's peculiar language was so fascinating. 'He exercises
quite a fascination on me, and makes me feel quite sick at the
end, but perhaps that is only if one knows Sicily.'

Lawrence has never had full credit as a translator. He
had a similar gift to that of the late C. K. Scott Moncrieff.
He could enter into the meaning of a highly individual outlook on life that was other than his own and expressed in a
difficult idiom. Had he not been novelist and poet in his
own right, he might have earned good money, an easy fame
and high ungrudging acknowledgment as a translator. He is
of the first rank.

That month of November, Seltzer was bringing out
Sea and Sardinia and the illustrated chap-book of *Tortoises.*
And there was word of Seltzer doing another chap-book of
the poems 'Evangelistic Beasts,' for which we were asked to
look for a medieval cover design among the British Museum
missals. Lawrence had received, as yet, no good word of
the *Aaron's Rod* MS. except from Seltzer, and though he
took this as probably no more than 'a publisher's pat,' it was

anyhow 'better than a smack in the eye, such as one gets from England for anything.' Some of the worst smacks in the eye had come from the *Athenaeum*, where Murry in the December of that year, with Katherine Mansfield behind him,[1] had attacked *The Lost Girl* at length under what he has himself designated the 'characteristic' heading of 'The Decay of Mr. D. H. Lawrence,' (December 17th, 1920), an attack by which he still stands, though he is obliged to admit that his conclusions were based on a chronological error. So far as I can discover it was in the *Athenaeum* that such words as 'tortured' and 'neurotic' were first applied to Lawrence's work. These were used as early as February, 1919, in the brief and unenthusiastic review of *New Poems*, while in the reviews of Murry's play *Cinnamon and Angelica* and Lawrence's play *Touch and Go*, the former is given twice the space and four times the respect.

In the same letter Lawrence makes an interesting forecast of Italian affairs—

I shouldn't wonder if before very long they effected a mild sort of revolution here, and turned out the king. It would be a clergy—industrial—socialist move—industrialists and clergy to rule in name of the people. Smart dodge, I think. If the exchange falls again they will effect it. Then they'll ally with Germany, Austria, and probably France and make a European ring excluding England. That seems to be the idea.

Lawrence believed, however, that this would come from a victory for the Communists.

[1] Murry has told us that Katherine Mansfield was 'unable to review it,' implying that her inability was due to illness. Yet in the same moment he admits that she had the book sent to her, presumably for review, and that she returned it 'with two pages of unfavourable comment.' As one who writes two pages of comment could surely have written a review, had she wished, the inference is that she passed on a disagreeable but not impossible task to Murry, who duly executed it, using her unfavourable comment with a slight change of phrasing.

All the while he was watching the birds and longing to know when he could set off on his journey.

There are crowds of all sorts of new birds in the garden, suddenly come south. And the storks are passing in the night, whewwing softly and murmuring as they go overhead.

He was scraping up hard for his fares to sail farther away. Not only the full blown hostility in England, but the growing sympathy in America, strengthened his conviction that there was his virgin soil. Already, as we have seen, Amy Lowell had stretched out a hand of practical helpfulness of a kind that could be taken without humiliation. Now came a letter from another rich and strange American—'a woman called Mabel Dodge Sterne,' offering them the loan of a furnished adobe house for themselves at Taos, New Mexico, and all they could want in addition if only they would go there.

She had told them, wrote Lawrence to me, that 'Taos is on a mountain—7000 feet up and 23 miles from a railway—and has a tribe of 600 free Indians who she says are interesting, sun-worshippers, rain-makers, and unspoiled. It sounds rather fun.' He wanted to know if we knew 'anything about such a place as Taos?' And he made inquiries about tramp vessels to New Orleans or Galveston so that he might go direct, missing out 'that awful New York altogether.'

Till at least the end of December he was thinking of going off in this way. At Christmas, when he sent me an American novel, he said that he was 'unbearably tired of Europe.' For New Year he sent me a copy of *Tortoises* and the further assurance that he was 'seriously thinking of sailing to New Orleans and going to Taos in New Mexico, to try that' in January or February. But he had spent Christmas in bed with what he called an influenza, which was hardly shaken off by January 24th, and I could feel that he was most reasonably afraid of disobeying doctor's orders by going to America in midwinter.   In Sicily, as it was, they were having 'vile, . . . really wicked . . . weather' and he was trying to 'possess his soul in patience.'   Of the influenza which had been epidemic in England again (I had just been down with it) he wrote me 'I believe it is partly an organic change in one's whole constitution—through the blood and psyche. We are at the end of our particular tether, and the breaking loose is an uncomfortable process.'

It was indeed uncomfortable for Lawrence.   He had just heard that his sisters 'loftily disapproved' of *Tortoises* and that his English publisher did not care for *Aaron's Rod*.

That Rod I'm afraid it is gentian root or wormwood stem. But they've got to swallow it sooner or later: miserable tonicless lot.

He hoped that my novel, then in proof, having found a new publisher, was bitter too, though he suggested that *Gingerbread* or *Rose Hearted Camellia* would have been titles more pleasing to publishers than *The Camomile*.

But the chief piece of news in this letter, written on January 24th, was that the Lawrences were leaving Europe. Having almost booked their passages to America, however, it had suddenly 'come over' Lawrence that he must first go to Ceylon.   His friend Brewster, who was studying Pali and Buddhism at the Buddhist Monastery in Kandy, had written asking him to come and had offered hospitality. The Lawrences were to have to themselves a 'big old ramshackle bungalow there.'   So they were going.

I have once more gone back on my plan. I shrink as yet from the States. Ultimately I shall go there, no doubt. But I want to go east before I go west: go west *via* the east. . . . I think one must for the moment withdraw from the world, away towards the inner realities that *are* real: and return, maybe, to the world later, when one is quiet and sure. I am tired of the world, and want the peace like a river: not this whiskey and soda, bad whiskey too, of life so-called. I don't believe in Buddhistic inaction and meditation. But I believe the Buddhistic peace is the point to start from—not our strident fretting and squabbling.

Mabel Sterne (as she has told us) was projecting her strong American self-will—her will to *use* Lawrence for ends of her own—across the Atlantic to draw Lawrence to Taos, but her will was as nothing to what Lawrence called the 'Balaam's ass in his belly.' What he had always felt concerning the 'over-riding of life' in U.S.A. had taken concrete form in Mrs. Sterne's letters. Americans would be better 'when the hand had fallen on them a bit heavier.' He would go there, but not until he had been 'fortified by a country with religion for one that had none.' To face America one must be strong. To be strong one must be 'cured' of sick Europe. So he would withdraw for a breathing-space, would try if 'the old, old East' would 'sweeten the gall in his blood.' He thought he might stay in the East for a year. Anyhow he would go and see.

In the midst of his preparations for departure he found time to write at length to me about (and no doubt to give other help to) a middle-aged and very poor Finnish writer, once the captain of a tramp steamer, who was struggling to support his wife and child on a small and severely depreciated pension. This man had written short stories of seafaring life which had already been translated into German, and Lawrence wanted me to read them with a view to making English translations and placing these in the English magazines. Unfortunately the stories, which I read as carefully as my inadequate German permitted, did not interest me; and in any case I knew I could not place them as I had no influence where any magazine was concerned. Lawrence had further admitted that they needed putting 'into proper literary shape.' This was no task for me. So I sent them back to the author with my regrets, hoping that the English-woman in Finland to whom he had also applied would be able to do better than I could. T. W. Nylander was the author's name. I never heard how he fared.

On February 18th came a post card from Taormina to say that they were leaving 'on Monday for Palermo, *en route* for Naples,' and that they would sail for Colombo from Naples on the 26th by s.s. *Osterley*, of the Orient line, the passage taking about fourteen days. Lawrence in 'throes of packing' was feeling thrilled and glad. 'I want to go. One day you and Don will come. I dream'd of elephants.' A further post card, dated the 25th, from Naples, told us that they were off next day, and begged us to write to Ceylon. No Columbus ever stood more in need of valour or was less informed as to what awaited him overseas. This may sound silly or exaggerated. It is strictly true.

PART FOUR

Aet. 36–40

Prose

Kangaroo
The Boy in the Bush (with M. L. Skinner)
The Plumed Serpent
Mornings in Mexico
The Woman who Rode Away, etc.
St. Mawr, etc.

★

'Rip the veil of the old vision across, and walk through the rent.'

PART FOUR

I

We are here and settling down—very hot at first—but one soon takes naturally to it—soon feels in a way at home—sort of root race home. We're in a nice spacious bungalow on the hill above Kandy in a sort of half jungle of a cocoa-nut palm estate—and cocoa—beautiful, and such sweet scents. The Prince of Wales was here on Thursday—looks worn out and nervy, poor thing. The Perahera in the evening with a hundred elephants was lovely. But I don't believe I shall ever work here.

This was Lawrence's first letter from Ceylon, written on March 25th, 1922. Already he was beginning to realise that the tropics, in spite of their interest and loveliness, were 'not really his line'—'not active enough,' a realisation that was sharpened by an attack of malaria—his first.[1] The careless-ness of Italy was one thing, but the immense not-caring of the Orient was another. Though beautiful to look at, the East was 'queer—how it seems to bleed one's courage and make one indifferent to everything.' This was an indifference which the Englishman in Lawrence rejected. It belonged to an order with which he had neither blood contact nor other affinity, so he must get away from it. It was not what he sought—though he had to see it. Nauseous to him were the tropical scents and sounds, and the 'boneless suavity of the East' did not offer that 'last dark strand from the previous pre-white era' which by joining with 'our own thin end' would, Lawrence believed, establish a new flow of life. He found that the dark Oriental was 'built round a gap—a hollow pit. In the middle of their eyes, instead of a man, a sort of bottomless pit.' As for the Buddhist monks

[1] So, at least, Lawrence and his doctor took it to be.

with their 'nasty faces' and 'little vulgar dens of temples,' theirs was 'a very conceited, selfish show, a vulgar temple of serenity built over an empty hole in space.' Within a month of his arrival he had planned to go on to Australia. 'If I don't like Australia I shall go on to San Francisco. Now one is started, nothing like keeping going.'

In the course of that month he saw a good deal, including the celebrations for the Prince of Wales, who was just then on the tour during which he made his celebrated gesture towards the 'Untouchables.' Though I never heard Lawrence comment on this gesture, I can guess that it fitted well with his high notions of princeliness. But I did hear his critical comments on the Prince's visit, and I think they merit record. He would have had the King of England's son splendidly apparelled and dazzlingly escorted in such a way as to strike both worship and terror into his Indian subjects. The frail, sensitive, simple-mannered, well-meaning, but too often weary-looking boy would have gained a thousand-fold, thought Lawrence, by the very frailty and simplicity of his bearing, if he had been framed in a magnificence symbolic of England and England's throne. Here were millions of men and women who could understand glory and submit to it joyfully, but only if the glory was conveyed to them by the eye and ear, by the richness of material stuffs and sounds and odours. It is a sophisticated, moreover a Western imagination that can be moved to the perception of the greatest earthly glory by the figure of a slender, clean-shaven youth with a pale gentle face, who wears the tailored jacket and creased trousers of Savile Row. The Prince's outfit for the hottest day in Canada ought, in Lawrence's opinion, to be fundamentally different from his outfit for a public appearance in Kandy. I would have backed Lawrence to stage-manage the public appearance of his own Prince to the best advantage for any given populace.

The Lawrences sailed for Australia at the end of April. In Australia—to be exact, at Thirroul, South Coast, New South Wales—Lawrence found a different kind of indifference from any he had met with before. It was neither Oriental nor Mediterranean but of the whitest kind, all English in its origins. This fascinated, even while it repelled him. 'A raw hole,' but wonderful for its freshness, its rough carelessness and its unfamiliar skies. It held him for three months, fruitful months too, that saw the inception and the writing of *Kangaroo* and the re-writing (planned at least) of *The Boy in the Bush* from the unlikely MS. brought forth for his inspection by his hostess, Miss M. L. Skinner, when he went upon an expedition inland.

If you want to know what it is to feel the 'correct' social world fizzle to nothing, you should go to Australia. . . . In the established sense it is socially nil. Happy-go-lucky, don't-you-bother we're-in-Austraylia. But also there seems to be no inside life of any sort: just a long lapse and drift. A rather fascinating indifference, a *physical* indifference to what we call soul or spirit. It's really a weird show. The country has an extraordinary hoary, weird attraction. As you get used to it, it seems so *old*, as if it had missed all this Semite-Egyptian-Indo-European vast era of history, and was coal age, the age of great ferns and mosses. It hasn't got a consciousness—just none—too far back. A strange effect it has on one. Often I hate it like poison, then again it fascinates me, and the spell of its indifference gets me. I can't quite explain it: as if one resolved back almost to the plant kingdom, before souls, spirits and minds were grown at all: only quite a live, energetic body with a weird face.

They were very happy, Frieda especially so, in the 'awfully nice' bungalow forty miles south of Sydney they had hired at the rent of 30s. a week, with living 'about as much as England.' It was a typical Australian bungalow, I imagine, with ' one *big* room and three small bedrooms, then kitchen and washhouse—and a plot of grass'; but the sovereign attraction was what lay directly beyond the plot of grass 'a low bushy cliff, hardly more than a bank—and the sand and the sea.'

It was the Pacific that Lawrence found lovely and stimulating—

A lovely ocean, but my, how boomingly crashingly noisy as a rule. To-day for the first time it only splashes and rushes, instead of exploding and roaring. We bathe by ourselves—and run in and stand under the shower-bath to wash the *very* seaey water off.

It must have seemed as if the constant roar and wash of that sea could empty a man of his consciousness as it emptied the shells that tumbled about its beaches.

His novel half done by June 22nd ('funny sort of novel where nothing happens and such a lot of things *should* happen: scene Australia'), Lawrence was already planning to sail upon August 10th to San Francisco, *via* Wellington and Tahiti, *en route* for Taos. All he waited for now was money for their fares, which he hoped to have from Mountsier. But he would be looking back at Australia over his shoulder as he did not look back on the East—

Australia would be a lovely country to lose the world in altogether. I'll go round it once more—the world—and if ever I get back here I will stay.

On the same day that Lawrence posted me a copy of *Aaron's Rod* in the American edition he received a copy of my second novel *The Camomile*. He thought it 'amusing, well written and better made' than my first novel and approved of its 'drift' as well as liking the letter diary form.

One simply must stand out against the social world, even if one misses life. Much life they have to offer! Those Indian civil servants are the limit: you should have seen them even in Ceylon: conceit and imbecility. No, she [the chief character of my story] was well rid of her empty hero and all he stands for: tin cans.

He hoped it would 'flourish without being trodden on.'

When they came to sail from Australia (Frieda told me this long afterwards), though enough had come for the fares, there was so little over and above that it became a nice question whether they might economise by laying in half a dozen pairs of socks for Lawrence. Socks would be far dearer in America—meat and wool were the only cheap Australian commodities—and Lawrence already stood in fair need of socks, and would soon stand in urgent need. But having considered carefully, he decided that socks must take their chance. The economy was not worth the risk of running out of cash before they reached America. He was right. For a dollar in hand was worth much, and in America, though unknown to him, the sales of *Women in Love* were even then running into 15,000 copies.

August 15th saw them in New Zealand for the day and going on to Raratonga and Tahiti. Tahiti he found beautiful, but Papeete 'a poor, dull, modernish place.' In any case there was little time for looking round. On September 4th, with exactly 20 dollars in their pockets, and not very much more in the bank, they reached San Francisco—'quite pleasant but very noisy and iron clanking and expensive.' And after four days there they went on to Santa Fé. He would write to us from Taos where he was to find his mail.

II

That summer of 1922 we stayed at the Tinners' Arms at Zennor—the same inn at which Lawrence and Frieda had stayed in 1916 when they were getting their cottage in order. I had written to Lawrence from there, addressing him at Taos.[1] He replied the day after my letter reached him:

I always think Cornwall has a lot to give one. But Zennor sounds too much changed.

Nevertheless:

In the spring I think I want to come to England. But I feel England has insulted me, and I stomach that feeling badly. *Pero, son sempre inglese.*

So much for Cornwall and England. What of Taos and America?

Taos, in its way, *is* rather thrilling. We have got a *very* pretty adobe house, with furniture made in the village, and Mexican and Navajo rugs, and some lovely pots. It stands just on the edge of the Indian reservation: a brook behind, with trees: in front, the so-called desert, rather like a moor but covered with whitish-grey sage brush, flowering yellow now: some 5 miles away the mountains rise. On the North—we face East—Taos mountain, the sacred mt. of the Indians, sits massive on the plain—some 8 miles away. The pueblo is towards the foot of the mt., 3 miles off: a big, adobe pueblo on each side the brook, like two great heaps of earthen boxes, cubes. There the Indians all live together. They

[1] My knowledge of Lawrence's life in America is derived mainly from his letters to me and from conversations with him and Frieda during their visits to England. Those who want a first-hand account will do well to read *Lorenzo in Taos* by Lawrence's hostess there, Mrs. Mabel Dodge Sterne. It is a book of great interest, being clearly an attempt to set down with care and honesty a personal impression. As an objective record, however, it must be regarded with caution. Where I have been able to check Mrs. Sterne's statements from my own knowledge I have found her inaccurate in her facts and wrong in her conjectures. She often fails also in understanding the idiom used in talk both by Lawrence and Frieda—especially Frieda. The great merit of the book lies in what may be read between the lines by the light of the admirable letters from Lawrence which are reproduced in full.

are pueblos—these houses were here before the conquest—very
old: and they grow grain and have cattle, on the lands bordering
the brook, which they can irrigate. . . . We drive across these
'deserts'—white sage scrub and dark green pinon scrub on the
slopes. On Monday we went up a canon into the Rockies to a
deserted gold mine. The aspens are yellow and lovely. We have
a pretty busy time, too. I have already learnt to ride one of these
Indian ponies, with a Mexican saddle. Like it so much. We
gallop off to the pueblo or up to one of the canons. Frieda is
learning too. Last night the young Indians came down to dance
in the studio, with two drums: and we all joined in. It is fun:
and queer. The Indians are much more remote than negroes.
This week-end is the great dance at the pueblo, and the Apaches
and Navajos come in wagons and on horseback, and the Mexicans
troop to Taos village. Taos village is a Mexican sort of plaza—
piazza—with trees and shops and horses tied up. It lies one mile
to the south of us: so four miles from the pueblo. We see little
of Taos itself. . . . The days are hot sunshine: noon very hot,
especially riding home across the open. Night is cold. In winter
it snows, because we are 7000 feet above sea-level. But as yet one
thinks of midsummer. We are about 30 miles from the tiny railway
station: but we motored 100 miles from the main line.

Interspersed with this was a brief description of the people
to gratify my curiosity, and the letter ended:

Well, I am afraid it will all sound very fascinating if you are
just feeling cooped up in London. I don't want you to feel envious.
Perhaps it is necessary for me to try these places, perhaps it is my
destiny to know the world. It only excites the outside of me. The
inside it leaves more isolated and stoic than ever. That's how it is.
It is all a form of running away from oneself and the great problems: all this wild west and the strange Australia. But I try to
keep quite clear. One forms not the faintest inward attachment,
especially here in America. America lives by a sort of egoistic *will*,
shove and be shoved. Well, one can stand up to that too: but
one is quite, quite cold inside. No illusion. I will not shove, and

I will *not* be shoved. *Sono io!* . . . Remember if you were here you'd only be hardening your heart and stiffening your neck—it is either that or be walked over, in America.

With this for the postscript:

> In my opinion a 'gentle' life with John Patrick and Don, and a gentle faith in life itself, is far better than these women in breeches and riding-boots and sombreros, and money and motor-cars and wild west. It is all inwardly a hard stone and nothingness. Only the desert has a fascination—to ride alone—in the sun in the forever unpossessed country—away from man. That is a great temptation, because one rather hates mankind nowadays. But *pazienza, sempre pazienza!*

This was the only letter I had till one that came too late for December 25th following a Christmas present of *England, My England!* and it was not from Taos, but from the Del Monte ranch, 17 miles away and 1600 feet higher up the Rockies. In September Frieda and he, busying themselves with the homely task of making wild plum jam, had in some measure settled down in the house hospitably put ready for them. It was near enough to Mrs. Sterne's own carefully artistic dwelling (upon first seeing the interior Lawrence had been rude enough to find it 'like those nasty little temples' in Ceylon!) for the Lawrences to be expected every night for supper. But this could not last long. Lawrence had quickly recognised what perhaps did not surprise him, that Mrs. Sterne wanted of him what he had made Gudrun want of Gerald in *Women in Love*—to use him as an instrument for the furthering of her own ideas and purposes—spiritual, political, artistic. One of the things she had set herself was to do salvage work for the Indians. This was not for Lawrence and he knew it. Her endeavour to make it so signified to him a kind of outrage. The man that yielded to such usage must die. Gerald had been made to die as surely by Gudrun's doing as if she had stuffed his mouth with snow to choke him. Lawrence would far sooner the woman died! Again, from its highly artistic-social nature, the existence was conducive neither to work nor enjoyment. So by the middle of December, finding Taos 'too much' for them socially—'Mabel Sterne and suppers and motor drives and people dropping in'—they had gone to the Del Monte ranch.

It extended over 1500 acres, 'mostly wild,' and held about 125 head of cattle. The house proper was occupied by a couple with whom lived the man's sister. They were more or less responsible for the place—educated, young, hard-working people called Hawk, to whom Lawrence took at once. Three minutes from the Hawks' house, in a fenced enclosure, were several log cabins. One was old and roomy and two-storied, and this—again by the kindness of Mrs. Sterne—the Lawrences occupied. Another, smaller and more modern, was inhabited by two young Danish artists who—need it be said?—had left Taos in the Lawrences' company. It was 'materially very fine.' Even it was 'very beautiful'—'the snow mountains behind—a vast landscape below, vast, desert, and then more mountains west, far off in Arizona, a skyline . . . trees all behind—and snow.' In the daytime Lawrence and the young Danish artists went chopping down trees for their own burning or 'riding off together.' So that it was 'altogether . . . ideal, according to one's ideas,' although to be sure in December the altitude (8600 ft.) took 'a bit of getting used to.'

But Lawrence was sober enough about it, and recorded even thus early that ' *innerlich*, there is nothing.'

It seems to me, in America, for the inside life, there is just blank nothing. All this outside life—and marvellous country—and it all means so little to one. I don't quite know what it is one wants because the ordinary society and 'talk' in Europe are weary

enough. But there is no inside life throb here—none—all empty—
people inside dead, outside bustling (sometimes). Anyhow dead
and always on the move. Truly I prefer Europe. Liberty—
space—deadness.

At the same time there *was* liberty and space, and there
lacked at least the same kind of deadness that Lawrence had
suffered from in Europe—the slow putrescence that vaunted
itself as life. It was what, if we look back, he had expected,
though realisation has always its difference. At least he got
out of it the conviction that he himself belonged to Europe
—'though not to England'—and that to Europe he must
return sooner or later whether he wished it or not. The
upshot was that he didn't want to 'live anywhere very long.'
He would stay for perhaps another three months where he
was, 'then come east—come to Europe—perhaps via Green-
land.' He might even like to go to Russia in the summer.
After America it made an appeal. But there was the difficulty of a moneyless Russia. He asked me to write to Ivy
Litvinoff asking her how it would be for Frieda and him to
spend a few months, even a year, there. At the moment, he
said, he was not writing. But *Kangaroo* was due for February,
and *Women in Love* had now sold 15,000 copies—there was
even talk of it being filmed! 'Why do they read me?' he
asks. 'But anyhow, they *do* read me—which is more than
England does.'

The Del Monte was too severe for the earliest months
of the year, so the Lawrences did some wandering in Mexico
proper. After the forgetful, physical life of the ranch, combined with the searching clashes of temperament and wills
(English *versus* American) at Taos, of which there had been
repercussions at the ranch, Lawrence was in the state to
begin another book.

On April 11th he sent me a postcard photograph of
himself with Frieda and an American poet, Witter Bynner,

taken on the top of the old Pyramid of the Sun at Teoti-
huacan. The picture shows him bareheaded, looking alert
and well. On the written side, under an address of Mexico
City, he acknowledged a letter of mine (by return) and told
me that they had been in Mexico for nearly three weeks and
liked it. The next day they were going to Puebla and
Tehuacan, and Orizaba, to see if they felt like staying the
summer. Two things only were immediately clear. He
was glad to escape the human complications at Taos, and he
was fascinated by Mexico. The rest was uncertain. 'Every
time I am near to coming to England, I find I don't want to
come—just yet. But I am never sure what I shall do in a
month's time.'

Russia, for the moment, seemed 'very far away and not
very desirable.' The money question could not yet be taken
for granted. As he put it himself—'my prosperity is only
relative—especially with so many relatives in Germany.' He
knew he must go on writing, and where he was he felt the
vivid interest that was the prelude to writing. This Pyramid
of the Sun, for example, he found 'very impressive . . . far
more than Pompeii or the Forum,' and the Indians there
were attractive to him. Though Mexico City was 'rather
ramshackle and Americanised,' there was 'a good *natural*
feeling—a great carelessness.' To me this meant that
Lawrence was either writing a book or about to do so.

Possibly the ramshackle and Americanised Mexico City,
made suddenly more hideous by the spectacle of the bull-fight
which Lawrence has described in the opening pages of *The
Plumed Serpent*, was responsible for the extreme but temporary
disgust which led him a fortnight later to feel he had had
'enough of the New World.' Another and much shorter
postcard made this announcement, and said that he expected
to sail for New York from Vera Cruz the following week,
arriving in England about June. He 'felt like coming back

now.' At once I wrote suggesting that he might like to take a floor of the old Hampstead house in which we now had rooms.

But meanwhile, in part perhaps out of that very disgust and that horrid bull-fight, the theme of *The Plumed Serpent* had announced itself. It was by far the most ambitious theme that had as yet called for treatment—the theme of men in a modern world who become gods while yet remaining men. A difficult undertaking, as Lawrence well understood. But he accepted it with his usual obedience to what chimed with his deepest desire. His next letter, dated June 7th, was from Lake Chapala, the scene of the novel. He had just heard from me and liked the idea of the rooms above ours.

But see, we are still here. I felt I had a novel simmering in me, so came here, to this big Lake, to see if I could write it. It goes fairly well. I shall be glad if I can finish the first draft by the end of this month. Then we shall pack up at once, go to Mexico City and sail from Vera Cruz for New York. Hope to be in England by early August. Where will you be then? I shall be glad to be back. But wanted to get this novel off my chest.

Auf Wiedersehen.

The novel, of course, took longer than Lawrence had calculated and, what was more important, the charm of Mexico grew upon him. He wanted to stay longer, to try it to the full. And though he accompanied Frieda—who was longing for Europe—to New York by boat from New Orleans (the latter 'a dead, steaming sort of place, a bit like Martin Chuzzlewit,' and the Mississippi 'a vast and weary river that looks as if it had never wanted to start flowing') with the idea that he might accompany her, he felt such a longing to be back in Mexico that he saw her off by the *Orbita* and returned alone. He would follow her—perhaps. He asked me to 'look after Frieda a bit' during the 'month or so' she was to be in London—probably in Mary Cannan's flat in

Queen's Gardens, Hyde Park—from August 26th, after which she would go to Germany, after which she would rejoin Lawrence wherever he might be—perhaps in Mexico, perhaps in England by the autumn. This, as it should happen. But, 'at present' he could not come to England.

To avoid confusion, it must be remembered that Lawrence felt very differently about Mexico and the United States. Murry has lumped them both together as America, and has conveniently said that Lawrence hated it. This is misleading. Mexico—horror and all—held something for Lawrence as a man and a writer that he needed. This he never disavowed. The United States on the other hand provided merely for his unhampered existence as a writer in the impersonal sense, and had to be visited on that account, much as he shrank from it. Even Mexico could never usurp Europe in the heart of the European Lawrence. But America was the medicine for England and there was no wantonness in his going. In Mexico he found something more than medicine—a sprig of the magic mountain herb for which he had gone on pilgrimage, a vestige of 'the last dark strand' from the pre-white, pre-Christian era.

But in the midst of these tastings and adventures there arrives by post for Lawrence a bottle of the latest London specific for souls. It is labelled *Adelphi*. Shake well. Contents to be swallowed monthly.

III

The story of the *Adelphi* and its connection with Lawrence has been told in the pages of that periodical by Murry himself with a running commentary. As he was the only begetter and the editor of the periodical we must accept his narrative, but we shall find that, extracted from his commentary, it appears in a different light.

Time and again he is obliged to accuse his 'great' man of self-deception—self-deception alike in small matters and in large. So much so indeed that, unless we take his bare word for it, we fail to see any greatness in the Lawrence of his narrative, just as we fail to see on Murry's part any true response to greatness. For one thing self-deception is surely not an attribute of true greatness. What does appear in the very turn of Murry's phrases is something for which self-deception is the most charitable word.

To go back a little. In spite of his ecstasy over *Aaron's Rod* as a 'fountain of life,' Murry does not seem to have written to Lawrence to tell him how much he and Katherine thought of the book. He left his review—his single favourable review, of a Lawrence novel, with the exception of a few lines commending *St. Mawr*—to speak for itself. The first friendly gesture came, he tells us, from Lawrence. He found the card from New Zealand 'unexpected'—as well as 'sudden.' It was none the less the kind of thing one might expect from Lawrence. His affection for Katherine, whom he now knew to be very ill, had always been great, and seeing her home land, he could not help remembering with tenderness his early hopeful association with Murry in her company.

There was nothing 'sudden,' however, about Murry's response. Not till the end of the year, when Katherine had definitely repudiated his guidance by going to Fontainebleau, did he write suggesting, 'he supposes,' that 'relations should be renewed.' Somehow this has the wrong sound, and judging from the short extract disclosed from Lawrence's reply, one may infer an appeal from which hysteria was not absent. Lawrence replied that it would be as well to wait and see. 'Heaven knows what we all are, and how we should feel if we met, now that we are changed: we will have to meet and see.' A kindly wave of the hand from New

Zealand had come naturally, but there was something which made Lawrence wary in this plea for a clasping of hands across the ocean.

When Katherine Mansfield died in December, 1922, Lawrence sent a message that was kind, eloquent and wise and, as was usual with his messages, free from any trace of emotional collapse.

'I wish it needn't all have been as it has been. I do wish it.' This, which was strictly true, was as far as he could go for the past. 'We will unite up again when I come to England.' This for a future hope. Lawrence was always willing to welcome a change for the better. As for Murry's present and his own, there was a frank warning but a steady affirmation of faith. 'We keep faith. I always feel death only strengthens that—the faith between those who have it.' Soon after this letter came a present of the *Fantasia*, published in America.

One spring night in a lovely part of the country, solitary and wrought up by that sort of 'half convalescent' emotion which in those who lack greatness can so easily take the form of spiritual self-abuse, Murry read the *Fantasia*. One may be pardoned for thinking that in this mood, and following the receipt of so moving a letter from Lawrence, Murry would have been in ecstasies almost equally over any new Lawrence book. A man of moods, this. Still, the *Fantasia* it was, and he has the benefit of the doubt. Its effect on him was twofold. It made him fall grovelling on his face before Lawrence, and it clinched his already 'half-formed' deter- mination—a determination which in the first place had nothing to do with Lawrence—to found the *Adelphi*. So he has told us. Why not launch the new venture with sorrow- ing praise of Katherine Mansfield and some essential chapters of the *Fantasia*, which was still unknown in England?

We can believe that he 'neither desired, nor intended to

remain editor' of the magazine, and that he was in his own
eyes 'simply *locum tenens*, literary lieutenant, for Lawrence,'
only by guessing how far he was swept away by his own
wrought-up condition. Except for a line of kindly encouragement from Lawrence (which could hardly have been refused,
elicited as it was by prepaid cable) the whole thing existed
merely 'in his own eyes.' In no real sense was Lawrence
consulted. Distance and time made that impossible, for the
first copy of the *Adelphi* appeared in June, 1923. Yet because he could infer from some remarks in Lawrence's letters
that Lawrence 'was in the throes of a revulsion from
America,' he concluded that the revulsion from England had
spent itself, and that he, Murry, had only to say the magic
word '*Adelphi*' for Lawrence to rush back and wait upon the
doorstep till such time as the founder and editor would vacate
his place at the office table.

    To anyone with any knowledge of Lawrence it seems
fantastic indeed to imagine him as the editor of a monthly
magazine in England: still more fantastic, had he founded
a magazine, that it should have resembled the *Adelphi*. No
doubt he was willing, even pleased, to encourage Murry and
to let him use the *Fantasia*. But in his very first letters after
the cable he made it clear that he had no intention of hurry-
ing to England. There were things more urgent than any
Adelphi that would keep him in America yet awhile. Besides,
'ghastly' and 'empty' as was the U.S.A., this was preferable
to plausible and stuffy England that made him feel as if he
had 'swallowed a lump of lead.' He would come—that
very summer, if he could, Murry might be looking out for
a quiet cottage for him. Meanwhile there was room for
improvement in the *Adelphi*. He did not like the first numbers. They were too accommodating by half, and apart
from the *Fantasia*, not to his taste. Murry must have
patience and show his mettle. In spite of his revulsion against

America he 'mistrusted his country too much to identify himself with it any more.' He even felt 'a certain disgust.' 'Something must *happen*' before he could return or regain his confidence. The editor of the *Athenæum* might, 'in his own eyes' be 'radically changed' by a spiritual experience in which the *Fantasia* had played a part. But how was Lawrence to be sure that such a radical change was necessarily for the better in *his* eyes (however convenient from a literary point of view) or even that it was not a case of 'plus ça change, plus c'est la même chose'? There was nothing in the *Adelphi* as yet to make him sure. While he praised what he could (for Lawrence in such things was both kind and courteous) and hoped hard for its future, and while he would give Murry of his best without expecting more than the minimum of pay, it was not to be thought that he would risk everything on Murry's intimation of a new partisanship and a new integrity.

If any reader has the patience to-day to read through those early numbers of the *Adelphi* he will see clearly what Lawrence must have thought of them—Lawrence who was himself without a touch of hysteria; Lawrence who was against precisely the kind of humble and emotional yet rationalised Christianity of which Murry now became the spokesman; Lawrence who, while recognising Katherine Mansfield's charming gifts, would never admit that she had genius or even that her work was quite honest; Lawrence who disliked anything in the nature of exploitation; Lawrence who was finding amid the horrors of Mexico the relief afforded by a 'good natural feeling' and was ready to begin writing *The Plumed Serpent*.

The reader, this is to say, will see what Lawrence must have felt about the *Adelphi* as a possible mouthpiece for his own thought, except in so far as he might be an outside contributor. Which is not, however, to say either (*a*), that he

did not wish Murry well in any venture that would help
him to think things out in his own way, or (b), that he did
not hope Murry's thinking might bring him and his magazine
round in time to something sufficiently harmonious with
Lawrence's own to allow of true collaboration.

Yet Murry was so 'perplexed' and 'bewildered' by Lawrence's letters, because they were doubtful and critical as
well as encouraging, that he wrote to ask if Lawrence had
really *meant* what he had said in *Aaron's Rod* and *Fantasia*,
about wishing for another man's help in the attempt to create
a new world! And when Lawrence decided that he must
stay a while longer in America—this time in Old Mexico—
Murry concluded either that he had misunderstood the
Fantasia or that Lawrence had *not* meant what he said, or
more probably both.

What Murry could not comprehend—or, being com-
prehended, drove him mad—was that Lawrence, with his
passion and his perceptiveness, stood between two worlds,
and not between economic worlds like those of capitalism
and communism, but between worlds of the human spirit—
the old world, rich and beloved but almost dead, which
demanded that he be 'faithful and faithless together,' and the
new world which meant nothing to his aching heart yet
claimed all his loyalty. But he would have no trumped-up
newness, no re-hash of the old, no fobbing off with economic
makeshifts of the moment. The new had to be most
delicately sought and perilously fought for. If England could
hold out the veritable olive branch of Spring he would take
it. Somehow the *Adelphi* olive branch did not meet his need.
By the side of the bare but quivering twig of the diviner
that he carried in his own hand it was suspect.

That his own twig had not lied in leading him to Mexico
was already proved. As he had written to me just then, in
the letter quoted earlier, there was 'a novel simmering in

him'—a novel of well over 100,000 words—which had
taken him to Lake Chapala, first to see if he could write it,
and then to hold him there till he should finish.

This then, and nothing more sinister was what, in Murry's
phrase, 'ailed Lawrence.' His 'strange instability' and the
rest of the fatal sounding phrases mean no more than that an
imaginative writer preferred the peaceful production of a
new novel in fostering circumstances to throwing in his lot
with a new magazine of which he was doubtful along with
a man whom he had no cause to trust.

Murry will have it that *Aaron's Rod* was the peak of
Lawrence's achievement in fiction.   I am against peaks—as
of an invalid chart—where Lawrence is concerned.   I see
him not as a waxing and waning but as a pulsing light, and
his life rather as a pilgrimage than as a pattern.   But, if there
must be a pinnacle, surely, so far anyhow as fiction is concerned, it is reached in *The Plumed Serpent*.   And surely
here is the most ambitious and the most impressive novel of
our generation.   If any has been more faultless, which has
possessed in the same degree the blazing virtue of potency?
Only the pinions of faith could have carried home such a
theme.   And more than faith.   For this tale Lawrence needed
not only all his genius, but all his long discipline and all his
savage pilgrimage.   So far from showing 'disintegration' it
creates.   In it Lawrence's powers as a novelist are established
and his thoughts as a man embodied to that extent that it
would have assured him his place without further production.
Indeed it may be said that all later works, such as *Lady
Chatterley* and *The Man Who Died*, are embroideries on
themes contained in the Mexican novel.

In relating how Lawrence delayed his coming Murry
makes no mention of *The Plumed Serpent*.   When it came
to be reviewed in the *Adelphi* in August, 1926, it was dismissed with humorous disparagement in a few lines as a

'disappointing' book that 'lets us down,' so much so that 'we cannot help suspecting that Lawrence has lost faith in his own imagination. . . . Alas! now that the miracle is here, we cannot grasp it either with our minds, our solar plexuses, or our tails.' Though he adds, of course, 'need we say that the book contains lovely and memorable things?'

While Lawrence was engaged in writing *The Plumed Serpent* Murry was 'giving himself away' in the magazine (which had been meant for Lawrence) to an extent that in his own words was 'past change, beyond all remedy.' In the editorial to his second number he quoted passages from two private 'letters to the editor.' One was from a woman who, all alone in Plymouth 'in the throes of a great bereavement, having come straight from the death-bed in the accident ward of a public hospital of a greatly loved friend smitten down under tragic circumstances in the prime of life,' had 'wandered into a public library where in an advertisement the arresting headline' of Murry's article in the *Adelphi* had caught her eye and thrilled her so much that she spent a shilling and discovered 'that ideals and aspirations are indeed spiritual potencies that here and hereafter demand our loyalties.'

As well as this Plymouth sister, Murry produced a male testifier. The two would seem to be closely related, like sufferers from kidney trouble, whose epistolary style in describing the benefits of a curative pill they exactly reproduce.

Somehow your advertisement had caught my soul—I was, and am still, troubled by this terrible enigma—life. I had tried in my way to satisfy my soul; but alas! what is my way? It had made me more miserable and unhappy. On the 28th I wandered the whole afternoon from newsagent to newsagent to get a copy of the *Adelphi*—[he failed owing to some fault in distribution] . . . and with heavy heart wandered—wandered aimlessly.

Though he knows not why, somehow or other the ideal

of the *Adelphi* had got hold of him, and he 'was like a moth, determined to whirl round and round the candle till he had either burnt his wings or understood the nature of light.'   Advertisers, reading this breathless narrative, must have been relieved to learn that the very next afternoon this most metaphysical moth procured a copy of the *Adelphi* and 'read it through from cover to cover including the advertisements,' with effects that are expressed in phrases of a like vague ecstasy.

It was not, of course, to Lawrence's *Fantasia* that these testimonials applied, but to Murry's first editorial, 'The Cause of it All,' in which Lawrence had no part, either alleged or conceivable.   It was a very catchy piece of work, before which, I am ashamed to say, I momentarily went down myself, though Donald condemned it at once as 'disgusting' and Lawrence, when I first met him afterwards, had no printable words in which to describe it.   It was in the emotional facetious vein—essentially the same flavour as we find in 'There was a Little Man,' Murry's contribution to the *Signature* in 1915.   It showed us Murry, aged thirty-four, sitting on the top of a Camden Town bus and describing himself with overflowing sympathy for our benefit.   He mentions his 'demon.'   But it is not what Lawrence means by a demon. It is merely the common little devil of doubt that, when Murry comes to earth after a heavenward caper of special emotional attainment, whispers in his ear that he may not be able to 'justify the *Adelphi*,' with the result that he feels impelled 'to write boldly, to unfurl and wave a flag.'

'What flag?'   I can hear Lawrence put this question, with dancing eyes.

Murry unfurls his banner.   It bears this device, 'The *Adelphi* is run for and by a belief in Life.'

'So,' replies Lawrence, 'might the editor of *John Bull* truthfully declare.   However, get on with it and good luck to you. I too believe in life. But it does not follow that our beliefs are not diametrically opposed, as indeed they have proved to be in the past. However, you *may* be getting by your own way to some plane where we can meet in agreement. You tell me that recent events have radically changed your outlook so that you enter into my position in *Fantasia* (notwithstanding that this book is a logical development from *Women in Love* and in perfect accord with *The Lost Girl* which you still hate). By all means get on with it. Possibly the nasty taste is only in my super-sensitive mouth. Again, possibly not.'

For the rest, in his opening number of the *Adelphi* Murry announced some taking features, named a small team of good men who were going to work for next to nothing for him under the banner of the idea, disclaimed the editorial chair for himself, and gave the usual journalistic venture 'send-off' by the good old stage-army band—Arnold Bennett, H. G. Wells, etc. In Murry's own words it was all 'the most frightful give-away.'

And it 'went with a bang.' So we learn in the second issue. But is Murry elated? Ah no, my friends. He is 'umble.' He fears only that he may not live up to his first number, or that he may 'fail' such people as his Plymouth sister and the male moth in their all too human appeal. He disclaims all notion of financial success, only initiating a scheme by which every three readers (already four times in excess of the number he had modestly counted on) shall bring him one new reader between them.

In this, his second number, he says nothing about vacating the editorial chair. He is indeed very much the editor, speaking in the first person, referring to his colleagues, his policy and his intended procedure, the last mentioned of which were as un-Lawrencian as can be. As between D. H. Lawrence and Mr. Horatio Bottomley they tended perceptibly, in regard to editorial flavour, towards the latter sage—wherein, no doubt, lay their appeal. Editorial matter apart, there was another long extract from the *Fantasia*; there were extracts from Katherine Mansfield's journal of a personal nature, which exhibited her mourning over her dead brother in language a thought too childlike; there was a poem by her to her dead brother, which, on the other hand, did not seem intended for the public eye; and there was the reproduction of a drawing by her, meant for her brother's pleasure when he was alive. Into this intimate At Home of the Murry-Mansfield family the *Fantasia* seemed to have strayed in unawares.

So thought the *Adelphi* readers, anyhow those of the type which Murry most feared to 'let down.' With Lawrence as even a single ingredient of this publication which was to have been all for him, there was going to be trouble. About the first extract nobody had felt impelled to write—not even the man who had read all the advertisements. But in the second Lawrence had stated—what Mr. Bernard Shaw had already stated quite a long time before—that Jesus was a failure.

It was now put beyond doubt for what section of the public Murry's magazine had made its bid. It 'passed the comprehension' of the Westminster Catholic Association how the editor of 'a responsible review' could have allowed the Lawrence matter with its 'studied insult to the Christian religion' to appear. Mr. Ellis Roberts in a letter took the same view. This was bad enough. But what really touched Murry to the quick was a protest from a private individual who at the risk of being 'very old-fashioned and narrow' bewailed the admission into this 'most delightful magazine' of 'sneers at the Founder of the Christian religion.' The inclusion of one who thus 'spat in the face of Christ' would 'drive out from the circle' of *Adelphi* readers 'the thousands of people who are alienated by this sort of thing.'

One might have thought that such a letter was predictable. But to Murry it was 'a shock,' and 'a bolt from the blue.' Recollect that the *Adelphi* now looked like being, all unexpectedly, a financial success.

Certainly here was a nice question, even a test one, though there were in fact, as there generally are, more than two ways of meeting it—*i.e.* three. Murry might have referred his critics to Lawrence—in which case the *Adelphi* would most likely have gone out on its third issue in a blaze of significant defiance, but would possibly have re-issued from its ashes at some later time. He might have referred them to the devil or—almost the same thing—ignored them, in which case he could never hope to recover the readers Lawrence had lost him. Or he might manage in such a way as to placate the 'circle' to which it was clear that his *Adelphi* personality appealed. While doing this he could stand on his dignity as an editor by *appearing* to stand by Lawrence, in which case, though readers might be temporarily dropped they could later be rounded up again.

He chose the third course. In the third issue of the *Adelphi* (to which I was one of the smaller contributors[1]) he told how the private letter from which I have quoted had 'deeply moved' him (as well as coming like a bolt from the blue) by its 'simple and exquisite sincerity.' At the same time (with Koteliansky sternly by his elbow) he made the utmost stand for Lawrence of which he was capable. He announced that in his opinion '*since Katherine Mansfield's death*' (the italics are mine) D. H. Lawrence had '*become* incomparably the most important English writer of his generation.'

If it had not been for that subtly misleading 'since

---

[1] In a letter written that August Lawrence told me (perhaps a doubtful compliment!) that he liked this—a note on Duse—better than anything else in the magazine.

Katherine Mansfield's death' it was really not so ill done. It saved Murry's dignity and it preserved the *Adelphi* to achieve good work of its kind and to publish, for a time at least, work by Lawrence. It is even doubtful if these ends could have been achieved by any other means: Murry, besides, had every right to manipulate for the maintenance of a magazine in which he believed.

But the inwardness of the matter lay in the fact that Murry was facing both ways and that Lawrence, perceiving this, lost any hope he might still have of identifying himself more closely with the *Adelphi*. The hands were the hands of Esau, but the voice was the voice of Jacob. If Murry could find a 'deeply moving' and 'simple and exquisite sincerity' in the sort of private letters from which he had quoted, and if he thought that only by reason of Katherine Mansfield's death Lawrence was become the most important English writer of his generation, he was far, very far from possessing the capacity to act as 'lieutenant' to a man whose essential creed was contained in the words 'never adapt yourself.' To put it more mildly, the *Adelphi* was not a thing to rush home for. It could wait. As usual Murry had underrated both Lawrence's subtlety and his clear-sighted arrogance.

IV

By August, as we have seen, Frieda was tired of being in Mexico and longed to be in England. For one thing she now had better prospects than ever before of seeing her children. She urged Lawrence to return, telling him among other ready half-truths that 'England was his place.' Like me she did not think so poorly of the *Adelphi* as Lawrence did. Like me she was even carried away by it, and what was more she could almost fancy a future in it for Lawrence. And almost he wanted to be persuaded. In August she got

him as far as the quay at New York.   But at that point the
'Balaam's ass in his belly' rebelled.   He would not go.
'Find I just don't want to—not yet.   Later.'   So he wrote
to me from New York after seeing Frieda off without him,
and this though he had no definite plans otherwise.

I think I shall go to California, and either pack with a donkey
in the mountains, or get some sailing ship to the islands—if the last
is possible.   Perhaps by the autumn I'll decide to come to England
—who knows!   At present I can't come.

On the quay Frieda and Lawrence had been through one
of the worst quarrels—perhaps the very worst—of their life
together.   And when they parted it was in such anger that
both of them felt it might be for always.   Because, of course,
if Lawrence felt that he must stay longer he wanted Frieda
to stay with him.   It was against his desire that she had
persuaded him this far.

Frieda, however, presently calmed and cheered by the
voyage, felt quite sure that the parting was not for always,
and immediately upon her arrival in England she sent Lawrence a wifely cable.   He must come to her because she needed
him.

Lawrence did not come at once, though no doubt he was
glad of the cable.   He went to Buffalo, to Tepic, to Jalisco,
which last he greatly liked, making a tour of some two
months, which must have had a strong effect upon *The
Plumed Serpent* when he came to re-write the MS.   In
some at least of these places he had acquaintances, at others
introductions.

Meanwhile, Frieda having paid her visit to her mother in
Germany, was in London;   and, thinking that she was preparing the way for Lawrence, was seeing much of Murry.
She kept writing enthusiastic letters to Lawrence about him
and the *Adelphi*.   Yet Lawrence held back.

'Frieda says she likes England now, and it is my place, and I must come back. I wonder.' So he wrote to me from Guadalajara on October 17th, having heard that I had just read *Kangaroo*. The letter continues:

We rode two days down the mountains, and got to Eztatlan. Mexico has a certain mystery of beauty for me, as if the gods were here. Now, in this October, the days are so pure and lovely, like an enchantment, as if some dark-faced gods were still young. I wish it could be that I *could* start a little centre—a ranch—where we could have our little adobe houses and make a life, and you could come with Don and John Patrick. It is always what I work for. But it must come from the inside, not from the will. And when it will be it will be, I suppose. It is queer, all the way down the Pacific Coast, I kept thinking: Best go back to England. And then, once across the barranca from Ixtlan, it was here again, where the gods may sometimes be awful, but they are young, here in Mexico, in Jalisco, that I wanted to be. And there is room—room for all of us if it could but be.

But let us watch : things, when they come, come suddenly. It may be my destiny is in Europe. *Quien sabe?* If it is, I'll come back.

Hasta el dia!

But by the middle of November Lawrence felt that he could, even that he must come to England. He need not stay, but he must look after Frieda. And he could see for himself if there was anything in the *Adelphi*, as Frieda, unlike himself, was so sure that there was. For the moment there was nothing keeping him in America as there had been three months earlier. He had got what he then wanted. As Frieda insisted, now that Murry was a free man, and was of a mind to accept Lawrence's leading as soon as Lawrence should come upon the scene, they might carry out the old scheme of going forth together.

Eight days after writing to me he wrote to Murry:

Yes, I think I shall come back now. I think I shall be back by the beginning of December. Work awhile with you on the *Adelphi*. Then perhaps we'll set off to India. *Quien sabe?*

The promise went no further than this. Yet Murry would have us believe that in the matter of the *Adelphi* Lawrence had let him down. Anyhow his 'nascent confidence' in Lawrence as his leader 'had already begun to wither.' It is with a peculiar sneer that he attributes Lawrence's return simply to his wish to rejoin Frieda.

Lawrence arrived in London at the beginning of December and Murry went with Kot to the station to meet him. Murry has described the meeting—how ill Lawrence looked, with a face of 'greenish pallor,' and how almost his first words were 'I can't bear it,' so that Murry 'supposes' he felt 'as though the nightmare were upon him again.'

Murry's supposition is correct. But this time it was a different nightmare. It arose from a conviction which had begun to form in Lawrence upon his arrival at Southampton, had hardened during the journey through the Southern Counties, and had been clinched as by a hammer stroke when he was greeted by Frieda and the others on the London platform. This conviction was that he had made a mistake in coming—that he ought to have waited for Frieda to come to him. If he could have been back in America at that moment, there would have been nothing but a fierce little greenish tongue of flame for Frieda and Murry to fetch from Waterloo to Hampstead. Now that he had come, however, he must see it through. From all this the reader is requested to make no obvious deductions. Lawrence had an uncanny and instantaneous way that was entirely his own, of 'sizing up' any situation. For him to see, for example, Murry and Frieda waiting for him so chummily together was enough to turn him greenish pale all over. 'Chumminess,' . . . 'palliness' between people was anyhow detestable to him.

Again, though Murry might be Lawrence's self-appointed lieutenant on a self-constituted *Adelphi*, Frieda was another matter. Here Murry would find himself up against the 'Unknown God' with a vengeance. In Lawrence's marriage there was no place for any kind of lieutenancy.[1]

Frieda had already been living for some little time before Lawrence's arrival in the same house as ourselves—not our own house but a large old one that a brother had divided up. He lived on the top. We had a lower part, and the Lawrences the flat above us. Murry had been Frieda's constant visitor and she was clearly prepared to back him up with all her strength (though why he should need her backing I could never understand) to Lawrence upon his arrival. 'After all,' she said to me one day, 'Murry is Somebody! And the *Adelphi* is Something!!' Her enthusiasm was childlike and infectious—at least it was childlike, and I should have found it infectious if I could have brought myself to believe in Murry, which I never did. I respected his talent, and admired his capacity for eliciting emotion in others. That was as far as I got. Yet I could see, and can now, why it was that for so long he made a special appeal to Lawrence. He seemed made to subserve another's compelling genius.

Before they so much as left the station, says Murry—or perhaps in the taxi—Lawrence laid it down that the *Adelphi* 'should attack everything, everything; and explode in one blaze of denunciation.' Murry could see nothing for it but to treat this as a joke, whereupon Lawrence could see no alternative but for Murry to give the *Adelphi* up and go back to Mexico with him to 'begin the nucleus of a new society.' Lawrence's lingering belief that his own scale of values might have any practical bearing on Murry should,

[1] Though the facts of the story 'Jimmy and the Desperate Woman' come from another source, there can be no doubt that the attitude of the husband is expressive of Lawrence's feelings at this time.

one thinks, have been the real joke of the occasion for Murry, had Murry been able to regard the situation with detachment. But of course he could not, and we hardly blame him. Strange as it may seem, Lawrence was the only one detached enough to see the true irony of events.

That afternoon I was asked upstairs while Lawrence bustled about unpacking. I cannot understand Mabel Dodge Sterne's description of him at such times, or when travelling, as fussy or inefficient. He always appeared to me as a model of neatness and precision, neither wasting a movement nor permitting even a temporary disorder. Perhaps as an onlooker Mrs. Sterne was upsetting. Some people are. And I have noticed that it is often the inefficient onlooker that most upsets the efficient worker.

On this occasion, while settling in, he talked with the greatest animation. And although he was thin I saw none of the 'greenish pallor' which struck Murry. Never had I seen him more vital. So much so that Frieda asked him didn't he think after the journey he ought to 'rest for a bit?'

But he turned on her. 'Rest!' he snapped. 'When Frieda says England is "so restful!" it gives me the cold shudders. I don't *want* to rest nowadays. I feel *full* of energy!' And he went on producing things for me to see— his Indian belt of plaited horse-hair, Frieda's snow-leopard skin, or a painted Mexican vase—fawn and pink and grey, with here and there a dab of light red or pale blue—all earth colours from a place where sun and earth were in close communion. He gave me one of these after warning me that I must never put flowers in it as even the egg-shell glaze was porous to water. But first he drew from it his sewing and first-aid kit, and unscrewing a pot of boracic he produced from the lid an engraved disk of metal — bigger than an English half-crown, and heavy and shining—a coin of

Mexican gold! Somehow, as he gave it to me to handle, it was as if he passed on to me the pristine magnificence of Mexico that had meant so much to him. By this he was to measure us in England and to find us wanting.

Already Frieda, who was great on making a place 'home-like,' had hung pictures about the walls, which Mark Gertler or Dorothy Brett, or both, had lent or given for this purpose. Enthusiastically she drew his attention to them. Lawrence inspected them very coolly. 'They want thinking about, I guess!' was his comment, uttered in that concise Nottingham speech of his that somehow agreed so well with his emphatic phrases; and Frieda subsided.

At the time I did what I wish I had done oftener. I noted down immediately what I could remember of Law-rence's conversation that first afternoon during his 'getting straight' as it ran on largely in the form of a monologue. I put it down now as it stands in my note.

'The spirits of everybody on board the boat just went right down into their boots when we first sighted the coast of Europe, at Corunna. . . . The English are no longer flower-ing . . . we are the seed . . . we should be scattered. We are the best-bred people on earth. But now we are caged and fearful.'

I asked him if he would rather have New York or London? 'New York,' he replied, without hesitating. 'London as a city—yes, I like it better, love it more. But it is locked away, out of touch. With New York one is in touch with the free outer world, and with the world of Mexico.' Of Mexico he spoke much, with loathing of many things about it, but saying that it had spoiled him, he feared, for Europe. 'Sicily?' he said. 'Never again!'

While he talked, he left all the letters that had collected for him in London unopened—did not even glance at them. He had liked it in Mexico, he said, that there had been no mail for him and no English newspapers. He described with delight how on the voyage home he had hung over the bows, watching a school of porpoises playing with the steamer in the translucent water. Then later the rain on the surface of black water . . . and the beauty of the flying fish. Then the shaking of the little English train—'so light, so light, as if it would fly to pieces long before we reached London.'

Between Southampton and London he had been oppressed by the hedged fields—'I feel I am a mouse—a net put over me—the network of the English hedged fields.'

Then suddenly, 'What do you think of the world these days?' he asked me.

I told him, what indeed I have always felt, that the world never seemed to come within my orbit. And that I was kept so busy endeavouring to keep a roof over our heads and food on our table that I never had much time to think about the world.

At this he laughed with a kind of mingled pleasure and disgust that it was so with me. It became a convention between us that I was attached to a little ship, which for me to leave would be infidelity. 'And how is the ship sailing?' he would ask, with a touch of mockery that I liked while I felt it was justified. Or again 'More bric-a-brac!' he would exclaim reproachfully, when I showed him some odd object newly acquired for the house. I pointed out that he himself found it hard to resist bric-a-brac, though he might not call it so. What about the snow-leopard skin, and the Navajo rings he had been describing to me? And he shook his head laughing. All the same he was in the right and I knew it, and he knew that I knew, though I fear he thought me incorrigible. He had ceased to collect things about him, and I had not.

It may have been Dorothy Brett—who now became as

constant a visitor as Murry to the Lawrences' rooms—who introduced the craze for modelling small figures and beasts and flowers, which seized upon us that Christmas, and upon Lawrence in particular. He and Dorothy Brett were by far the best at it—Murry worked hard, but without conspicuous success, making all the while little jokes at his own expense. Frieda and Donald and Koteliansky stood resolutely aside as spectators, when they troubled to look at us at all. To a richly herbaceous garden of Eden, which owed its very red Adam to Lawrence and its paler Eve to Dorothy Brett, I remember I contributed several species of wild-fowl, including a kiwi.

Again, I recollect seeing Lawrence sitting by the table, his head on his hand, reading with astonishing intentness (which made the activity seem so much more than mere reading) Conrad's then latest novel *The Rover*. Without once relaxing his concentrated attention he read it all through, then closed it and pushed it from him with the ejaculation that it was 'poor and sad stuff.' Conrad at his best in a sea-story, I gathered, he had never regarded as the equal of Herman Melville. As compared with the true sea literature of *Moby Dick*, Lawrence dismissed the storm in *Typhoon* as descriptive journalism. Still, *Almayer's Folly* was a fine book, and it was depressing to find the author of that declining into the author of *The Rover*.

It was at this time that I heard Lawrence take Murry to task in his rôle of propagandist of Katherine Mansfield. As I came in only for the end of the conversation I cannot tell what went before. The guess might be hazarded that Lawrence had not shrunk from denouncing the whole policy and atmosphere of the *Adelphi* in this particular matter, which I know he had found repugnant. On the other hand, it would be more characteristic if he let that be, and plunged straight to the quick of the subject. This was what he was doing when I entered. 'You are wrong about Katherine,' he was saying to Murry. 'She was *not* a great genius. She had a charming gift, and a finely cultivated one. But *not more*. And to try, as you do, to make it more is to do her no true service.' To this Murry made no reply, but turned away in a kind of obstinate mortification. Long before this, when I read her *Prelude* and praised it to Lawrence, he had said 'Yes, yes, but prelude to what?' It was his opinion that the author of *Prelude* would come in time to find a certain essential falseness so closely entwined with the charm in her literary fabric that she would herself condemn even the charm and would write nothing further until she had disentangled herself from the falseness.

Looking back now I find it extraordinary that I could live for so many weeks in the same house and realise so little what a struggle was going on, chiefly between Lawrence and Murry, but also between Lawrence and all of us. In spite of what critics—usually hostile ones—have said about his morbid sensitiveness, Lawrence was not the man to wear his heart on his sleeve. And when he forced an issue he did so with a kind of delicacy that easily concealed the crisis from those concerned. It was the issue, never the person, that he forced.

Murry, not long after Lawrence's arrival, had said that he would give up the *Adelphi* and go back to New Mexico with him. By those who knew that he had from the first no real intention of doing either, Murry was implored, even commanded, to make a clean breast of it to Lawrence, disclosing his mind in both matters. But Murry appears to have temporised.

It had come to this, that Lawrence's only purpose for staying a day longer in England, was to discover if all of us, or some of us, or even one of us, would feel the compulsion to go with him and Frieda to a freer and richer air where things 'could happen' as they could not in England.   The *Adelphi* was a proof to Lawrence of just *how* things happened in England.   But with Murry in a new atmosphere and away from the cloying influences of his past, Lawrence still felt that something might be done.   As for the rest of us, we were his friends of whose support he would be glad in a less crucial way.   It would neither be out of personal affection, nor to 'live to ourselves' in a pleasant spot, as Murry has suggested, 'rejecting the world, washing our hands of it altogether,' though something of both these things would naturally be included.   It would be to leave the associations of the old ideals that we might live and work freshly in the belief that of such a departure something good was sure to come.   Katherine could not come now, hiding her fun behind a solemn face, to prove by time-tables and guide-books that *Rananim* was impossible.   Lawrence had gone on and had found the very place for us.   There was nothing wrong with Taos except the Americans.   The Indian mode had sunk so far into forgetfulness, so far beyond the confident prying of the intellect, that it was almost one with nature and therefore ready to re-nourish human life.   We must get away from the white benevolence that spouted of 'life' and resulted in *Adelphies*, and learn instead something of the dark malignity that revealed the realm of death.   Our mode had come to an end.   The new mode must be from a different source.

Who shall say that Lawrence was wrong?   To him it was as clear as in old time it was to Noah or to Lot.   It may yet be found that before a new spirit can grow up in the world some men and women will have to get together and leave their homes in a special kind of faith.   However this may be, only one person in London went with the Lawrences back to New Mexico, and of all Lawrence's friends to-day she is probably the happiest.

For a day or two Lawrence had to stay in bed with cold

and a mild attack of malaria. He sent a message by Frieda that he wanted to speak to me. 'I assure you that it is a gr-reat Kompliment!' she said, opening her smiling eyes at me.

What she said was true, and I was flattered. I went upstairs at once. Still I did not really want to talk alone with Lawrence just then, a disinclination I tried to attribute to the fact that Frieda had come in upon me at a busy moment of some domestic sort.

A single bed had been moved into the living-room, and there was Lawrence sitting up all neat and trim and looking every bit as alert as if he were well. I sat down feeling distrait and uttering platitudes.

He asked me about things. Without, so far as I can remember, putting the question directly, he asked if there was any chance of my coming then or later to New Mexico. I said I was afraid it must be later. 'You see, Lawrence, unless a woman is going to leave her husband and child she can't go off without them, and I don't think Donald feels like going, anyhow not just now. I'd come, but I can't go without them. It would be no good.' A terrible sadness descended on me and I should like to have left the room. Lawrence quietly admitted the difficulty. 'No, a woman can't choose if she's really married,' he said. And although he had told me more than once that Donald was only a lover, not a husband, he let this pass to-day. And I knew he was only sounding me. He spoke of how free Dorothy Brett was—'a real odd man out,' he called her with approval. Then he asked if I was writing anything special. 'I could beat you that you don't write,' he said. And why was I pottering about with rubbishy articles for women's papers when I ought to be doing a book either of notes like my Duse note in the *Adelphi*—a book to be called *A Woman Looks at the World*,— or stories and sketches about the queer lot of people who were sheltering under the roof that covered us? There were at that moment five separate lots of us living in the old rambling house, and to amuse him I had sometimes retailed the gossip concerning them. I could see that he was casting about for the best way to help me, feeling somehow that I needed help.

Partly to fend off anything like a silence, which I could not have borne, I told him of a novel I had in mind to write. The theme had been suggested to me by reading of some savages who took a baby girl, and that they might rear her into a goddess for themselves, brought her up on a covered river boat, tending her in all respects, but never letting her mix with her kind and leading her to believe that she was herself no mortal, but a goddess.

I was almost taken aback by Lawrence's interest. He was never effusive, and seldom enough really engaged by what one said, but when he was engaged one knew it. I was not to guess, of course, at that time anything about the contents of *The Plumed Serpent*, or I should have understood his special interest in an allied theme. He would have gone on talking now, but I excused myself and went back to my paltry duty below stairs. As I went, I knew that in some essential I had turned away from what I most wanted in life.

It seemed quite a short time after my return downstairs that Lawrence sent Frieda again to fetch me. 'I like that story of yours so much, Catherine,' he said, 'that I've written out a little sketch of how I think it might go. Then, if you like the idea, we might collaborate in the novel. You do the beginning and get the woman character going, and let me have it, and I'll go on and fill in the man. Of course,' he added, 'you may not see it the same way, but I think this would be the *easiest* way to do it, easier than the way you thought of. Our only trouble will be the end. I'm afraid it can't be a happy ending. But have a look and we'll see.'

Here is what he had written out for me in these few

minutes. I began to work upon the beginning in quite the
wrong way, then I saw I was not up to it and lost heart. So
it remains as it was:

A woman of about thirty-five, beautiful, a little overwrought,
goes into a shipping office in Glasgow to ask about a ship to Canada.
She gives her name Olivia Maclure. The clerk asks her if she is
not going to accept the Maclure invitation to the feast in the
ancestral castle. She laughs—but the days of loneliness in the
Glasgow hotel before the ship can sail are too much for her, and
she sets off for the Maclure island.

The Maclure, who claims to be chief of the clan and has bought
the ancestral castle on his native isle, is a man of about forty-five,
rather small, dark-eyed, full of energy, but has been a good deal
knocked about. He has spent ten years in the U.S.A. and twenty
years in the silver mines of Mexico, is somewhat grizzled, has a
scar on the right temple which tilts up his right eye a little. Chief
characteristic his quick, alert brown eyes which seem to sense danger,
and the tense energy in his slightly work-twisted body. He has lived
entirely apart from civilised women, merely frequented an occasional
Indian woman in the hills. Is a bit cranky about his chieftainship.

Olivia arrives a day too soon for the festival, at the patched-up
castle. Maclure, in a shapeless worksuit, is running round attending
to his house and preparations. He looks like a Cornish miner,
always goes at a run, sees everything, has a certain almost womanly
quickness of perception, and frequently takes a whiskey. He eyes
Olivia with the quick Mexican suspicion. She, so distraught, is
hardly embarrassed at all. Something weighs on her so much, she
doesn't realise she is a day too soon, and when she realises, she
doesn't care.

As soon as he has sensed her, he is cordial, generous, but watchful: always on the watch for danger. Soon he is fascinated by her.
She, made indifferent to everything by an inward distress, talks to
him charmingly, but vaguely: doesn't realise him. He, a man of
forty-five, falls for the first time insanely in love. But she is always
only half conscious of him.

She spends the night in the mended castle—he most scrupulously sleeps in the cottage below. The next day, she is mistress of the absurd feast. And at evening he begs her not to go away. His frantic, slightly absurd passion penetrates her consciousness. She consents to stay.

After two days of anguished fear lest she go away, he proposes to her. She looks at him very strangely—he is just strange to her. But she consents. Something in her is always remote, far off—the weight of some previous distress. He feels the distance, but cannot understand. After being in an agony of love with her for six months, he comes home to find her dead, leaving a little baby girl.

Then it seems to him the mother was not mortal. She was a mysterious woman from the faery, and the child, he secretly believes, is one of the Tuatha De Danaan. This idea he gradually inculcates into the people round him, and into the child herself. It steals over them all gradually, almost unawares.

The girl accepts from the start a difference between herself and the rest of people. She does not feel quite mortal. Men are only men to her: she is of another race, the Tuatha De Danaan. She doesn't talk about it: nobody talks about it. But there it is, tacit, accepted.

Her father hires a poor scholar to be her tutor, and she has an ordinary education. But she has no real friends. There is no one of her race. Sometimes she goes to Glasgow, to Edinburgh, to London with her father. The world interests her, but she doesn't belong to it. She is a little afraid of it. It is not of her race.

When she is seventeen her father is suddenly killed, and she is alone, save for her tutor. She has an income of about three hundred a year. She decides to go to London. The war has broken out— she becomes a nurse. She nurses men, and knows their wounds and their necessities. But she tends them as if they were lambs or other delicate and lovable animals. Their blood is not her blood, their needs are not the needs of her race.

Men fall in love with her, and that is terrible to her. She is waiting for one of her own race. Her tutor supports her in the myth. Wait, he says, wait for the Tuatha De Danaan to send you your mate. You can't mate with a man. Wait till you see a demon between his brows.

At last she saw him in the street. She knew him at once, knew the demon between his brows. And she was afraid. For the first time in her life, she was afraid of her own nature, the mystery of herself. Because it seemed to her that her race, the Tuatha, had come back to destroy the race of men. She had come back to destroy the race of men. She was terrified of her own destiny. She wanted never again to see the man with the demon between his brows.

So for a long time she did not see him again. And then her fear that she would never see him any more was deeper than anything else. Whatever she wanted, she wanted her own destiny with him, let happen what might.

V

If I could help it I would never intrude upon Lawrence when Murry was there—and Murry frequently was there—because I could not bear the underlying sense of strain and dissatisfaction. Frieda was torn between her recent friendliness with Murry and Lawrence's belief that England held nothing for him any more in spite of all the *Adelphies* that were or ever could be. Lawrence, waiting in vain week after week for some reply to the letters and cables which he was sending to his New York publisher, had begun to be anxious about money. Where was the use of his books going well in the States if he received nothing for them? 'It was a painful time,' says Murry from his point of view. So it was from Lawrence's.

Of the 'painful things that happened in it' I was certainly witness to one. But on that occasion the special painfulness was created by Murry. Possibly from a conscious desire that Lawrence should be spared, he has not told the story in his *Reminiscences*. It has since been given, however, from mere hearsay and with the utmost inaccuracy by Mabel Dodge Sterne.[1] As the incident concerned neither Lawrence nor Murry alone, but inclusively nine of us, it seems imperative that it should be given here correctly to the best of my remembrance.

During this visit of Lawrence to London he was determined to make at least one attempt at friendly gaiety—a sort of 'well, well, now that we are here don't let's be too gloomy even if we have made a mistake' gesture on his part. He went with Koteliansky to the Café Royal, engaged a private room there and ordered a supper. (For which, to Lawrence's annoyance, the manager insisted upon having a deposit, and refused to take a cheque.) When Frieda first told me that they were giving a party in a restaurant, I took it merely as an announcement, not as an invitation. I knew that Lawrence had a considerable acquaintance in London, and it struck me as natural that we, living in the same house and seeing each other constantly, were not to be among the guests. But when I said I hoped they would have a good evening, Frieda shouted in amazement. 'But you and Don are coming! You are *invited*! It is a dinner for Lawrence's friends!'

Only then did I recognise my half-conscious withdrawal on the first reception of the news, as a too willing abnegation.

---

[1] *Lorenzo in Taos*, pp. 130-131. Mrs. Sterne states that Lawrence's English friends—'not one of whom had raised a finger to help him in the old days'—gave him a dinner party on this visit home; that he went unwillingly, but responded to the show of affection and the 'plentiful champagne;' that he was as happy and excited as a boy; that Murry leaped upon the table, glass in hand, and gave the toast, 'Lawrence, the greatest of us all;' and that after drinking it the company threw their glasses on the floor, while Lawrence 'just put his head down in his arms on the table and cried.' She proceeds: 'The next day he was simply raging at them in a passion of anger. "They betrayed me," he exclaimed over and over again.'

From the first I had felt a slight sinking of the heart at the notion of this supper, so far as I might have any part in it. And it was this that made me utter a feeble and ill-mannered protest even thus late. 'Are you quite sure that you want us?' I asked. 'There are so many people you must want to see and we can eat together any night.' 'No, no,' sang Frieda, quite shocked and hurt, I could see. 'This is for Lawrence's real friends. Are you not his real friends?' So it was settled. It was just the presence of some of those other 'real friends' that was saddening to me in the prospect. But we must try to enter into the spirit of the thing, and attend with goodwill this, the one and only formal gathering I have ever known Lawrence to initiate.

Soon enough we knew who the others were to be—Koteliansky, Murry and Mark Gertler for the men; Mary Cannan and Dorothy Brett for the women. The round table was attractively laid and the room intimate. Lawrence made a charming host—easy, simple and warm. There was something at once piquant and touching in seeing him receiving us, his friends, thus in surroundings so unlike those in which we had been accustomed to foregather with him these ten years past. It emphasised the lack of sophistication in him which, combined with his subtlety, was so moving a charm. 'Schoolboyish' is perhaps the last adjective that could justly be applied to this mature and refined, this disciplined and impassioned artist, that was D. H. Lawrence at the age of thirty-nine. But at any moment, surroundings like the Café Royal, or the rooms of some fine old house not in the cottage style, would bring out in Lawrence a boyishness that was as comic as it was lovable. 'You'll see I'm quite up to this,' he seemed to be saying. 'Mind you play up to me, so that nobody will have the slightest idea that we don't dine in marble halls all the year round.' It is never a thing to underline, but it *is* a thing to be remembered, that Lawrence was the son of a miner and spent his youth in a miners' row—no matter with how superior a mother or how sensitive a group of brothers and sisters. For him, for instance, to visit at a house like Garsington Manor, was a genuine experience. He coped with it admirably and he knew just what estimation to put upon it, both as an experience and as a phenomenon. He could add up the life behind it and 'see through' the persons belonging to it, without being in any way dazzled or shaken. Even the utmost of kindly patronage could not keep him from the eventual expression of his summing up. More even than Robert Burns in his adventures with the rich and the famous, Lawrence was the 'chiel amang them takin' notes.' Yet he never became sophisticated enough not to be superficially over-impressed at the first impact with personages like the Meynell family, or Bertrand Russell, or Lady Ottoline Morrell. With them this most un-schoolboyish man betrayed a kind of quiet schoolboy knowingness that is not unrelated to nervousness. And the reaction from his impressibility (as in the case of Robert Burns) was apt to be violent. People gave themselves away to Lawrence in an extraordinary degree. And as often as not, their 'giving away' was a subtle form of patronage, a fact that was by no means lost on the observer and writer of fiction who lurked with cool eyes behind the poet in Lawrence. It was naturally a shock when, out of what had seemed a pleasant friendship, there should spring such prodigies as *England, My England!* or the figures of Hermione and Sir Joshua in *Women in Love.* True, he did this with any or all of us. But one cannot escape from the touch of malice in certain instances, nor from the belief that it is there as a make-weight for the special sensibility of a man whose genius has lifted him out of his class.

To return to the Café Royal. Frieda as our hostess

purred loudly and pleasantly. Cafés Royal or Tudor houses
were not even child's play to her! She wore, greatly to
Lawrence's approval, something that was both gleaming and
flower-like—anyhow petal-like, as she delightedly pointed
out. I forget how Dorothy Brett was attired except that
her afternoon dress seemed a thought dowdy. Mary in
décolleté black, with a large black picture hat, *à la* Mrs.
Siddons, looked like the heroine from a forgotten novel by
John Oliver Hobbes. My dress was black velvet barred
with gold like a bee's back. The men wore their everyday
clothes. Kot, in his dark clothes as ever, looked both the
most conventional and the strangest.

The food was excellent, but somehow the feast did not
go well. Gertler was silent and looked watchful, even con-
temptuous. Kot conceived a murderous dislike for Donald,
next to whom he was placed. Mary had nothing to say. I
too was stricken with dumbness. Lawrence did his best to
enliven us all with wine, bidding us to drink our fill and
rejoice in a festive occasion. He set us a good example and
drank level. There was *no* champagne. We drank claret.
And never before, nor since, have I swallowed so many
glasses and remained so heavily sober. With the coming of
the dessert a mistake was made. What was the wine to be?
asked Lawrence. Murry and Donald both said port. They
had forgotten, or had not known, that port was a drink
Lawrence could not well tolerate. He immediately hinted
very gently that port was not his drink, but his remark was
either missed or good-naturedly overruled. 'Port is a man's
drink,' I remember either Murry or Donald announcing in
solemn tones. So port it was. And Lawrence drank it with
the rest of us.

It had the effect of loosening at least some of the mute
tongues about the table, though none of us women were
perceptibly elevated. Lawrence began to talk in Spanish

(which he had learned in Mexico). Donald, who prided himself on knowing a bit of Spanish (enough to read *Don Quixote* and to reply to simple questions), endeavoured to engage in Spanish conversation with Lawrence. This, for some reason, infuriated Kot to such a degree that he looked like taking the unwary Donald's life had not Murry tactfully placed somebody between them. Kot's idea seemed to be that the Spanish language was Lawrence's special perquisite. Gertler drank, or possibly refrained from drinking, in silence, looking on, always looking on from a cold afar. Both he and Mary Cannan seem to have left early.

But not before this strange incident. It began with a speech by Kot in praise and love of Lawrence, the speech being punctuated by his deliberate smashing of a wine-glass at the close of each period. As—'Lawrence is a great man.' (Bang! down came Kot's strong fist enclosing the stem of a glass, so that its bottom came in shivering contact with the table.) 'Nobody here realises how great he is.' (Crash! another good wine-glass gone.) ' Especially no woman here or anywhere can possibly realise the greatness of Lawrence.' (Smash and tinkle!) 'Frieda does not count. Frieda is different. I understand and don't include her. But no other woman here or anywhere can understand anything about Lawrence or what kind of being he is.'

We women were silent. We felt, I think, very sympathetic to Kot. Anyhow I did. Sympathetic to his jealous, dark and overpowering affection. Even inclined to agree with what he said.

Lawrence looked pale and frightfully ill, but his eyes were starry to an extraordinary degree. It occurred to me then —and I have since had no reason to change my reading, which was revealed as by the appearance of clear writing on the wall—that the deep hold of the Last Supper on the imagination of the world is not unconnected with the mystery

of Bacchus.   Given a man of genius; more especially given
a man whose genius runs to expression by means of symbol,
his essential utterance may well be achieved only when his
genius is acted upon at a crisis by the magic of the fermented
grape.

Anyhow, Lawrence who, like the others present, was
habitually temperate, revealed that night at the Café Royal
his deepest desire to all of us simply and unforgettably.   And
in doing so he brought about some other revelations, as will
be seen.

Without making anything approaching a speech, he caught
our attention by the quiet urgency of his request.   What he
said, in effect, was that we were his friends here, each and all
of us people he had been very fond of.   He could not stay in
England.   He must go back to New Mexico.   Would we,
would any of us, go with him?   He asked each of us in turn.
Would we go with him?   Implicit in this question was the
other.   Did the search, the adventure, the pilgrimage for
which he stood, mean enough to us for us to give up our own
way of life and our own separate struggle with the world?
Though his way of life must involve also a struggle with the
world, this was not—as we well knew—its main objective.
Rather was it a withdrawal of one's essential being from that
struggle, and a turning of what strength one had into a new
channel.

Essentially the appeal was not a personal one.   Though
it was to his friends, it was not for his sake or the sake of
friendship that he made it.   It was because of something in
himself which we all acknowledged.   But it had never before
come so near being a personal appeal.   It certainly had a
personal element that told of his overwhelming loneliness.
It was far less 'follow me,' than 'come with me.'   It was
even—to my thinking at least—'come, for a time, and support me by your presence, as the undertaking is too much for

me alone, yet I must not stay here with you.' I give my own reading, but I think something very like it was in the minds of all the others.

Remember we had just supped, and our glasses had been replenished with port and, as I have said, we were all normally very abstemious people.

Mary Cannan was the only one to return a flat negative to Lawrence's question. It was as plump and plain as she herself was slender and pretty. 'No,' said she hardily. 'I like you, Lawrence, but not so much as all that, and I think you are asking what no human being has a right to ask of another.'

Lawrence accepted this without cavil or offence. It was a clear, hard honest answer.

What Gertler said, I can't remember. I rather think it was a humouring but dry affirmative, which we all understood to mean nothing. Kot and Donald both said they would go, less drily, but so that any listener guessed they were speaking from goodwill rather than from deep intention. Dorothy Brett said quietly that she would go, and I, knowing that she would, envied her. Murry promised emotionally that he would, and one felt that he wouldn't. I said yes, I would go. And I meant it, though I didn't see how on earth it could be. anyhow for a long time. Unlike Mary and Dorothy Brett I had neither money of my own nor freedom from responsibility. Dorothy Brett, who loved to serve, was always coming to a loose end. I, who did not particularly like serving, was always having fresh responsibilities put upon me by life. Mary, disappointed with her 'freedom,' had yet got used to its little self-indulgences and could not give them up. All the same, I felt that Lawrence had somehow the right to ask me to go. And I feel to-day equally the impossibility of my going and the wish that I had gone.

As for the supper, what I next remember is Murry going

up to Lawrence and kissing him with a kind of effusiveness which afflicted me. He must have been sensible to my feeling, because he turned to me.

'Women can't understand this,' he said. 'This is an affair between men. Women can have no part or place in it.'

'Maybe,' said I. 'But anyhow it wasn't a woman who betrayed Jesus with a kiss.'

At this Murry again embraced Lawrence, who sat perfectly still and unresponsive, with a dead-white face in which the eyes alone were alive.

'I *have* betrayed you, old chap, I confess it,' continued Murry. 'In the past I *have* betrayed you. But never again. I call you all to witness, never again.'

Throughout all this Frieda remained aloof and scornful—excluded. Her innings would be later. She reminded me of King David's wife looking down in derision from an upper window. One could not but admire her.

It must have been almost immediately after the strange episode with Murry, that Lawrence, without uttering a sound, fell forward with his head on the table, was deadly sick, and became at once unconscious. The combination of the port (which when he had said he could not abide, he said truly) and the cruel loneliness which was brought home to him by the responses he had elicited from us, his friends, was too much for him.

In his sickness Lawrence was more like a child than a man. There was nothing disgusting about him. Frieda, however, remained stonily detached, while Dorothy Brett and I ministered to him as best we could—the Brett especially, who did not want me to help.

It must have been now that Mary and Gertler left us. What with the glasses broken by Kot, and Lawrence's sickness, I was sorry for the waiters who would have to clear up. But they behaved as if they had noticed nothing out of the

way. Donald, as the soberest man, was handed money to pay
for the wine and the damage. The bill, he tells me, struck
him as wonderfully moderate.

We left in two taxi-cabs, Lawrence being still unconscious
so that it was difficult getting him down in the lift. But Kot,
even in liquor, was powerful. I recall that his legs seemed to
fill the cab in which I was. I had been given all the hats of the
party to hold, and I lost my own—a little real Russian cap of
black astrakhan, which I liked better than any head covering
I ever had, though I gave only three shillings for it in an
antique shop, and it had a bullet hole through it.

Arrived at Hampstead the problem was how to get
Lawrence up to the first floor. Kot and Murry had to carry
him. But in their enthusiasm they went on with their
burden, up and up, till my brother, asleep on the top story,
was awakened by the trampling, stumbling sound, and ran out
in alarm to the little landing. He told me afterwards that
when he saw clearly before him St. John and St. Peter (or
maybe St. Thomas) bearing between them the limp figure of
their master, he could hardly believe he was not dreaming.
However, he conducted the party downstairs again.

Next morning soon after breakfast—certainly not later
than 9.30 A.M.—I was passing the open door of the Lawrences' sitting-room, when Lawrence hailed me and bade me
enter. He was fresh and serene. 'Well, Catherine,' he said,
'I made a fool of myself last night. We must all of us fall at
times. It does no harm so long as we first admit and then
forget it.'

At such times he was an overwhelmingly attractive human
being. That light and easy, yet not flippant manner of his
for dealing with such an incident, bespoke an underlying
steadiness that begot trust in the onlooker and was—it seems
to me—incompatible with any neurotic condition. Although
the fullness of his admissions, and the sensitiveness of his

abandon to the impulses of life might give to the superficial
observer the impression that he was a sufferer from a neurosis,
Lawrence was emphatically no neurotic. Of this I am
convinced. If I add that he hated neurotics, even while he
had the misfortune to find in them more immediately than
in others a kind of response which sprang from superficial
understanding, I suppose I shall call forth the gibe of the
analyst—'thou sayest!' 'The real neurotic is half a devil,'
said Lawrence, 'the cured one' with his 'perfect automatic
control,' is 'a perfect devil.' And again 'spit on every
neurotic and wipe your feet on his face if he tries to drag
you down.' Yet I know that what I say is true. Lawrence
hated, he feared, he fought and he was obliged to consort
with neurotics. But he was himself untainted.

When I told him that I had lost my astrakhan cap he
insisted on giving me two pounds to buy myself a hat.
Unfortunately he did not like the one I bought, though he
was too kind to say so. He liked a hat to be a hat and to
have a proper brim. This small black felt was brimless. He
gave it a single glance and looked away. 'Quite saucy!'
he said. I felt crushed.

VI

Before returning to New Mexico the Lawrences were
going to Baden-Baden, and there was some talk of my meeting
them in Paris. But from Paris he wrote to say he did not
think it would be worth the effort and the money I should
have to expend to get there. One of these days he would
give me, he said, 'a *real* holiday in place of this.' He advised
me to do as he was doing—to 'lie low' and to 'save oneself
up for something better, something real later on.'

I understood that he did not really wish me to come—
bringing with me reminders of his unsatisfactory visit to
London. Besides, as things were, he was right: it was

hardly worth while. In less than a week he was going on to
Baden-Baden, and was in the mood of wanting to get it all
over so that he could get back to New Mexico. In London
he had felt more ill than he said to any of us.

It was, I realised, his first visit to Paris, and he had arrived
'almost stupefied from London' to find—after one rather
lovely day of sunshine and frost—something of the unreality
of a museum; a museum, moreover, under rain and dark
skies. He admitted the beauty, but found less life than in
London (not that he liked the life there was in London!) and
when in the Louvre he kept wondering whether the museum
was more inside than outside. Somewhere he has written
an amusing and characteristic essay on either the Louvre or
the Tuileries, in which Frieda saw herself living in peacock
state, a desire from which he dissociated himself with
the utmost violence. His own notion was for a life of
rough and austere and simple beauty, without the trappings
of state.

Meanwhile, said he, he wanted only 'to sleep a good bit,
and let the days go by.' In fact, however, refreshed im-
mensely by two days' rest alone with Frieda, he was 'trying
to amuse himself by writing stories.' It was like him that
on a first short visit to the famous capital he should feel compelled to fall back upon short-story writing from sheer lack
of amusement. I imagine that the story in question must
have been 'Jimmy and the Desperate Woman,' which
certainly gives us Lawrence at his most amusing, though
the *Adelphi*, not unnaturally, selected it later in a review as
a demonstration of Lawrence at his worst.

From among the letters and packages which I had to
forward Lawrence told me to keep back and read the MS.
of his introduction to Magnus's *Memoir*, after which I was
to hand it to Koteliansky. I have said already what I thought
of this. Koteliansky, however, disapproved of it and bluntly

told Lawrence so. Lawrence was angry and hurt, the more so because, during his stay in London, both Dorothy Brett and Murry had made the situation between him and Koteliansky a difficult one, and Koteliansky had felt obliged to withdraw his friendship from them both, while he remained devoted to Lawrence. He withdrew himself also from the *Adelphi* into a special and respectable kind of solitude. As an honest man he could see no other way open to him. He was definitely unable to accept or approve of Frieda, and so it was useless for him to think of going to New Mexico, as Lawrence well knew. His great love for Lawrence, however, remained always. He was a critical unbeliever in Lawrence as a 'philosopher' but a profound believer in Lawrence as a man and an artist. Among those who were drawn to Lawrence he was the doubting Thomas. I question if any suffered more from being Lawrence's friend.

After a day at Strasburg, and less than a fortnight at Baden-Baden, Lawrence wrote asking me to find him a quiet hotel in London as he was coming on February 26th to stay for one week before sailing for New York. There was still no word from his New York publisher, and no money, so that the sooner he saw to his affairs out there in person the better. I was to tell nobody that he was coming, as he didn't want 'to see people.' On the way back he wasted five days in Paris hoping to get a reply to his cables from New York. None came.

For six days he stayed at Garland's Hotel, Haymarket. He liked this place because of its quiet old-fashioned, very English ways. Then, with Dorothy Brett to make a third, he and Frieda sailed. After a good journey (which, however, he hated) they reached New York on March 11th in 'a sort of blizzard' that presently gave way to 'strong American sunshine.' In New York they found that owing to heavy losses his publisher there could only with difficulty scrape together the few hundred dollars needed to take them west at the end of a week. In spite of the large sales of *Women in Love* and the respectable sales of other books, there was now no money at all in the bank. Lawrence had spent—for him —a large sum in London and on the Continent. So here he was, actually poorer than on his first arrival from Australia. If England did not read his books, the United States did not pay for them! Friendly relations, however, had been preserved: and Lawrence's agent would collect the money that was due, 'bit by bit.' All this in his letter to me from New York, where he was doing his best to avoid 'people.' As a place it was 'of course no better than London,' but the climate suited him better—'even the cold wind gives one one's energy back again. It's just that.'

Travelling down through Kent to Southampton on what happened to be a lovely spring day, he had deeply felt the beauty of England, and he was anxious to hear all about our venture in the country. He knew we had thoughts of a small farm. He would let us know what it was like in Taos when he got there again. It seemed anyhow that there were 'plenty of houses going begging there.'

Our farm idea dissolved into a very small cottage in Bucks where we reckoned we could live better than in town. When I next heard from Lawrence—towards the end of April—we were shortly going there. He wrote from Santa Fé, to which place he had come down for a day or two to see the Indian dances. This must have been when he saw the 'Dance of the Sprouting Corn,' of which he wrote for the *Adelphi*, although the article did not appear there until August, and was, in fact, the first Lawrence contribution, except for two translations of Verga, since the excerpts from the *Fantasia*.

During the first weeks of May he was very happy. To

begin with, he was deeply affected and cheered by the sight
of the Indian dances; also by himself joining in at times
(not in one of the great ritual dances, of course, but in the
casual smaller affairs) with some two dozen Indians. It was
the first dancing he had ever in his life enjoyed, for he hated
ball-room efforts. It was further the first time he had ever
felt in physical touch with men who had a traditional religion
that still meant something to them. There can be no doubt
of this. Though 'superficially' he admitted that he did not
like the Indians, and though he knew that there was no breaking down the barrier of alien blood: though here was only
the faintest shadow of what he might have felt had he been
able to dance with men of his own blood under an English
moon (remote consummation of life for Lawrence!): yet
here was the nearest he was ever to get to 'the dragon's den
of the cosmos,' and the farthest (save in spirit and in solitude)
from the outworn and now accursed ideal of a primal, perfect
godhead and a lost perfect paradise. In New Mexico, and
for the first time, he found physical relief from the 'cheerful,
triumphant success' which was killing the white races with
ennui. He became a partaker as well as a spectator. Not by
the abnegation of the Christian saint or the Oriental fakir,
not by the psychic powers of the yogi, not by the short-cut
by which a modern world contemplates the conquest of the
cosmos by science, not by any victory over matter by either
the spirit or the intellect did Lawrence see the possibility of
our salvation from boredom and sterility. We were all starv-
ing in the midst of plenty. Nothing was needed but for us to
perceive religiously that the cosmos itself was alive, and to
enter into the richness of that perception. In wrestling with
a live cosmos men would immediately become themselves
gods of a kind—fallible still, but potent with cosmic energy.
Then, and only then, could man properly solve his great
problems. But to do so we had to 'destroy our own concep-

tion,' our accustomed consciousness. Because 'a man can belong to one great way of consciousness only.' [1]

It was when Lawrence was thus soothed and restored, that Mabel Dodge Sterne made him a present of the Del Monte ranch. Strictly speaking, it was to Frieda she gave it; but this was because she thought this the best, perhaps the only way of conveying it to Lawrence. Lawrence joyfully accepted it, and at once set about paying for it—with the MS. of *Sons and Lovers*. Even at that time this was said to have a high market value, and Mabel could afford, as Lawrence knew, to hold on to it. She was in no need of ready cash. He gave her many other presents and did her substantial services. As usual, Lawrence insisted upon paying his way.

Few things could have delighted him more than to feel that the ranch was his—a hundred and sixty acres high in the skirts of the mountains and with the long summer before them. If his friends would not come, at least he had prepared a place for them, and paid for it! Here he could work off the benumbing and degrading influences of London. And work he did—'like the devil.' He rather hoped now, that Murry would *not* come.

To help restore the log cabins which were falling down, they got three Indians and a Mexican carpenter. But as always Lawrence did the work of two, inside and out, at the same time undertaking the direction of everything and everybody. In three weeks he and Frieda and Dorothy Brett had rebuilt the whole of the three-roomed house, except the chimney, making all the adobe bricks themselves. Then the roofs of all the cabins had to be re-shingled. The three-roomer was for Lawrence and Frieda, the two-roomer for Mabel when she cared to come, and the little one-roomer for

[1] For what Lawrence got from America the reader must consult *Mornings in Mexico*, which is, among other things, its author's apologia and manifesto to Middleton Murry.

Brett. Besides these, there was a nice log hay-house and corral, and there were four horses in the clearing.

Now it is our own [he wrote in May], so we can invite you to come. I hope you'll scrape the money together and come for a whole summer, perhaps next year, and try it. Anyway it would make a break, and there is something in looking out on to a new landscape altogether. I think we shall stay till October, then go down to Mexico, where I must work at my novel. At present I don't write—don't want to—don't care. Things are all far away. I haven't seen a newspaper for two months, and can't bear to think of one. The world is as it is. I am as I am. We don't fit very well. I never forget that fatal evening at the Café Royal. That is what coming home means to me. Never again, pray the Lord.

Down in the valley, where they often had to ride for necessaries, the spring was—

. . . so lovely, the wild plum everywhere white like snow, the cotton-wood trees all tender plumy green, like happy ghosts, and the alfalfa fields a heavy dense green. Such a change, in two weeks. The apple orchards suddenly in bloom. Only the grey desert the same.—One doesn't talk any more about being happy— that is child's talk. But I do like having the big unbroken spaces round me. There is something savage unbreakable in the spirit of place out here. The Indians drumming and yelling at our camp-fire at evening. But they'll be wiped out too, I expect—schools and education will finish them. But not before the world falls.

Remember me to Don. Save up—and enjoy your cottage meanwhile.

Lawrence, of course, did not stop writing for so long as he thought he would. In August he went down to the Hopi land in Arizona and wrote his marvellous account of the Snake Dances which appeared four months later in the *Adelphi*. He wrote also the short novel *St. Mawr*, and the two novelettes, *The Woman Who Rode Away* and *The*

Princess—'all sad,' as he told me, but 'after all, they're true
to what is.'

In October, with the coming of the first snows he was
ready to go down to Mexico and revise *The Plumed Serpent*.
Brett would go with them, but not to share the same house if
they took one. ' Not be too close. . . . It's so much easier that
way.'

He now knew the worst as well as the best of life at the
ranch. Probably he had never felt so well anywhere, but the
altitude made the place intolerable to his lungs for longer
than five, or at the utmost six months of the year. Already
by October his bronchials felt 'raw.' Also it was 'very *hard*
living up against these savage Rockies. The savage things
are a bit gruesome, and they try to down one.' These things
he recognised. At the same time, 'better, far better they
than the white disintegration.' In April he hoped to be back,
and he wondered if I would be able to get over.

For anybody who wishes to know about Lawrence's life
it will be necessary to compare his own letters and actions at
this, as at other times, with the account given in Murry's
Reminiscences, remembering always that these provide the
basis for *Son of Woman*, remembering too that Lawrence in
his letters admitted every passing mood. The simple fact is
that it was impossible to remain at 8600 feet once the snows
came. But Lawrence fully intended to return in April
after that fruitful and economical summer, and he adhered
to his plan. In his October letter he hoped I might be able
to get over by the following spring.

For the winter in Mexico he had saved 2000 dollars. *The
Boy in the Bush* and the introduction to Magnus's *Memoir*
had just appeared in England. But of his American publisher
he wrote, 'He still hovers on the brink of bankruptcy and
keeps me on the edge of the same.'

His bronchials felt better at Oaxaca at a height of 5000

feet, but 'he took it out of himself' over the final revision of
The Plumed Serpent, so that Frieda was afraid for him, and
when the book was finished he fell dangerously ill. He was
very near death and himself believed for a time that he must die.
But Frieda kept her head and he came round—very slowly.
The doctor poured quinine down his throat, but his own
treatment—which Frieda carried out—was to surround himself with bags of hot sand. Once, at a critical moment, he
told her that she must have him buried in the little local
cemetery. He would have her make things as easy for herself
as possible. But stifling her fear she rallied him by refusing.
It was much too ugly a place to be buried in, she protested, and
he really must not put that upon her! Frieda was brave, and
she had a marvellous power of putting strength into Lawrence
when he was ill. This, though in the ordinary sense she was
a bad nurse, as both she and Lawrence freely admitted.

In describing his malady to me he called it 'malaria, 'flu
and tropical fever.' But though any or all of these may have
set the thing going (as it would seem from the huge doses of
quinine which permanently increased his deafness) the true
danger lay in the active presence of tubercle. This the
doctor told Frieda privately but plainly, and she knew from
what he said that Lawrence would never be the same man
again.

The letter of 'pure denunciation' which Murry received
from Lawrence must have been written during the short
interim between the completion of *The Plumed Serpent*
and this illness. At a loose end for the moment, he had
become acquainted with a group of people—tired Europeans
and sophisticated Americans—of whom he was soon weary.
He then saw Mexico at its worst—the town and tourist and
political sides, the horrors of which engendered home-sickness.
Because he admitted this, Murry concluded that he was
'done with America,' Mexico, New Mexico and all.

But this was not the case. Hateful as the modern aspect
of Mexico appeared, so that by the side of it the virtues of
Europe shone out like the lights of home, the trend of English
thought, as exemplified by the *Adelphi*, was yet more hateful.
Lawrence could just tolerate Murry on Keats. Murry on
God or Jesus or humanity or Katherine Mansfield he could
not stomach. At the same time he had still some hope that
Murry might be brought to understand. Was not the drift
of his Indian Dances clear enough to one who was so intelligent, given a good will? And about himself, as usual, he was
perfectly open. His problem was still how to live. He would
return to the ranch for the summer. But what when October
came again? Perhaps he ought always to cross the Atlantic
for the winter. His illness had shaken him. He must keep
in touch with any at home who called themselves friends.
Lawrence needed to go to America, and in America he met
with much friendliness, which he returned; but I doubt if
he ever made a friend there. For a friend he needed one of
his own blood.

That April, still weak, staying at Orizaba, he certainly
was tempted to come home. But he thought better of it,
carried out his original plan and struggled up to the ranch.
After ten weeks there he was 'beginning to be himself again.'
That was to say he was milking his black cow night and
morning, riding his black horse, Aaron, on the more tiresome
errands to the valley, sowing pansy seeds, and irrigating without help a twenty-acre field to which the water had to be
brought from two miles off. Frieda's nephew, a boy still
in his teens, had arrived from Germany to be with them.
For other help they now had only a Mexican boy who came
up occasionally for two dollars a day.

My description of our Bucks cherry trees in bloom made
him a little homesick. They were 'lovely to think of,' he
said; 'here the country is too savage, somehow, for such

softness.' But he would come to Europe in the autumn, he wrote. He hoped to find 'a warm place for the winter.'

In August he wrote to say he would be seeing us 'in one place or another in early October.' There was no hint in this of anything melodramatic such as a 'final farewell to America.' The melodrama is of Murry's imparting. Lawrence was never dramatic, much less melodramatic, though he was usually emphatic. 'We are running to the end of our stay here,' he put it to me:

. . . leave about September 10th. I suppose we shall be in England in early October. . . . Frieda talks of staying some time in England, seeing her children. But I dread the tightness and stuffiness of England—feel I shan't be able to breathe. But I may like it better this time. I expect I shall suffer a bit anyhow, being shut up in houses and towns, after being so free here. I am as well as ever I was—but malaria comes back in very hot sun or any malaria conditions.

PART FIVE

Aet. 40–41

Prose

THE VIRGIN AND THE GIPSY
ETRUSCAN STUDIES (*in part*)

★

'*For now I am fully a man, and free above all from
my own self-importance.*'

PART FIVE

I

The Lawrences arrived as planned, and went first to Garland's Hotel for a couple of days.   Coming up for a half-day from the country, I saw them there, and arranged that they should have the loan of my younger brother's flat—then unoccupied—in Gower Street.   Leaving their luggage at the flat, they would pay a visit to the Midlands, and would return to see a few friends before going to Italy by November. Lawrence did not speak of his health, and, as usual, there was nothing of the invalid about him; but under his big-brimmed Mexican hat his face looked pinched and small, and one easily guessed that he could not face London in the winter.   Neither could he yet afford the sort of comfortable house somewhere on the south coast where he might have stayed safely if there had been enough interest or friendship to make England attractive to him.   On this occasion he seemed very solitary in London.

This particular solitude was of his own making, as he had told hardly anyone of his arrival.   He could not bring himself to do so.   However, as our cottage was only three miles from High Wycombe and he could break his journey there on the way north, he said he would spend a day and night with us.

We both met him at High Wycombe Station and travelled uphill in the country bus.   Either Frieda had gone before him to the Midlands or—more likely—she was visiting alone elsewhere.   Why he was by himself I don't remember.   But here he was, and not in a cheerful mood, though as always well-disposed towards me.   I was not, just then, very cheerful myself.   Things had not gone as well as we could wish, and we were poor and anxious.

He was disappointed with the look of the immediate country, which is not particularly attractive, and on Sunday we all four walked under grey skies in the beech woods, while I thought how poor and tame it must seem to him after the pine slopes at Taos. Then, as we sat over a log fire and were near getting to some real talk, unexpected visitors came from London and robbed the occasion of its intimacy.

What with these visitors, my own domestic cares (which just then were pressing), and the sadness I divined in Lawrence, I was in a distracted state, and only two incidents of the visit stand out clearly now in memory. One was pleasant, the other the reverse. While we stood by the garden gate to see the London people off, John Patrick, then aged seven, made some sudden and unsolicited gesture of love towards me, and as quickly broke away again to his play. We continued with our adieux, paying no attention to the child, but I noticed Lawrence looking keenly at him, and later he referred to the boy in a letter in a special way, which I took to be connected with that remembered glance. 'Wait and see,' he wrote, 'this will be *ein seltsamer Mensch.*'

By the other incident I felt wounded and taken aback. But as it shows once more how scrupulously Lawrence insisted on paying his way through life, I give it also. As we sat round the tea-table he produced a five-pound note, and in a manner half shy, half careless, threw it across to John Patrick. The child had never seen such a thing before, and did not know what to make of it. Neither did I. I remembered unhappily that it was precisely the sum I had given to Frieda for a travelling coat once when they were leaving England and she badly needed such a thing. Possibly I was wrong, but I don't think so, when, with a pang, I felt that this symbolised the sort of squaring up of accounts that goes with a long farewell. True, we were now rather poorer than

Lawrence and with less prospect of growing richer, which he knew. But equally well I knew that he had not any spare five-pound notes to throw across tea-tables. Though he was now fixed up with a new American publisher he was still mainly dependent upon what could be 'squeezed out of' the first unlucky one. However, there was nothing for it but to take it, as he would have it so.

II

From Derbyshire he sent us one of the famous Midland pork pies, with apologies for its not being so big as Midland pies—according to him—ought to be. He had intended to stay a week at home and then to go with his sisters to the Lincolnshire coast. But instead he remained ten days at home and fled again south. He would always be fond of Ada, and would feel kindly towards his 'own people.' He was pleased, he wrote me, to find them in 'comparative opulence—*comparative*, of course—judging by old home standards.' But he hated more than ever 'past things like one's home regions,' and when I saw him soon after his arrival in London he told me how, especially on that visit, the horrors of his childhood had come up over him like a smothering flood. Glad he would have been if the place thereof 'were puffed off the face of the earth.' The weather too had been atrocious and continued so. He must get away or a 'cold' would lay him low.

Only then did he write to Murry—first a postcard to say that he was in England; and then—a few days later when he had seen Frieda off to Baden-Baden—a letter to say that after all he could not prolong his stay, and would Murry come to Gower Street for his last night in London. Two things seem clear: he could only bring himself to meet Murry this time without Frieda and at the last possible moment.

Murry has told how he went and how, after a dispute about his book on Jesus, which Lawrence disliked and condemned, he and Lawrence parted the next day. Murry congratulated himself on not having accompanied Lawrence to New Mexico. He 'could not help thinking in what a hopeless position he should have been at this moment if he had really gone.' But as at no time had he shown any serious and visible intention of going, these meditations seem to be neither here nor there. They gave him, however, the sensation of having at last 'burned his boats.' Still there was no quarrel. Lawrence asked if Murry and his wife would visit them in Italy. And Murry, lacking the hardihood to burn so new a boat, said they would. When the time came there would be—indeed there were already—excellent reasons for not being able to go. Before they parted, Lawrence nearly blew his lungs out running to buy a present of fruit for Murry, and Murry, faced by one of life's revealing moments of 'pure choice,' found it not worth his while to see Lawrence off at the price of spending the night in London. It was natural that he should spare himself so painful a farewell.

In the November number of the *Adelphi* appeared the article by Murry called 'A Simple Creed,' by which he stands to-day, even as he stands by his review of *Women in Love*. Lawrence hated the article and wrote in vehement protest. Murry, on the other hand, held that Lawrence had missed the point of it. One hopes that by the publication of Lawrence's letters, those who are sufficiently interested will be able to place Lawrence's commentary by the side of Murry's 'Simple Creed' and judge of the matter for themselves.

Leaving what must have seemed to him like the ghosts of his old friends in London—and not glad ghosts at that—Lawrence reached Baden-Baden in the first days of November to find it almost as ghostly: '. . . unbelievably quiet and deserted—really deserted. Nobody comes any more: it's nothing but ghosts from the Turgenev period.' This is not an exaggerated description of the Baden-Baden I was to visit two summers later. A happy exception, however, was provided for Lawrence by his mother-in-law, who, though she belonged to the past, remained always fresh and alive for him, with a genuine sturdiness as well as a sensitive vitality—real, bright and alive to the last. In all his returns to this, his other home, Lawrence was more soothed and happy than in his dutiful visits to the Midlands—so long as Frieda's mother was alive. This time he wrote to tell me that she was 'looking older, slower, but still very lively, walks uphill to us in our hotel. She asks for news of you.'

After a fortnight there, he and Frieda went on to Spotorno where they hired a four-storied villa. It was not much to their liking, but would serve, especially as they hoped for visitors, beginning with Frieda's two daughters.

Frieda's long insistence had been rewarded. Already in Hampstead, two winters before, she had managed to break down in a great degree the reserve between Lawrence and her children. Her son still remained aloof and refused to see the man who had taken his mother away, but the two girls had often called and, having made his acquaintance, had found themselves vanquished. Now, as young women, they came to Spotorno of their own wish and for the first time lived under the same roof with their mother and Lawrence. The younger of the two, who was then seventeen or eighteen, became particularly attached to Lawrence, and he to her. Here at last was a new and pleasant relationship. These young people were not ghosts, and they felt the greatest admiration, liking and respect for Lawrence, both as man and as writer. *The Virgin and the Gipsy* probably belongs to this time at Spotorno in the four-decker villa.

It is nevertheless the case that Lawrence in this houseful of women, that yet was not his own, grew restive. Possibly

too, while he had to accept it, he was irritated by the flaunt-
ing of Frieda in her rôle of *mater triumphans*.   She had
squared her circle, and was now having her cake and eating it
with a relish that must have been overwhelming to witness.
While allowing her achievement with a wry male smile, and
even while taking her daughters to his heart, he felt the need
of male support.   He wrote to Murry reminding him of his
promised visit.   Two might perhaps play at resuscitating
ghosts from the dead past and finding them transformed into
healthy flesh and blood.   To a woman her children: to a man
his comrade.   Hope was slow of dying in the heart of Lawrence.   In a moment he could brush aside all intellectual
differences, all past lapses and disappointments, and look to the
miraculous renewals of life.   Murry claimed that in the past
he had undergone profound spiritual changes.   There was
anyhow something mobile in him, and he might yet be
moulded by experience to something nearer to Lawrence's
heart's desire.   Belief in impulsive life tends to weaken belief
in the more static aspect of character.

In reply to Lawrence's letter Murry said that he would
come—he and his wife—for a fortnight in January.   Mrs.
Murry was then expecting a child, and her husband was fully
aware of her condition; but it was not until *after* he had
promised to go out to Lawrence that he chose to take medical
advice as to his wife's fitness for the journey.   He would
have us believe that this was by way of afterthought and a
'simple matter of precaution,' so that the doctor's veto came
'rather to his surprise.'

Lawrence, anyhow, did not believe it.   Such a precaution, when it is truly 'simple'—*i.e.* when a journey has
been seriously contemplated and an honest friendship is concerned—is taken beforehand, not afterwards.   The manipu-
lation was of a kind that is allowable between acquaintances
but not between friends.   If friends permit it to themselves

they yet feel it to be a transgression. But to this day Murry
continues to represent himself as the hapless victim of circumstance—as 'not being able to do something which I
really wanted to do,' while in the same breath he makes the
strange excuse that Lawrence, after writing from America
to say that he would visit him in his country cottage, had
later changed his mind.

The parallel does not emerge. Murry was hurt because,
in a changed mood, Lawrence refused to come. Lawrence
was hurt because Murry denied that his refusal was a refusal
at all. Such a lack of candour and of courage argued that
the face of friendship might be trampled upon with impunity.

Lawrence was not merely hurt: he was outraged.
Murry was 'really amazed' upon the receipt of his letter.
He found that it 'missed the point' and was 'preposterous.'
It had suggested, as a proof of good faith, that Murry should
come alone! To have one's bluff called is never pleasant.

Yet the affair was not quite finished. Perhaps Lawrence
came to question if he had not been too hard in refusing what
in social usage amounted to a legitimate excuse. Perhaps
he wished to push things to a more definite conclusion.
Perhaps he was merely moved by loneliness. Anyhow, at
the turn of the year—always his worst time in health—he
wrote, to use Murry's phrase, 'as though nothing had happened,' to say that he felt oppressed, unwell and unfriended.
He had hated the editorials in the recent numbers of the
Adelphi. Murry had demonstrated that his way in life was
very different from Lawrence's way. Yet they were two
men and there had been a personal sympathy between them.
Might not the storm of hostile beliefs be weathered, given a
staunch and sound personal relation?

What reply, if any, was elicited by this advice Murry
has not shown us. We learn from him only that a week
later Lawrence wrote, repudiating the *Adelphi* once and for

all. In view of the editorials it had become for him 'a sort of self-betrayal' to appear in its pages, and not again would he do so willingly. Either, in view of Murry's reply, he had changed his mind as to the possibility of friendship with hostile aims, or he was carrying out his determination to force the matter to a clear issue. He gave Murry a final choice. Let him stand by the *Adelphi* or by Lawrence. It could not be both.

Had it been truly the case, as Murry has told us, that the *Adelphi* was started on Lawrence's behalf, and that he acted therein 'simply' as Lawrence's lieutenant and *locum tenens*, there would seem to be nothing unwarrantable in such a request. It was, indeed, the same request that Lawrence had made on his arrival in London a year before, when Murry had acceded to it without, however, acting upon it. But Murry, just as he had closed his eyes to the demand for frankness in friendship, now refused to see that he had any choice in the matter of the *Adelphi*. Now he would even throw doubt on Lawrence's honesty in suggesting that there was a choice. In his own trite phrase he 'accepted the inevitable.' (It is notable how many vague banalities occur when Murry writes of Lawrence — 'simply,' 'curiously easy,' 'strangely enough,' 'irony of fate,' 'bolt from the blue,' 'out of his ken,' 'accepting the inevitable,' and the rest.) That is to say he admitted no responsibility towards Lawrence. The *Adelphi*, as we have seen, had been designed —unconsciously perhaps at first—as the mouthpiece of his own egoism, and in a state of egotistic emotion he had found himself provided with an opening fanfare to the public by Lawrence's *Fantasia*. Even at the beginning Lawrence's strictures upon the tone of the paper had not been allowed to count, and as it took on ever more clearly the imprint of Murry it had become increasingly the enemy of Lawrence. Now, in the January issue, there appeared an exposition of the aims of the paper, running to eleven pages, of a kind which was unthinkable for any publication sanctioned by Lawrence. In the February issue Murry undertook to discuss the outlooks of living novelists and poets, yet he made no reference to that 'most significant' one of heretofore.   In the March issue Lawrence was found to be at his worst in his contribution[1] to 'The Best Short Stories of 1925.'   And not long afterwards *The Plumed Serpent* was dismissed in a few lines of facetious contempt.   To round things off the July issue announced the Prologue to the *Life of Jesus*.

So Murry 'accepted the inevitable,' and with an 'acquiescence' that was 'curiously easy,' told Lawrence that if private feelings were to be dragged in, future co-operation was certainly impossible.   Lawrence too had now to accept the inevitable, although it was of a different order from Murry's and had about it no 'curious ease.'   From that day, until, when he was safely dead the *Adelphi* rushed for the time into a new existence on his name, he ceased to contribute.   Only a belated and brilliant review by him of *Saïd the Fisherman* (which must have been a hold-over) was printed in the January issue of 1927.

Illness, and a visit from Ada to Spotorno — Ada and Frieda having different, and to Lawrence equally obnoxious theories on the subject of sick-nursing, together with bedside technique—brought this unhappy winter to an end.   For other visitors there had been Martin Secker and, I think, Curtis Brown.   To recuperate Lawrence fled south to Capri.[2]   In Capri he fell in with Millicent Beveridge, whose company was always pleasant to him, and with her and Mabel Harrison, another painter who was her friend, he made the long ago planned Etruscan tour.   The trip lasted

---

[1] 'Jimmy and the Desperate Woman.'

[2] While there he sent me *The Plumed Serpent*, which he feared I might find 'heavy.'

from March 22nd till April 2nd. They visited Ravello, Rome, Perugia and Assisi: then went by way of Pisa to Florence, where Lawrence was by way of hearing of a country villa. On then to Ravenna, at which town he took ill, so that they had to wait a day or two in a place none of them liked. From there, on to Milan.

In Rome Lawrence had seen Dorothy Brett, who had returned alone from America some time before. But she had fallen in love with the life in New Mexico and wished to go back. Lawrence told her that she must go, by herself. She went, and I am told she has never regretted it.

III

Now Lawrence was joined in Florence by Frieda and her daughters. Through his friend Pino Orioli, he had found a house—the Villa Mirenda—at the familiar rent of £25 a year. Frieda saw it and heartily approved. For a time the four stayed at the Lucchesi pension. Then the girls returned to England and the Lawrences moved in. By the middle of May—a May long remembered in France and Italy for the cold ferocity of its rains—they were established in the new house.

At first the idea of the Mirenda, as described by Lawrence in his letters, was that it should serve as a *pied à terre*, so that they might come and go, and lend it (to us and others) when they were away. But in fact it became their much loved home till the summer of 1928, and they were there for a time as late as April 1929. That it could not be the permanent, nor the all-the-year-round home for which Lawrence was then beginning to long, he knew fairly soon. The rooms which formed the upper part of an attractive old farm villa were fine and large in good weather, but bare and cold and comfortless in bad. It stood in good country, lovely country in the spring, but it was a mile and a half from the tram terminus at Scandicci and then half an hour's journey by tram from the Duomo. It was a good place in which to write and paint—especially paint—but a bad place in which to be ill.

And unhappily from this point onwards Lawrence's plans and movements were to be dictated more and more arbitrarily by illness. That he might bring to fruition the findings of his pilgrimage, he must bend himself to seize and seek every chance of health. He had the strongest hopes that he would be restored; but he had to admit that he was a fugitive, and he never ceased to face the fact that death might overtake him. When Murry identifies him with his own reading of Herman Melville—as a man with 'a long thin chain round his ankle' while he tries frantically to run away, he appropriates a tempting simile and conveys an easy half-truth. But he has omitted two essential elements in Lawrence's life, the elements of art and of illness. And surely he is confusing the needful pilgrimage across the world of a young and delicate, but comparatively sound man, to whose art and aims pilgrimage was a first necessity, with the later and different restlessness imposed upon an experienced man by the struggle for physical existence.

Lawrence was the first to confess that his trip round the world and his visits to Mexico, New and Old, were 'a kind of running away.' But he needed absolutely to run from the world he knew and to see the world he did not know. It was his initial quest to see if the two ends of humanity might not be brought together—'our own thin end, and the last dark strand from the previous, pre-white era'—for the beginning of a new life-mode. And to do this he had to see with his own eyes the Buddhist priest in his temple and to hear with his own ears the Indian drum-tap on the *mesa*. He must subject his own body to the 'boneless suavity' of the East, to the rawness of Australia, to the 'over-riding of life' of U.S.A.

If it was only that in his own person he was the representative of Europe in thus subjecting himself, he had to do it, discovering and condemning himself in the process.

I've been a fool myself, saying Europe is finished for me. It wasn't Europe at all, it was myself, keeping a strangle-hold on myself. And that strangle-hold I carried over to America; as many a man, and woman worse still, has done before me.

So he wrote in an article called ' Europe versus America,' for America in April, 1926.[1]   It goes on:

Now, back in Europe, I feel a real relief. The past is too big, and too intimate, for one generation of men to get a strangle-hold on it. Europe is squeezing the life out of herself, with her mental education and her fixed ideas. But she hasn't got her hands round her own throat not half so far as America has hers; here the grip is already falling slack; and if the system collapses, it'll only be another system collapsed, of which there have been plenty. But in America, where men grip themselves so much more intensely and suicidally—the women worse—the system has its hold on the very sources of consciousness, so God knows what would happen if the system broke.

This is confession, but it is also discovery, and it is the kind of discovery that comes only by pilgrimage, and by pilgrimage of the savage kind. It is far removed from the musings that emanate from editorial arm-chairs. It is indeed removed from any mere musings. In the making of such confessions and discoveries Lawrence fulfilled his paramount duty and his essential destiny.

But there might, and there should have been more, had he lived. There is every indication that, his pilgrimage fulfilled, Lawrence was not the man to live unsettled and rootless. He knew that every sane creature, man as well as bird or beast, is tied in the long run to a place or compelled to a rhythm

[1] In the 'Lawrence number' of *The Laughing Horse*.

by an invisible chain, be it long or short. He believed in
natural phases, in the changing needs of age, and in vital pro-
gressions and recessions, as strongly as he disbelieved in evolu-
tion, as commonly understood. He was quick to know when
youth was over, and to make ready for the different richness
of age, which to youth can seem so poor and maimed a thing.
Even as a boy it was the faded quietness of the married woman
that moved him, and September was his favourite month.

As surely as he had genius Lawrence had the capacity
for serene and fruitful old age. In the best sense of two
hackneyed but correct expressions, he was already mellowing
into a true pontiff of life and letters who could not have failed
of widespread acknowledgment. This is not to say that he
failed to do his work. Neither is it to suggest that his ultimate
influence would have been increased by established acceptance. I do not think it would. The pontifical voice echoes
less hauntingly and long than the voice of one crying in
the wilderness. This is merely to say that the potentialities
were there—the wisdom, the sanity, the fine incalculableness,
the incorruptibility and the passion that is never all spent—in
short the capacity to accept responsibility and to blossom afresh
in bearing it. Like Mr. George Moore, Lawrence would
always have remained an artist, yet like Mr. H. G. Wells
he would always have realised that our age needs most of
all a certain life activity in the artist which forbids his pre-
occupation with artistic perfection. Abundant evidence for
these conclusions will be found in his latest works—in
Assorted Articles, Etruscan Studies, and the magnificently
measured *Apocalypse,* with its profound understanding of
Christianity, such an understanding as true repudiation re-
quires. Also in the poems—not yet published—which he
wrote shortly before his death. Not one of these works is
marred by a trace of shrillness, decay or impatience. Thanks
to his own valiant diligence he had won the recognition and

the moderate financial prosperity that were needed for him to set and spread his roots. And he knew it. By 1927 at latest—more probably by 1926—he was ready to stay quietly productive in some chosen home, or anyhow, as the swallows do, to abide in some steady rhythm between two homes.

By now he had seen what he wanted to see in the world, and he was home-loving by nature. Lawrence was far from being of that omnivorous tribe that must ever be fed with new travel by way of excitement. It might even be said of him that he was the most incurious of men. In the summer of 1926 he said to me—and I knew he spoke truly—that except for the nuisance of being blind, he would not care now if he were to lose his sight. He had looked his fill, and now there was something other than looking to be done. Certainly he cared not a straw about his greatly increased deafness, which was doubtless the reason why one never thought of noticing it as an affliction. As often as not, one felt that with his outward ears he was hearing rather more than he wanted, and that some degree of deafness was to be desired as a protection against the wearisome chatter of the world. When Dorothy Brett would re-charge her listening-machine, I have heard him laugh and ask if *any* human conversation was worth the three shillings needed for a fresh battery. He was, of course, nothing like so deaf as she, but, had he been past the aid of acousticons, it would not have mattered beyond the practical inconvenience. This will sound exaggerated only to those who did not know him. To those who did he conveyed— quite unconsciously—the strange conviction that if all five senses were to desert him (or anyhow all but the sense of touch) he would still be able both to apprehend and to express the life about him by some direct magic of the blood. The trouble was that in his very blood he now had to grapple with the enemy illness.

IV

At the Mirenda in May, 1926, he was at first undecided
and unwell, though not actually ill. Pressing invitations from
Taos inclined, but did not persuade him to go there again
for the summer. The effort was too great. It was too far.
He could not forget how the altitude in October had torn
at his bronchials. Also he was tired of 'straining with the
world'—the world of U.S.A. He would come to England
before the summer was out. For the first time he was chary
of inviting me. 'If only the weather cleared up,' he wrote,
'you might come and see us: and if Frieda feels like having
a visitor. We'll see later.'

I thought I understood well enough. In any case I could
not have come, as we were making a difficult experiment
of our own. I was living in a French village on half-a-crown
a day, with John Patrick at school there and Donald with
friends in London. Lawrence, who approved of the move,
wrote me encouraging and sympathetic letters, offered to do
anything to help, and sent me an introduction I was glad of
to Mabel Harrison in Paris. At Jouy-en-Josas (our village)
I was for days on end without a soul to speak to.

Although the years 1926 and 1927 were 'bad' and
'muddled' and 'unsatisfactory,' largely because of illness,
he came to the Villa Mirenda. He painted happily there,
and in so doing developed the passion of his teens. The
severe, but sensual and non-intellectual discipline of colour
and canvas opened up a new field of activity and a different
mode of expression. Not that he stopped writing. But he
took writing more easily and watched the Tuscan seasons
pass.

It was at the Mirenda, however, that he had his first
bronchial hæmorrhage, and though he made light of it, the
symptom was a new one. When we saw him in London

that autumn, he said that the year had been spoiled for him by 'bad colds.' No more than that. As usual he did not dwell on the subject of his health, but his thinness was alarming.

This time we saw him only twice. When he and Frieda arrived at the end of July, after a fortnight at Baden-Baden, we were still in France, and we could not return until within a few days of their leaving. They had hired Mildred Beveridge's flat in Chelsea, and it was there, I believe, that they first met Aldous Huxley. His wife, Maria, they had known before her marriage in the early days at Garsington Manor where she had lived with the Morrells. It was there too that he met and became at last on good terms with Frieda's son.

But the Chelsea flat was chiefly for Frieda, as Lawrence himself wished to be in London as little as possible. So, leaving her there, he had gone first to Inverness-shire for some twelve days to visit the Beveridges, who were at Newtonmore for the summer; and then for over a fortnight to his sisters at Sutton-on-Sea and Mablethorpe, places where he had been on holiday four years before the death of his mother, when he was a youth of nineteen. Scotland, as he saw it at Newtonmore, made no appeal to him. He found in the typical North Highland scenery none of that touching or moving beauty which I believe he would have found either in the Hebrides or in Galloway. Perhaps too, the weather was bad, though for this I cannot say. Again, though he was glad to see his family, with the children lively and growing, the Lincolnshire coast was too full of sad ghosts for careless enjoyment. When he came back to London in the middle of September the old weariness was upon him, and he was longing for the rich and glowing autumn of the Mirenda vineyards.

This time they were in rooms in Hampstead, whither

even then, we were returning, having taken a studio there. He came with Frieda to lunch, and I was so horrified by his delicate looks that I could think of little else. Our talk, however, so far as I can recall, was chiefly of money—the difficulty of making a living. He had always declared that Donald would never make any money, as money did not really enter into his scheme of things, and that therefore I must. 'You should go on a lecture tour in America,' he now said, scolding a little. 'Now don't say you can't. That helpless air of yours would just be the very thing. You'd have all the Yanks scrambling about to do things for you.' I laughed, partly at this fancy picture and partly relishing his malice. But he insisted, and we argued. 'Well,' said I after a while, 'shall I go on tour and expound D. H. Lawrence and his works?'

He thought this a good plan. Yes, this was what I must do. And immediately he mapped out my tour and gave me all sorts of practical hints about the Americans and how to treat them. Then I would come home with bulging purse and we should all three be able to go and live near the Mirenda or at the ranch, or both. 'Have you never thought of lecturing yourself?' I asked. But this he seemed to regard as an unnecessary question. Excellent as Lawrence could be as a fireside or roadside expositor, it was certainly difficult to imagine him as a platform lecturer.

He had brought me a typescript to read, saying that he much wanted to know how it struck me. This was a section of Mabel Dodge Sterne's autobiography, beginning with her earliest memories and carrying her well into adult life, which she had sent to Italy for Lawrence's advice about possibilities of publication. His own opinion, as I remember, seemed to be that publication would have to be deferred until after the deaths of all the people who appeared in the narrative.

All autobiographies are interesting, and I found this one

especially so. But it was so full of personalities and so un-
reserved that it struck me as unfit for publication for many
years to come. When I told this to Lawrence he agreed.
'But I don't care,' he added with a grin, 'so long as she dies
before she gets to Frieda and me!' When he had said a
thing like this Lawrence would set his teeth in his lower lip,
drop his head and look up at you sideways, his eyes dancing
with a special kind of malice. Perhaps he was never more
himself than just then, and if you did not like him thus you
did not like him at all.

That day, having some other engagement, they had to
leave early. I went out to the street to say good-bye, and
though I saw that Lawrence sped along as swiftly as ever—
not like any town walker—with Frieda careering in full sail
beside him, I looked after him with a sinking heart. It was
a shivery afternoon. He had told me how depressing and
void he found the faded eighteenth-century charm of Hampstead, even at its best. How long ago it seemed since in the
summer of 1914 we had all gone for a picnic on the Heath!
How far, far beyond our reckoning Lawrence had shot in
experience and achievement! Now, by being still in N.W.3,
I felt that somehow I had failed myself and him; that all
the while he had sat talking so gently and stimulatingly by
the studio fire, he had done so merely out of the kindness
that was in him; that really he hated being there. And yet,
when I had boasted that John Patrick was 'a good traveller,'
he had shaken his head and said, 'Nay, Catherine, but I want
to hear of good stayers at home!' All of which contradictory
things came with a truth of their own out of Lawrence's
richness of spirit, and none of which things would have made
my heart sink so badly but for Lawrence's dreadful thinness
of body. He had alarmed me by mentioning for the first
time that he had had a 'bronchial' hæmorrhage. But immediately he had brushed my alarm aside. 'It's nothing

serious,' he had assured me, 'not lungs, you know, only bronchials—tiresome enough, but nothing to worry about, except that I *must* try not to catch colds.'

I next saw him a day or two later, on what I think was the night before he left for Italy. He had invited us and a few others to his lodgings. Koteliansky was there, and my brother from Gower Street, whose war novel, *The Natural Man*, had greatly interested Lawrence. It was, for some reason, a harmonious evening with nothing much else to remember it by. Once more we talked of money. Koteliansky maintained that *any* unearned income must alienate the possessor hopelessly from the large portion of mankind who had to earn its bread. I still had £50 a year, and it was discussed whether I was therefore alienated. Kot insisted that I was.[1] Then my brother held forth on the advantages of great wealth, telling us what he would do if only he were 'really rich.' 'Will neither of you people *ever* face reality?' asked Lawrence, shaking his head over my brother and Koteliansky alike. 'Of *course* Catherine ought to have her £50, only it ought to be £300 instead. And *of course* Catherine's brother would do none of the things he thinks he would do if he were really rich. Because the moment he was really rich he would be a different person. A lot of money has an influence on the nature of a man that is not to be resisted. I *feel* of myself that I, at least, should be able to resist it. But that's just how everybody feels, and I suppose I'd be not so different from the rest of mankind. Money, much money, has a really magical touch to make a man insensitive and so to make him wicked.'

I am glad we were all gay and friendly that night. Because I never saw Lawrence again.

---

[1] Recently I reminded Koteliansky of this conversation, adding that I was now completely removed from the state of alienation which he had deplored. He had forgotten the discussion, but admitted that he had once held such views, though he had since found reason to change them.

PART SIX

Aet. 41-44

Prose

ETRUSCAN STUDIES (*unpublished*)
DAVID, A PLAY
LADY CHATTERLEY'S LOVER
APOCALYPSE

Verse

PANSIES
NETTLES
LAST POEMS (*unpublished*)

★

*'But never mind, the tragic is the most holding, the most
vital thing in life and as I say, the lesson is to learn
to live alone.'*

PART SIX

I

In Tuscany they had a quiet and splendid autumn. The vintage, though not abundant, was unusually fine in quality. The white oxen plodded at their leisure with wagon-loads to fill the Mirenda cellars. After misty mornings the sun came hot, and throughout the cool nights the thick stone walls of the villa held the daytime warmth. The woods were dotted with the small wild cyclamen—the hovering yet downward-looking flowers that perhaps Lawrence loved best next to the open-faced rock rose and the luminous white campion. Lawrence, who never minded not working for a time, took things easy, went for walks alone among the hills and pondered on the lost Etruscans. He seems even to have gone on another gentle little Etruscan tour, this time with Mr. Brewster. For neighbours he had the Gair Wilkinsons— Mr. Wilkinson of the puppet show and the red beard, 'king of all the beavers,' as Lawrence wrote to me,—gentle and pleasant folk to drop in upon. It was his usual state before the inception of a new undertaking.

And of course the Lawrences had visitors. When did the Lawrences not have visitors?—except in Australia, and there only because they did not stay long enough. The Aldingtons came to stay. And towards the end of October, 'Aldous Huxley, a writer, and his wife came for the day, in their fine new car,' as he put it in a letter to Ada.

It was the beginning of an important friendship—emotionally important for Huxley, practically important for Lawrence. And it began with Huxley's offer of a car—the kind of car that is a friend's bargain, being both sound and cheap. Here was Lawrence in the very situation where to Huxley the owning of a car would seem to be a necessity. And he could just afford it. But Lawrence refused. 'I won't bother myself learning to drive, and struggling with a machine,' he wrote to Ada. 'I've no desire to scud about the face of the country myself. It is much pleasanter to go quietly into the pine woods and sit and do there what bit of work I do. Why rush from place to place?'[1]

But in November, coming up the long road from Scandicci on foot and laden with provisions, Lawrence got wet through and had to take to his bed in consequence. There followed the kind of weather he most dreaded—everything 'steamy, soggy wet' with 'great pale brown floods out in the Arno valley' and nothing to do but to 'grin and abide.'

He would have liked well enough to have seen the Stage Society production of *Mrs. Holroyd* in December, but did not feel equal to the journey—perhaps shrank too from the double trial of the theatre and the 'miserable ending' which belonged so much to his past.

For Christmas the Mirenda had rare celebrations which included the peasants of the *podere* and their families—twenty-seven souls. These all came in to see their first Christmas tree, decked by Lawrence and Frieda in best German style with candles and shining trinkets from Florence. And there were little toys and sweets and dates for the children, and wine and Tuscan cigars for the grown-ups.

So Lawrence all his life grasped every natural chance that offered for cheerfulness and peaceful gaiety. And he did so without a trace of fuss or spouting, sweet posing or exaggeration. His Christmas tree was without the too common

---

[1] In such fundamental matters Frieda was entirely like-minded with Lawrence. I remember someone once trying to commiserate with her over the nuisance of house-work and other homely duties. 'But what else is there to do?' asked Frieda blithely. For her, as for Lawrence, life was richly in the everyday things.

adjuncts of vanity and frivolity, and so was a truly sacred symbol, a tiny fountain of life for all who could feel it.   There was absolutely no nonsense, emotional or æsthetic, about him. He liked and respected the peasants, for example, and he envied them their physical strength, but he broke into no rhapsody of preference which would put their life above his.   As he wrote to Ada:

Sometimes I think it would be good to be healthy and limited like the peasants.   But then it seems to me they have so little in their lives, one had better just put up with one's own bad health and have one's own experiences.   At least they are more vivid than anything these peasants know.

I have said that Lawrence that autumn was in the condition common with him as precedent to a new undertaking. After Christmas he wrote the first draft of the novel that was later to be known as *Lady Chatterley's Lover*.   As usual, therefore, he was less idle than one would have guessed from his letters of the period.   His constant productiveness, like his constant courage, fits badly with Murry's picture of dislocation and degeneration.   From England during the early months of 1927 came nothing but news of strikes and troubles and illness, which he felt badly, yet he worked firmly on.

'Eh, one wishes things were different,' he wrote to an old friend in the Midlands, a woman who was faced with a serious operation.   'But there's no help for it.   One can only do one's best, and then stay brave.   Don't weaken or fret— while we live, we must be game.   And when we come to die, we'll die game too.'   In essentials Lawrence never weakened and never fretted, and though no man ever felt the trials of life more keenly than he, both for himself and others, he never either plumed himself upon his sensitiveness nor wasted his strength in a leaking 'sympathy.'   For that he was too much alive and too shrewd a fighter for his own life.   His sympathy was like a signal from the very heart of his own courage.

He needed it all too, if only for the repudiation of that sweet and suffering ideal of courage that has become associated with Christianity—the courage that is playful about symptoms of illness, or that vaunts itself as ready to die 'for a trick not worth an egg,' the courage that is not simple, the courage of the victim, that is so easily reversed into what it demands for its existence, namely, the bullying of the persecutor. Because, what Murry finds with his little intellectual chop-logic to be Lawrence's failure, is precisely what emerges as his most victorious endeavour.

In practice [writes Murry] Lawrence's belief seemed to mean pretending a harmony between impulses which were verily contradictory; to mean denying the spiritual consciousness and asserting it, to mean loving the world and hating it at the same moment, to mean nailing the flag of the civilised consciousness to the mast and hauling it down in a single operation.

Precisely. But it should not be set down as a jibe or a regret. If for 'seemed to mean pretending' we substitute 'established,' and for 'were' put 'hitherto have seemed,' and if we continue, 'he has enabled us to deny the spiritual consciousness and to assert it in the same breath, to love the world and hate it at the same moment, to nail the flag of the civilised consciousness to the mast and to haul it down in a single operation,' we have said one of the most important things about Lawrence that can be said. And if we can apprehend it, even a bit, we understand a lot about Lawrence. It is not, strictly speaking, an intellectual apprehension as yet, though it will become so in time. Then we can go on to something else.

As we have said, Lawrence needed all his courage. The spring came beautifully at the Mirenda, with sky-staring daisies and earth-gazing violets, with blonde narcissi and dark anemones both air-trembling, and 'under the olives all the pale-gold bubbles of winter aconites.' But it brought also the *tramontana*. Colds went about, and Lawrence caught one by infection, which first drove him to bed, and then— with a change in the weather to damp heat—turned into an attack of malaria. This, by his own account. Whatever the cause, the effect was no doubt an active tubercular attack, and it was accompanied by bronchial hæmorrhage. It seems not to have been so very bad, however, and upon becoming convalescent, he might have gone in May to London to help with the Stage Society production of his play *David*,[1] that is, if he had much wished to go. The first performance was to be given towards the end of May. But he was both doubtful of his strength and reluctant about the undertaking. His refusal caused, I understand, some natural resentment in London, where much hard voluntary work and a considerable sum of money was being expended on the production, and it was felt that Lawrence ought to make every effort to encourage and direct the enterprise. But Lawrence would not risk the strain and disappointment. Though he always had a half-hope that one of his plays would succeed on the stage, I doubt if he had much belief in them as stage plays, or if he felt their failure acutely. So he held to the 'take-it-or-leave-it attitude.' Actually *David*—in theme and scope a far more ambitious play than either of the others published, and containing magnificent passages—was less successful as staged in 1927 than was *Mrs. Holroyd*. The critics were not kind to either, and Lawrence was obliged to make the best, or the worst, of kindly reports from friends. He could only hope that it was 'really quite a success,' knowing well enough what this meant. As I write now, I hear that there

[1] This play had already been translated into German, Lawrence himself typing the translation in June, 1926.

may shortly be another production of *David*. Personally,
had I the choice, I would rather see an experimental performance of *Touch and Go* than a repetition of the Biblical
play, unless the production was transformed from that
accorded to it in 1927.

In April, though summoned by letter and even cable, not
to mention the invisible transatlantic summons of Mabel
Dodge Sterne's 'will,' Lawrence had refused to go to Taos
for the summer. Taos was vastly more attractive than
David. But Lawrence measured the effort and decided
against it—as he had done also the previous spring. One
day he would like to go again. For the present, the demands
of life there were not equal to what he could get from it.
The Plumed Serpent was written. He hoped one day to
revisit the ranch. Never would he forget the beauty of its
daily life. But I think he knew that now there could be
no second blooming for him except in old Europe, in his
real home to which he had come back wise and enriched—
assuaged.

Besides he could not afford it. There was no new full-
size book newly out or coming—nothing but the little
Mornings in Mexico, which would not bring much money.
Thus he was rather short for the moment. He could just
hope to keep going with the help of the improved exchange
in Italy. He therefore went quietly on with the Mirenda
life, painting the 'Finding of Moses' and writing at intervals
about the Etruscans. He was forty-two now—'getting on,'
as he recognised. It was time to settle, if only he could
get more 'solid' in health. 'Why can't one make oneself
tough!' he sighed.

In vain. That same spring, as Millicent Beveridge[1] has
told me, although he did not consider himself as ill, he had

[1] In February, 1927, Miss Beveridge had taken a villa in the neighbourhood of the Mirenda.

to pause for breath every fifty yards or so when they walked out together.   And in June, when the heat on those slopes became too fierce, he allowed Maria Huxley in the kindness of her heart to drive him down the hundred miles to Forte dei Marmi, bathed once in the sea, and came back to the Huxleys' house with severe congestion.   In any case he was oppressed and enervated by the dead flat sea at Forte.   So back to Florence again till he was able to travel to Austria, there to take an inhalation cure.

Lawrence resembled the Christian Scientists in one respect alone.   He preferred not to name an illness precisely, disliking the jargon and finding it unhelpful in the fight for health.   But he never denied the existence of the illness, nor ignored the nature of the fight.   And though he fought and hoped to the last, he always admitted that he might be beaten.

'I'd rather be penniless and struggle, than not *quite* penniless and sick.   *Sporca miseria!*' he wrote to me that autumn.   And again, early in 1927, 'If only I could be really well.   What a mercy!   It's my one refrain.'

His one refrain it certainly was not.   One is struck in his letters, even from now on, by the rarity of its occurrence. But it must have become the undertone, the tolling ground-bass of existence for him.   And one of its effects was an unwillingness in him to return to any place where he had suffered from a severe attack.   All he could do to live he must do.   The scene of a defeat would only weaken his resistance.   Accordingly, as time went on, the distant ranch grew more and more attractive.   There he had never been really downed by illness, and he had felt full of lightness and energy.

But till he could grow stronger, the journey, the altitude, and the strictly seasonal nature of the spot, forbade it as Eden was forbidden to Adam by the flaming sword.   Lawrence

distrusted the verdicts of doctors as much as the scientific
descriptions of illness.   He was not rabid on the subject, but
rather sceptical.   Upon the very few regular practitioners
whom he consulted from time to time he must have spent
little of his hard-earned money.   As to quacks and the great
army of the specialists, he was immune from their wiles.
He could listen to good advice and put it patiently into
practice, but this only when the doctor showed signs that
he could collaborate with the undoubted, almost uncanny
knowledge that Lawrence had of his own body.   Such a
doctor he found in Dr. Giglioli at Florence, who, though
he recognised the gravity of Lawrence's symptoms, was
equally impressed by his patient's 'splendid healing power.'
I believe the strictly medical verdict by those who had occasion
to make a thorough examination at any time since 1914
is that by his own vitality and skilful courage Lawrence
prolonged his life—a working, vivid life—by a good five
years.

As Lawrence's less comprehending critics have been
disposed to connect what they take to be his 'pathological'
or 'morbid' or 'diseased' state of mind with the tuberculosis
that was unhappily lodged in his flesh, it is necessary to dwell
upon his illness with an emphasis that would otherwise be
superfluous.   Before long it will be realised, I believe, that
as the mind of Lawrence was not morbid, not pathological
and not diseased, but rather full of new health, nothing that
is unpopular about him can be explained away by saying that
he was ill.   This will come about of itself.   Meanwhile a
clear distinction may and must be drawn.   Lawrence is
not explained by his illness.   Yet in any examination of
his life his illness is important because it *was* important.
Though it did not cause his pilgrimage, it helped to make it
savage.

In one truly helpful and illuminating statement Murry

has disposed of the contamination-by-disease criticism.   Here
he speaks of what he knows.   He says:

> Tubercle does have strange effects.   Chief among them is its
> tendency to make infinitely more intense the spiritual character of
> the person who suffers from it.   Whatever he intimately is, he
> becomes to the *n*th degree.

If you remove from this some of the exaggerated and over-
charged expressions such as 'infinitely' and '*n*th degree,' you
get an indisputable truth.   Experience goes to prove that the
victims of tuberculosis, so far from being temperamentally
changed or intellectually undermined by the disease, are
rendered the more intensely themselves.   Keats was never
more himself than when he wrote 'my heart aches, and a
drowsy numbness stills my sense': Tchekov was never more
himself than when he noted down his symptoms in medical
detail: Katherine Mansfield was never more herself than
when she dared to break her lovely and long-drawn fantasy
and to seek her woman's honesty through submission to a
male dominance external to her fantasy: Lawrence was never
more himself than when he wrote *Lady Chatterley's Lover*,
refused to seek the diagnosis of specialists and went on calling
his attacks by the name of 'colds,' and 'scratchy' or 'unhappy
bronchials.'
     At the same time, to put Lawrence's illness out of the
reckoning seems to me as grave an error as to account for the
obnoxious in him by it.   It was a force that he fought against
in a special way as well as a force that made him the more
himself.   He differed from almost all the other famous con-
sumptives in refusing to make any sort of 'copy' out of his
illness.   He proved his strength by never becoming an invalid.
And—most valuable of all—the inherent consistency of his
life was vindicated by his manner of dying.   He wanted to
live longer, but not to change his life beyond the changes

imposed by age.   Disease is not merely the revealer of a man:
it may also be subdued by a man to his own likeness, and this
in the moment of his defeat.[1]

II

At Villach, Karuten, in Austria, he was at first hardly able
to walk.   But though the weather was variable, he rejoiced
in the coolness after the gruelling heat of that July in Florence, and he grew quickly stronger.   In September he went
with Frieda to Germany, returning to the place from which
he and she had started on their perilous mating more than
fifteen years earlier — Irschenhausen in the Isarthal, near
Munich.   Here, in the very same little wooden house at the
corner of the forest, and even attended by the very same
servant as before, they stayed the month out quietly.   Frieda's
sister Else (of *The Rainbow*) visited them.   The forest was
behind, the open country in front, with the mountains beyond, all still unspoiled.   Lawrence drank goat's milk and
rested.   They were both happy, but I think it was Frieda's
hour.

Sadly for me I missed seeing them at Baden-Baden where
I was able to call one day that September.   In circumstances
wholly unforeseen I had been despatched by my brother-in-
law by aeroplane to be with my sister who was having heart
treatment at Nauheim.   I did not know of the Lawrences'
whereabouts, and — taking my chance — missed seeing even
Frieda's mother.   In October I should have caught all three,
but by then I was back at home.   A letter from Frieda at
Baden told me that Lawrence was doing some more inhaling

---

[1] All that follows, so far as it concerns Lawrence's illness, became
known to me only after his death.   Neither his letters nor Frieda's gave
me any idea of its severity.   It was the same, I think, with all his correspondents.

there, and that he was very 'mild and tame,' the utmost of
excitement being a game of whist in the evenings with the
'old excellencies' at the *Stift*, whose darling he was.

When Lawrence wrote soon after, it was to assure us that
it was only 'a question now of putting on weight and getting
the general condition up again.' He had been badly shaken
by this last bout, and even while he felt better he could not eat.
Still he believed that all would yet come right. 'We really
must all chirp up, and have one of the jolly old times,' he
wrote. 'We *must* chirp up, all of us. *Sempre!* D.H.L.'
Incredible as it now seems I was not seriously anxious about
Lawrence at this time. I had always known that he was
'delicate.' Equally I knew that he recovered from every
upset and was never very long knocked out. I am sure that
most of us felt the same—more anxious to hear of his expected
restoration to his normal state than we were afraid of not
hearing of it.

He enclosed a number of photographs, taken at the Mirenda,
of the pictures he had been painting during the past two years.
On the back of each was a pencil note of the dimensions and
colours. One of these days, he said, he might think of exhibiting them.

There was a shy but eager note in every mention by Lawrence of his pictures which I never found in any reference to
his novels, though there was something like it in the case of
certain poems. In painting he was at once more playful and
more exposed than in the writing of prose. He had tremen-
dously *enjoyed* the making of his pictures, and at the same time
he felt that he was expressing by means of them something
both personal and fundamental to himself. But he had kept
very quiet about it, regarding it for long as little more than an
amusement. He had, in fact, begun through having by chance
at the same time both a number of canvases left by somebody
at the villa and a collection of oddments of ordinary house

paints left over from re-decorations. But of course the careful copying of pictures had been one of his favourite pursuits as a boy, and he had always taken a great interest in drawing.

By then the larger and more memorable of his pictures— the 'Holy Family,' the 'Expulsion from Eden,' the Boccaccio illustration and the men bathing by the willows—were all in existence, besides most of the smaller ones.

I am no judge of paintings, especially not of paintings by Lawrence. Some who are said to be good judges have told me they are worthless. Others again whose judgment is equally estimable have contradicted this verdict, I certainly liked the look of those in the photographs, as I did when I later saw them at the Warren Gallery. They seemed to me work that could have been done by nobody but Lawrence, and like everything by Lawrence they opened windows and let in fresh air. Simply as compositions I found the Boccaccio piece and the willows landscape lovely. And I was delighted by the true believer's touch of mockery in the rendering of the Eternal Triangle of Father, Mother and Child posed in front of their cottage crocks—that cheeky, clever little Jesus who was going to upset everybody's apple-cart, that mindless, smiling, big-breasted mother Eve, and that moustachioed Father and Husband who was so clearly the master in his own house! Who but Lawrence would have seen them just so?

III

November saw them back at the Mirenda and Lawrence writing his third draft of *Lady Chatterley*.[1]

Just then, after having spent some time on getting up the subject, I was starting to write a life of Robert Burns. Lawrence applauded the project. He wrote to Donald (whose

---

[1] Lawrence always re-wrote the complete MS. from end to end.

book *Brother Scots* he had just read, enjoyed and helpfully criticised):

Cath's idea of a Burns book I like very much: I always wanted to do one myself, but am not Scotchy enough. I read just now Lockhart's bit of a life of Burns. Made me spit! . . . If Cath is condescending to Burns, I disown her. He was quite right, a man's a man for a' that, and it's *not* a bad poem.[1] He means what he says. My word, you can't know Burns unless you can hate the Lockharts and all the estimable bourgeois and upper classes as he really did—the narrow-gutted pigeons. Don't, for God's sake, be mealy mouthed like them. *I'd* like to write a Burns life. Oh, why doesn't Burns come to life again, and really salt them! . . . don't be on the side of the angels, it's too lowering.

Not long afterwards, liking very much Burns's letter to Ainslie, which I had sent to him, he suggested that somebody might like to re-issue *The Merry Muses* (of which I had told him but which he had never seen) with an introduction—'a little essay on being bawdy'—by himself.

For that Christmas a German friend had offered us her little house in the Harz Mountains, and we managed to get together our fares and go there. My friend was a Doctor of Philosophy, and her husband a medical doctor, the head of a *Klinik* at Frankfurt-on-Oder which specialised in lung cases.

Like so many other cultured Germans, our friends were keenly interested in Lawrence and his work, and they questioned us eagerly about him. Hearing of his delicacy, they assured me of what I could well believe, that the air of the Harz possessed in their experience a softness which often rendered it more healing than the air of Switzerland to troubled lungs and bronchials. Very gladly, they said, they would treat Lawrence for nothing, or for what he could afford without a strain. I felt that this doctor, a man who

[1] I had never said it was, but Donald had made a rather slighting reference to it in *Brother Scots*.

had come through the horrors of the Russo-German front and was quiet and sensitive and gentle, would have known better than most how to deal with a patient to whom the word sanatorium was almost synonymous with suicide. I even elicited from him his opinion that in a case such as Lawrence's, the prescription of sanatorium treatment *in* a sanatorium was usually a mistake.

But it came at the wrong moment. Lawrence, though greatly attracted by our descriptions of the place and of the doctor, wrote that it was 'too far, too far.' He was supposed, he said, to be going 'up to the snow in January' but was 'shirking it' and would see when January came. He hated the chopping and changing about. He would prefer to wait where he was, if that were possible, till the spring, and then perhaps, having saved his energy, try another summer season at the ranch before deciding to sell it. The doctor who had examined his lungs at Baden had not been against altitudes. There was a chance that the high dry American mountain air might set him up again. Anyhow he was tired to death of crawling about and being driven to consult new doctors whose prescriptions varied strangely. Money was not exactly pouring in. On what he did earn, there was his agent's tax of ten per cent besides the new foreign commission on visitors of twenty per cent.

I still have the unhappy feeling that with more pressure on my part or with very slightly altered circumstances on his, and if we could have outstayed the holiday period there, Lawrence might have joined us; and Dr. Dege and the lightly moist air of the Harz might have helped toward healing him. But such are vain imaginings. As it was, Lawrence stayed at the Mirenda, provided a second jollification for the peasants, in which he joined on Christmas Eve, and for Christmas Day he allowed the Huxleys to motor him to friends of theirs in Florence.

It has been said that since their meeting in the summer of 1926 a dependable and fruitful friendship had sprung up between Lawrence and Huxley. One day this friendship will no doubt be enlarged upon as one of the most remarkable of our time. I can give no more here than my own reading of it, as formed from my very limited knowledge and observation.

As early as 1916, when he was in Cornwall, Lawrence said to me, 'Young men ought to wish to come to me of themselves, I ought not to need to ask them to come.' Already he was sure of himself,[1] and sure that he could make young men surer of themselves by what he could tell them. And even then young men were drawn to Lawrence after a fashion. They were attracted, and some of them came. But they came timidly, half unwillingly, and most of them withdrew in a strange fear—a strange but quite comprehensible fear—and a grave misunderstanding. At the same time these young men — Koteliansky, Murry, Gertler, Cannan, Heseltine, Gray, Aldington and others—were without exception sensitive and gifted persons, unusual men who were potentially or actually capable of contributing a creative share to their epoch. While they were still as yet untried and unknown, Lawrence divined this of them. It was also this in them that made them find in their first contacts with Lawrence a stimulant as well as an irresistible charm. And although in turn they were repelled by his entire refusal to adapt himself, and discovered in his intention something at once uncompromising and hard to understand, each one went his way marked for life. Their conversation with Lawrence might result in nothing better than a lasting

---

[1] So sure was Lawrence that, in 1916, when I heard him say, 'I profoundly believe that a single individual may prove to be of more worth than the whole generation of men in which he has lived,' I knew he was referring to himself.

dissatisfaction, a feeling of guilt or a frantic spite.   It never lacked results.

Lawrence on his side remained wholly untouched in the sense of being influenced.   If he was incomparably more innocent than any of them, he was also of incomparably superior attainment as an artist and as a man of vital experience in life.   Already 'never to adapt himself' to humanity was a first requirement and proved his certainty.   But he loved these friends as long as he might, bore with them, debated with them patiently and passionately, went to endless trouble over them, and gave them handsomely of his best.   It must be borne in mind that of the established men of the day, even those who had stated early admiration or accorded some practical help (such as Beresford, Garnett, Russell or E. M. Forster) held themselves at a cautious distance from the author of *The Rainbow*.   Either they did not care, or did not know how to approach him, and in the peculiar circumstances the approach would have to come from them.   Patronage, frigid, advisatory or uncomprehending, of the kind that urged him to write another *Sons and Lovers*, was useless. He needed a grown man's hand stretched out in warm equality and comradeship.   There was no such hand.

Not until Aldous Huxley arrived at the Mirenda with his sensitive goodwill and his second-hand car to sell.   But then it came—better late than never!

In Huxley, taking first the externals, Lawrence was offered a man still young, who was yet of established reputation, with nothing in the worldly sense to gain or lose by seeking a friendship.   As regarded the practical aspects of life, which must always count, Lawrence and he met on an equality.

Less externally, Huxley came before Lawrence as a writer of exquisite perceptiveness who was both perfectly honest and perfectly sceptical.   He was indeed so sceptical as to be almost without opinions, certainly without what can be called religious opinions. If Lawrence was our Eager Heart, Huxley was our Scandalised Spectator. He was so perfectly open-minded that intellectually he stood for nothing. But he had looked at life and his heart was appalled. And he had a heart to be appalled.

This is the inmost point. Huxley could suffer cleanly and warmly, without self-seeking or shrieking, but none the less acutely. Unlike Murry, he could feel simply and with the heart. And what he had not been able to get over was that suffering was one of the major facts of life. 'Be brave!,' 'bear it!,' 'endure!,' 'swallow it!,'—So we are obliged to address the baby boy from birth as the terrible equivalent of 'be a man!' Why?

The Japanese, the Chinese, the Red Indians and other peoples take full cognisance of this fact in their education. The boy must learn to bear pain without flinching, perhaps in the process to come by a species of useful self-hypnosis. If less pain falls to him than he may expect, this will be a bonus to his life. If it falls in its plenitude he will deal with it un-surprised. There is much to be said in practice for some such imposition of ardours and endurances. But the true inward-ness of the imposition is that it is religious in its origin. The initiation ceremonies enacted by the savage on the threshold of virility are not mere cruelties, they are inspired by the sacredness of manhood and by the recognition in the soul that suffering is something irremediable which must be met without repining.

That is to say, at a certain stage in life they are conven-tionally inflicted, first in recognition of what man may expect from a live, unknowable, partly malicious cosmos, and second, to endow each individual with the power to defy the cosmos when need be in his own sacred person. The conception is profoundly religious and it meets one of the deepest of human needs.

The modern European, however, has no such vitalising way out. He combats pain with science, denies it with Christian Science, bears it with intellectual stoicism, or accepts with regard to it the Christian ideal.

Concerning the first, non-religious ways—stoicism and modern science go badly together, and in spite of our many pain-destroying inventions it is, I suppose, a debateable question as to whether suffering—taking things all round and including mental suffering—has not rather increased than decreased in a nerve-ridden modern world.

By the Jewish-Christian ideal again, we suffer either as a punishment for sin or in furtherance of our spiritual purification, this being undertaken by a loving God for his own inscrutable ends. In either case we are victims. As it works out in practice, we can become godlike only by welcoming suffering, not by resisting it. The more a victim, the nearer to the divine. When pushed to this extremity the flesh will get some of its own back by such means as flagellation. But the whole of the ascetic practice is an exact antithesis to the hardships undergone in the non-Christian initiation to adult life. The first seeks to weaken the flesh which already it has ideally degraded: the second seeks to strengthen an ideally potent flesh in the conflict between man and the unseen. Both would have man partake of the divine, but submission is the secret communion of the one, while the other communicates by way of a challenge which is none the less worship.

Once I told Lawrence a story I had thought of writing. A bishop, as I fancied, was obliged to preach in a district that had been ravaged by some awful plague. As he sat in his chair preparing a sermon full of adjurations to the faithful, bidding them endure gladly that their souls might be refined in the fires of suffering and so be fitted to glorify their Maker, he dropped asleep. And in his sleep he dreamed that the Lord, clad in a mantle of pure and sumptuous fur, came and asked him to have a walk through the universe. The bishop went, and he found that the universe was a vast stockyard for fine-skinned animals, such as foxes, hares, ermines and the rest. In each section the beasts—which were the souls of men—were progressively tortured, plagued and beaten, in such a manner as to refine to the utmost the gloss and quality of their pelts. Only the finest, which incidentally suffered more excruciatingly than the rest, were fitted to adorn at last this God who rubbed His hands over the crucifixion.[1]

Lawrence shuddered over this tale. 'You can't write that,' he said. 'It's too horrible. Yet, oh yes; it is what thousands of us were brought up to believe. The flagellation of the Christian Saint. Yes, you'd better write it, if you can bear to.'

On the other hand, when I was shocked by the old Japanese play *Bushido*, in which the adoring parents of a talented and beautiful only boy, tell him that they must cut off his head to save that of his Emperor, and the boy, like his parents, purifies himself and is willing for the sacrifice, Lawrence told me I was wrong to be offended. 'It is the only way to happiness,' he said, 'the only way for life to be rich, for people to have something apart from their own little individual souls that is worth the sacrifice of life itself.'

Again, though in Lawrence's phrase we were 'between the hammer and the anvil' and life was 'full of wonder and surprise and mostly pain,' pain with him was always magnificently balanced by wonder and surprise. In spite of accounts to the contrary, accounts marred by the hidden hysteria of their writers, he was the least hysterical of men. He was sensitive less in an extreme than in a special degree, maintaining

[1] Those which did not respond suitably to the treatment, being merely damaged by it, were thrown out to rot.

his responses to life at every point, yet accepting his own share of suffering in a manner that in practice had almost the appearance of stoicism. This was because his sensitiveness was so far removed from self-importance. During the War it was not primarily the physical or mental agony, or even the wastage of humanity, that engaged his passion. It was the initial outrage on manhood inflicted by a mechanised conflict for something deeply felt to be not worth fighting for. What he entered into, as perhaps did no other man at the time, was the smothered horror of soldiers who feared neither death nor wounds. Thus he never fell into that self-persecuting and impotent 'suffering-with' which only too often begins as a form of masochism and ends as an excuse for lack of life in ourselves. No one I ever met responded more spontaneously or acted more gently in case of illness or pain. But he never worked himself up by *imagining* the sufferings of another, nor of the world as a whole. Once when we heard of an acquaintance who had lain exposed and wounded for three days in a shell-hole in Flanders, Lawrence checked my horrified fancy. 'He didn't suffer as sitting here we think,' he said. 'He wasn't there as you and I are here. In an experience like that, the being, the *man*, is almost gone, is at one remove. Bad enough, of course, but not the kind of sharpness you are imagining.' That this was true was proved when the same man, in hospital later, was cheerfully vague in recounting his sensations. Lawrence indeed exposed for me the wastefulness and the spiritual conceit that for so long have racked the nerves of our northern world in the guise of 'Christian sympathy.'

To return. In Huxley we get a man whose awareness of suffering had led him to pillory in his books each form of cruelty in turn. But this awareness was no neurosis with him as with so many writers of to-day who wallow in horrors, but a real heart wound that made him aloof and gentle. He was

therefore immediately attracted to Lawrence, both because
Lawrence admitted suffering and because Lawrence in some
way had freed himself from its trammels.   The effect is
apparent in everything written by the younger man since the
two became acquainted.   It has been so deep that, at this date
and in his last book, Huxley finds that a painless life might
well be intolerable.   Murry has spoken at length in *Son
of Woman* of Lawrence's 'greatness.'   But he has neither
permitted to his great man any of the qualities of greatness, nor has he himself been modified by contact with
greatness.   The capacity to take a step that should betoken
genuine apprehension remained for the true perceptiveness
of another.

As for Lawrence, he was in certain respects past the stage
when he could give himself in friendship.   But he was glad
and grateful to find an Englishman to whom he could talk
and a heart on which he could rely.   For the time that
remained Huxley was simply and charmingly devoted to
him, and proved dependable to the last.

IV

After Christmas, Lawrence was perplexed as to how best
to scheme for health throughout the difficult coming months.
The Huxleys, marking the seriousness of his condition,
pressed the wisdom of an escape from the uncertainties of a
Florentine mid-winter.   They were themselves going in
January to Les Diablerets.   A separate little flat could be
found in the snow there for Lawrence and Frieda.   Lawrence
hated the snow.   He was now told, however, after a re-
examination by his doctor, that the altitude of Les Diablerets
(4,000 feet) was just right for his healing.   At the same time,
in the doctor's opinion, the altitude of the ranch, even in
summer, had become dangerous and must be put out of all

question.   Upon this Lawrence reserved his own judgment, but he would follow the immediate counsels of doctor and friends.   He promised to go to Switzerland shortly after the middle of January.

'I want really to try and get myself better,' he wrote to me on the 10th. 'Cough still troublesome—and I want to lay hold of life again properly.   Have been down and out this last six months.' It was the second time he had used this phrase 'down and out,' and it came now at the end of the longest passage concerning his health that had ever occurred in a letter to me.   We knew he must be ill then, though still we did not take it as really serious.

But he had finished *Lady Chatterley*, keeping quiet about it as usual till it *was* finished.   This was the first I heard of it.

I wrote a novel last winter and re-wrote it for the 3rd time this —and it's very *verbally* improper—the last word in all its meanings! —but very truly moral.   A woman in Florence said she'd type it— she's done 5 chapters—now turned me down.   Says she can't go any further, too indecent! . . . But will you find me some decent person who'll type it for me at the usual rates?   You'd do it, I know, if you were a person of leisure.   But you're *not*.   So turn over in your mind some decent being, male or female, who I could trust not to let me down in any way and who'd do the thing for the proper pay, and write me soon.

Then I think I shall publish my novel privately here in Florence,[1] in March—April—1000 copies, 2 gns. each; and so, D.V. earn myself a thousand pounds, which I can do very well with—rather low water.   I'll call it *Tenderness*—the novel.

But please don't talk about it to anybody—I don't want a scandal advertisement.

---

[1] Before Lawrence came to this determination the book had been refused by two English publishers to whom—surprisingly—he had submitted it.

I do hope I'm not bothering you. But I feel I must get another blow in at the lily-livered host. One's got to fight.

To someone else he wrote of this book 'It'll infuriate mean people: but it will surely soothe decent ones.'

When Lawrence said this of *Lady Chatterley* he meant, as I understand it, that the book was a manifesto to a modern world which doubts the sufficiency of bodily love even at its best. It is not, Lawrence would say, the body that fails. It is the modern man and woman who despise or fear or exploit for sensational ends the subtle simplicities of nature. The intellect and spirit have tried by turns to deny the flesh, and degrade it, and the flesh has had its revenge by turning physical love into mere frictional excitation, of which the fruit is apples of Sodom.

Four days later he sent a postcard to say that an attack of influenza had driven him to bed and postponed his journey to Les Diablerets. It was 'misery' but 'not bad,' he insisted. 'Seems to me I always decide to go away a bit too late—or the flu gets me a bit too soon. It's my unhappy bronchials that lacerate so easily.'

The delay, so that he was caught again by the dampness of Florence, was probably due to a variety of causes—to his shrinking from the snow, to his arrangements for the Florentine production of *Lady Chatterley*, which had to be made at once, and to his growing dislike of moving. 'One gets older,' he had written to Ada a week earlier, telling how he longed to find a place in which he could really settle. He even thought of trying 'Devonshire or somewhere there for a time, and if it suits me, really make a home there.' The Mirenda, though he loved it, provided a home neither for midsummer nor for midwinter. Nor was it a place in which to take to one's bed, even for a short spell.

By the end of January he was able to 'creep up' to Les

Diablerets with Frieda. He did not like it, finding himself
unable to walk the slopes, still more debarred from the mildest
of winter sports. But in a very few weeks he felt greatly
the better for being there.

Though much wishing to do it I had been unable to
undertake the typing of *Lady Chatterley* myself for Lawrence. But I had arranged to have it done for him, and he
had sent the first half of the MS. to me, retaining the last
chapters to be typed by Maria Huxley. He wanted to know
which title I preferred. *Lady Chatterley's Lover*, *My Lady's
Keeper* or *Tenderness*. I did not care much for any of them,
but have forgotten my own alternatives. Actually, owing
to an unforeseen delay, I was obliged to sit up two nights
typing the last few thousand words myself. Lawrence was
in more of a hurry than I had realised. The typescript was
in his hands, however, by the 1st of March.

At Les Diablerets, with the breaking of the snow in March,
the atmosphere had gone 'warmish and cloudy.' Lawrence
dreaded the descent 'to the levels and the germs,' but it was
time to go. Everybody up there was starting a cold anyhow.

He went down alone to Florence on the 6th; and though
it was to find the Mirenda veiled in sleet after a frost that
had killed outright the first crop of peas and beans, he felt
so much better that five days later we find him writing home
to say he was thinking of the ranch for the summer. Up at
Les Diablerets he had spoken much of it to the Huxleys, and
he believed that they would go with him, and Brewster as
well. The doctor was not necessarily right on the subject
of altitudes. What could an Italian doctor know about the
air of the Rockies in summer?

Meanwhile the weather in Florence convinced him that
he must give up the Mirenda. Throughout the latter part
of the month it poured cold rain upon him; and if it had not
been for *Lady Chatterley*, he would have given his landlord

notice there and then and fled the place. His term was due
to expire at the end of April. He must see the book through,
however, and of course there were delays. The little
Florentine printer knew no English: he was short of type:
he ran out of the special paper, which had to be hand-made.
But, except for the difficult question of copyright,[1] prospects
were encouraging. Order forms had been sent out earlier:
now they came back filled in with cheques attached. For
the first time one of his books was going to bring a solid
sum safe to his pocket.

During the difficult printing he took ill. Frieda, who
had gone from Les Diablerets to see her mother, was not
yet back from Germany. But Pino Orioli, who was acting
as publisher and distributor of the book, came out every
night all the way from Florence at great inconvenience
(though with his accustomed cheerfulness, which nothing
ruffles) to sleep at the Mirenda, bringing with him a load
of comforts, material and otherwise. On the news Frieda
returned. Lawrence was soon up and about again. But it
meant the end of the Mirenda for them. He could never
live there now. At the same time he must have seen that
the ranch would be impossible, for that summer at least.

It is not too much to say that he had sacrificed it to his
book. Because, upon first leaving Les Diablerets, he had
felt quite strong enough for the journey to New Mexico,
where he believed he would re-establish his health. But the
task of production was not completed till the middle of June.
This obliged him to take on the Mirenda, though he would
not stay there himself once *Lady Chatterley* was launched.
Friends could have the house if they cared to come for the
holidays. I do not think that it was occupied that summer

---

[1] This was not adequately met, with the result that ten to twenty
pirated editions (mostly American) appeared soon after the authorised
edition, many of these complete with forged signatures of Lawrence.

after the Lawrences left, but during May, while they were still there, they had a fortnight's visit from Enid and Laurence Hilton, who came out from London. Enid Hilton's mother had been Lawrence's mother's dearest friend long before at Eastwood, and her father a staunch friend since Lawrence's boyhood. Later she and her husband were to be of great service to Lawrence in London over the *Lady Chatterley* troubles.

A second small trip with Millicent Beveridge, for which he had hoped, had to fall through because he was not strong enough for it. Better obey the doctor and go to Switzerland again. After a couple of months there to 'fix up his chest,' he would go to England in August. The question of exhibiting his pictures that autumn was under discussion.

'. . . make a few more enemies,' as he wrote to me. 'But you'd like some of them. I'll tell you.' Dorothy Warren thought highly of those he had sent for her to see and she was willing to undertake a one-man show for Lawrence at the Warren Gallery. She was a good friend whom he had known since the Garsington Manor days.

v

Soon after the middle of June Lawrence and Frieda were at Chexbres-sur-Vevey. I had a postcard to say that he did not like it much but found it 'good for his bronchials' so they would stay awhile.

They stayed about a month, after which they went for two months to a peasant chalet up on the mountain-side at Kesselmatte. It was like a little, double-decked wooden ship that sailed high above the valley, and they had it entirely to themselves. Lawrence was unable to walk the mountains, but he began to paint again, and the intelligent young Swiss postman came and stared at his pictures, wondering at them,

sometimes liking them very much, never at all shocked.
And the peasant proprietors of the chalet, who lived during
the summer in their hay-hut across the valley, brought
over baskets of bilberries and cranberries. And sometimes
Lawrence and Frieda drove across the pass to revisit Les Diablerets, which in summer was quite a different
place.

August came and went. England would have to be postponed as Lawrence did not feel up to it.

For the first time he was frankly despondent about his
health as surveyed over 'this last year,' and found that it
was 'useless thinking of going anywhere till his cough
went.'

But in September they must move on. The signal came
with the cow-bells as the beasts moved down from the high
Alps. Summer was over. Where next? There was some
talk of trying the French Alps near Grenoble, this time with
Brewster. But, as so often before when no definite step
presented itself, they went to Baden-Baden. From there
Frieda could visit England by herself, see the picture show
now fixed for October, and bring back the reports. She was
to have our studio.

Lawrence wrote to Ada advising her in good time not to
visit the Warren Gallery. 'You won't like the things. Best
leave 'em alone.'

The show, however, was put off and Frieda did not come
to England. After little more than a week at Baden, Lawrence left her there, and with her elder daughter Elsa he
went to where the Huxleys were at Le Lavandou, near
Toulon. When Frieda had seen to things at the Mirenda
she would follow them there.

The place and the sea agreed with Lawrence. He felt
well, anyhow much better, and when Elsa and the Huxleys
left, and Frieda arrived bringing old friends with her—

Richard Aldington and others—they made a good company. Together they crossed the ten miles of sea to the Island of Port Cros, there to picnic in the little rooms of La Vigie, fortified and moated on the top of the highest hill. The only trouble was that Lawrence 'with his cold' could never make one of the daily bathing expeditions. La Vigie was an hour's climb from the sea,—the wonder was that he had got there at all!—and even had he been able to accompany the others he could not have bathed. The experience at Forte dei Marmi had been enough of a warning for that.

If I know anything of Lawrence his disabilities in such a party must have been hard to bear, for he hated to be a mere onlooker, and alone with Frieda he was always very much the leader. Possibly this had something to do with the fact that the beauty of the green island, with its umbrella pines and 'the blue sea and the other isles,' while he admitted it, did not much move him, and as the others disported themselves he kept thinking of the strikes that were forward in the Midlands. At the same time the notorious *John Bull* article on 'Lady Chatterley'—'Famous Novelist's Shameful Book'— 'A Landmark in Evil' (this time unsigned) appeared in London, together with a picture (unrecognisable) of the 'bearded satyr' and 'world-famous novelist, who has prostituted art to pornography.'

Upon re-reading that article now, one finds in it, as before in *John Bull*, a phrasing which at times recalls Murry's reviews of *The Lost Girl* and *Women in Love*,[1] and there is no doubt that the writer was every bit as 'sincere' as Murry (while having more excuse for his obtuseness), also that he would 'stand by' his review to-day if anybody bothered to ask him. It was, of course, to be expected. Yet, as we know in actuality, a writer who sees clearly the pure intention of

---

[1] Murry seems to have avoided reviewing *Lady Chatterley* as successfully as he avoided *The Rainbow*.

his work will always be astonished, and even wounded by the accusation of dishonesty and disgustingness.

. . . the most evil outpouring that has ever besmirched the literature of our country. The sewers of French pornography would be dragged in vain to find a parallel in beastliness. The creations of muddy-minded perverts peddled in the back-street bookstalls of Paris are prudish by comparison. . . . Unfortunately for literature Mr. Lawrence has a diseased mind. He is obsessed by sex. We are not aware that he has written any book during his career that has not over-emphasised this side of life. Now, since he has failed to conquer his obsession, the obsession has conquered him. He can write about nothing else, apparently.

Lawrence, 'Great' but 'sex-sodden,' artist out of 'the turgid vigour of a poisoned genius,' had created a 'fetid masterpiece,' an 'abysm of filth' and 'the foulest book in English literature.' So *John Bull*, on the work that Lawrence would have called *Tenderness*—expressing, it would be idle to deny, the view of the majority of Lawrence's countrymen. Equally idle to deny that it did not help him to enjoy his little spell of relaxation at the Île de Port Cros.

Still he would not let such a thing affect him deeply. The neighbourhood of Le Lavandou had seemed to suit his health. And when the weather broke, with such gales that no boat could bring bread, and the fortified walls proved no defence against the wet, and the holiday party had to pack up and at the first opportunity make for the mainland, the Lawrences thought they could not do better than try that coast for the winter. On November 14th they went to the Hotel Beau Rivage, Bandol, where, as it chanced, Katherine Mansfield had stayed during an early stage of her illness.

In noting this coincidence Murry appears to have made yet another mistake in his dates. According to his *Reminiscences* he had written through Curtis Brown in March after a silence of two years, to ask a trivial favour of Lawrence; [1] and he gives us to understand that without undue delay Lawrence replied from the Beau Rivage. But as Lawrence in March was first in Switzerland and then in Florence, and did not reach Bandol till mid-November, Murry, if correct, must have waited eight months for any response, by which time the response would not be of the practical use he sought. Neither was it like Lawrence that if he were going to answer at all, he should have waited so long. What seems most likely is that Murry did not write until the following March (1929), which would make the silence between him and Lawrence longer by a year, and incidentally would emphasise the heartlessness of writing then to ask for a trumpery material service. It would also fit with the fact noted by Murry (as if in support of his 'pattern' of Lawrence's restlessness, though actually it deranges that pattern) that the Mirenda had already been given up. However these things may be, Lawrence remained at the Beau Rivage from November 28th till the first days of March, 1929. The poems in *Pansies*, which he designated as his 'rag-poems,' were all written before Christmas.

At Christmas he had a visit from Ada. On the whole this brought sadness. As always, Lawrence was glad to see her; but he knew that now, save in his affections, he was out of touch with this dearest member of his family who was also the sole remaining link with his youth. Such a situation is always most sharply realised upon a face-to-face meeting. And in this case it was no doubt aggravated by Ada's restrained sadness at the sight of her brother's increased fragility. Lawrence hated restrained sadness, and he disliked any

---

[1] Murry wished Lawrence to inform him if any edition of *The Rainbow* was obtainable abroad, as a friend had asked him for the loan of the book and he feared to risk his own copy (the now valuable first edition given to him for review by Lawrence in 1915) in the post.

sisterly attempts at treating him as an invalid. That winter
he did not spend a single day in bed, and on Christmas day he
spoke hopefully of starting for the ranch in spring, if only for
six months there. The hope persisted throughout January
and February until on March 2nd he confessed that it was
'no good,' that though he *was* better and never needed to lie
in bed, he was 'not well enough,' and that it would be best
to sell the ranch. It was then that he uttered one of his rare
complaints before quoted: 'O why can't one make oneself
tough?'

With Ada, as with most others who loved him, Lawrence
had to stand up against the knowledge that while she delighted
in his gifts and himself, she wanted him to be the sort of
'great man' that she and the world were accustomed to.
She wanted for him the acceptance and honour which she
felt were his due. Again she could not help resenting the
awful discomfort of Lawrence's genius, which was brought
about by just that 'demon' of his, to which obedience meant
everything to him—that 'Balaam's ass in his belly,' that
would not let him move along the path of accredited success
and loving ease. So he was obliged to break deep down with
Ada, or rather to withdraw from her in essentials for the time
being, causing a suspension of vital contact. At the same
time the bond of affection would always hold between them.
On her side there was the goodwill that can exist without
understanding, eternally if need be, and on his a tenderness
that could forgo understanding while it went on hoping. It
was only where, as in the case of Murry, there was neither
understanding *nor* natural warmth, but only the jargon of
love, that Lawrence could make an absolute break, as we
shall see. Indeed what Murry called 'love' was that very
thing that stank in Lawrence's nostrils as the festering of
lilies—the emotional collapse due to the Christian ideals,
which bore a noble name, but was false and death-dealing

and the cause of the war.   Because of it, said Lawrence, we must give up using the word.   *Tenderness* would do for a change.   In *tenderness* there was still a living test of a man's fidelity while *love* was heavy with generations of betrayal.

As ever, with Ada as with myself, he was patient, hopeful, wise and extremely gentle.   Almost immediately after she had left to go home, he wrote a letter as unconquerably kind as it was free from egotism.   He faced the situation squarely and intimately, making none of the familiar excuses of self pity decked in playful or touching phrases which are so often the last vanity and refuge of the consumptive.   Neither by his illness nor by his gifts did he put her at a disadvantage. The phrases are light and quivering with real sweetness.   It is among other things a vital refutation of Murry's picture of Lawrence in his last phase.   And as such, though it appears also in Ada's book, it may be reproduced at least in part here:

. . . But don't be miserable—or if you must be, at least realise that it's because of a change that is happening inside us, a change in feeling, a whole change in what we find worth while and not worth while. The things that seem to make up one's life die into insignificance, and the whole state is wretched. I've been through it these last three years—and suffered, I tell you. But now I feel I'm coming through, to some other kind of happiness. It's a different kind of happiness we've got to come through to—but while the old sort is dying, and nothing new has appeared, it's really torture. But be patient, and realise it's a process that has to be gone through—and it's taken me three years to get even so far. But we shall come through, and be really happy and in touch. You will see, the future will bring great changes—and I hope one day we may all live in touch with one another, away from business and all that sort of world, and really have a *new* sort of happiness together. You'll see—it will come—gradually— and before not so very many years. This is the slow winding up of an old way of life. Patience—and we'll begin another, somewhere in the sun.

Ada wrote to say that she was hurt because she felt that Lawrence was 'hiding some part of himself' from her. He replied frankly and firmly:

You say you think I've hidden some part of myself from you. Not at all. I am always the same. But there is something you just refuse to see and refuse to accept in me. You insisted on a certain idealisation and there it was . . .

Incidentally it was Frieda's supreme virtue that she did not refuse to see or accept, even if her acceptance was by way of open combat. Neither did she insist on 'a certain idealisation,' so from her Lawrence never needed to withdraw himself, except in those moments of ultimate loneliness which are for every man and were for him in particular.

In March, though all thoughts of summering at the ranch had to be put aside, he felt well enough to think of prospecting for a real home. He had not liked the French Riviera enough to wish to make his home there:

Somehow here there isn't enough to it to make one want to live—the country is a bit no-how, and the French mess up their sea-side coast worse than anybody—fearful hotch-potch of villas almost as bad as a slum.

But he agreed he might have to do so, as it was 'good for him,' which Italy was 'not just now.' There was much to be said for Bandol. Before committing himself to a villa there, however, he might have a look at Spain. He had wanted to make 'a little tour in Spain' as early as December, but had deferred it.

VI

What was immediately urgent was that he should use his strength to go to Paris and make arrangements there in person for the private issue of *The Escaped Cock*,[1] which he

---

[1] Another title for *The Man Who Died*.

had finally re-written at Bandol that winter, besides painting four more pictures for the postponed exhibition in London. So from early March—accompanied on the journey by Rhys Davies—Lawrence was in Paris on business for about a month. He stayed with the Huxleys, who were then living at Suresnes, and Maria Huxley, distracted by his looks, arranged for his examination by a specialist. Frieda tells me that Lawrence did not go to be examined. Whatever happened, or did not happen, a rumour reached England that he had only a few days, possibly only a few hours to live. Several of his friends, including ourselves, were rung up on the telephone by unknown editors, while the sound of the sharpening of obituarists' quills made itself heard. We could only hope that it was a scare and say so. I wrote at once to Frieda asking how Lawrence was.

Murry, too, had heard the rumour and had written, not to Frieda, but to Lawrence. It was his third letter since the estrangement. A second had followed Lawrence's 'sad and tired' response to the request about *The Rainbow*. Because, in that response, Lawrence had said that he might write again later but had not done so; 'after a month or two' Murry had written opining that so far as he was concerned (I use his own phrasing) there seemed no reason why they should not write occasionally to one another. But to this Lawrence had not replied. It was an omission so unusual as to be significant to any who knew him as well as Murry did.

The rumour that Lawrence was dying, however, gave Murry another chance, and he wrote his third unsolicited letter. In it he said he had heard that Lawrence was passing from this world. Would not Lawrence therefore like him— Murry—to come out and hold his—Lawrence's—hand? He could manage, it seemed, to make out a few days for this pious purpose.

This time Lawrence replied. His business being finished

in Paris, he had gladly fled, and since the middle of April
he and Frieda had been staying at the Hotel Royal, Palma de
Mallorca.

I have often fancied that rage, coupled with a sort of
bitter amusement, may have acted upon Lawrence like a
strong tonic when he read Murry's missive. Talk about
'deathly messages' and 'death miasmas!' Murry gives us
only a part of Lawrence's reply, and that in paraphrase. But
it would seem to have been short as well as trenchant. No,
said Lawrence, in effect. He wasn't passing out just yet,
but if he was, it would not willingly be with Murry's hand in
his. Death-bed reconciliations were not his line. Leave such
things to the editor of the *Adelphi*. Once and for all Lawrence hoped never to see Murry again, in this world or the
next. 'Even when we are immortal spirits,'—Murry allows
himself to quote this much—'we shall dwell in different
Hades.'

One might have thought that upon a heart capable of
loving, no heavier sentence was ever passed by one who was
once regarded as a dear friend. Not so Murry, however.
He finds it 'not so poor an end to a friendship as it may
appear to be.'

My letter to Frieda brought an immediate reply from the
Hotel Principe Alfonso, Palma de Mallorca, where they now
were. 'No,' she wrote, 'I am thankful to say Lorenzo is
better; in Paris he got worse again after a good winter on
the Riviera. No, we are really enjoying this. . . . This is
just a line to let you know that we aren't on the downward
slope!'

She begged me to go and see the picture show when it
should open, told me of the Mandrake Press book of the
pictures which might be expected shortly, and said that before
long she and Lawrence were going to find a house for themselves in one place or another. Ten days or so later Lawrence

was writing to Ada in the same tone, dispelling the 'silly rumour that he was ill' and giving her his news. *Pansies* was about to appear minus about a dozen censored items, but he hoped to issue a small unexpurgated edition as well. And the Mandrake people were expending £2000 in the production of the picture book, including ten copies in vellum at fifty guineas, which last had already been ordered six times over. 'Seems to me a bit absurd, but there's this collecting craze nowadays,' was Lawrence's comment. When the proofs arrived he was not greatly pleased with them, finding them 'very dim, vague and disappointing,' but, as he philosophically put it to Ada, 'Of course other people don't know them as I do.' As usual he had begun to set aside copies for his family, and for friends who might like to have them but could not afford to buy. The original pictures he was not anxious to sell. He therefore put high prices upon them, and most of them are still Frieda's property.

At midsummer the show opened. It had a mixed reception from the critics and from the public who flocked to see it. Towards the end of the run Frieda came to London, and we went to the party given for her at the Gallery. She wore a gay shawl, red shoes and a sheaf of lilies—the last to symbolise Lawrence's purity! Ada came from the Midlands, and other old friends of the Lawrence family travelled up to see 'Bert's pictures.' These were no more shocked than had been the peasants at the Mirenda, the postman at Kesselmatte or the proprietress of the hotel at Bandol. Ada, who HAD been shocked by *Lady Chatterley*, genuinely liked them. I too liked them. But undoubtedly, as Lawrence knew, 'people who called themselves his dear friends were not only shocked but *mortally offended* by them.' Millicent Beveridge was one friend who was shocked, though I think not mortally offended.

Unhappily for Frieda there was something much worse

than hostile critics or offended friends to be withstood. Lawrence, who had returned to Italy *via* ship to Marseilles and had been in June at Forte again with the Huxleys, had gone on to Florence in July. There, staying with his Italian friend and publisher, Orioli, he had fallen alarmingly ill so that Frieda was sent for by telegram.

When Frieda arrived Lawrence, thanks to Orioli's devoted nursing and his own recuperative power, had pulled through the attack. To the astonishment of those who were with him he managed to greet her as if he had scarcely been ill. Huxley has told me how, at a later period, if Frieda was away, the mere expectation of her return would enable Lawrence to get up and dress himself, though before he knew she was coming he could not so much as lift his head. On this occasion he was joking and easy and interested in her eager news, and then he sent her off to an hotel as there was not room for her in Orioli's flat. Probably she concluded (as he intended she should) that the telegram had been a matter of mere precaution or expediency. Really he was extremely feeble, and Orioli had feared the worst.

The police raid on the Warren Gallery, with the confiscation of all the pictures and the books of reproductions, came very soon after Frieda's return. It was a blow—especially a blow to a man in great physical weakness. But Lawrence did not noticeably blench. What he felt was chiefly disgust. Perhaps it had also a tonic effect. Anyhow he wrote *Nettles*, and as soon as he could travel—early in August—got away from the intense heat of Italy to Baden-Baden.

'Yes,' he wrote to Ada, 'one feels very sick about the pictures. I suppose they won't let them burn them. Well, it's an unpleasant world—but I shan't let it worry me more than it need—and don't you either. The dirty swine would like to think they made you weep.'

After a few days at Baden itself, where it was still too hot for them, they moved with Frieda's mother to a hotel in the hills some 2000 to 3000 feet up. Here it first thundered and then rained so hard that they were obliged to hug themselves inside their greatcoats for warmth. After little over a week of this they fled back to Baden. Re-examined by the same German doctor who had seen him two years before, Lawrence was told that he was 'in several ways better,' and that his lung was 'much healed up.'

But his condition was admittedly 'still bad' and he was plagued with asthma. Accordingly, even the altitude of 3000 feet prescribed earlier was now said to be bad for him. He must go to the sea. Once more the Mediterranean was indicated. For the winter they must choose between the sea-coasts of Italy, Spain and the French Riviera.

In spite of his determination not to let the affair of the pictures disturb him unduly, the constant receipt of letters and telegrams and newspaper extracts with reference to the 'trial' at Marlborough Street Police Court,[1] which was then proceeding, was undoubtedly prejudicial to health. He was bound to feel it and he did.

Disgusting how one is insulted! [he wrote to Ada]. I shall not forgive it easily, to my white-livered lot! Thank God I needn't live among them, even to hear their beastly mingy British voices. . . . However the best will be to forget it as soon as possible.

And to me from Baden on August 12th:

The police case business bores and disgusts me, and makes me feel I never want to send another inch of work to England, either paint or pen. Why are those morons and *canaille* allowed to insult one *ad lib.*, while one is defenceless? England is a lily-livered country when it comes to purity.

And in the same letter:

---

[1] We were among those present at the hearing.

These people are nastier than you imagine, and it only needs a little more to start them putting pressure on the French or Italian Govts. to prosecute me for producing and issuing obscenity. I do not want to find myself in gaol, as a final insult—with a little vague sympathy in the far distance.

His post was again being tampered with, and I had suggested that it might be good if the police were tempted to seize as obscene some extracts from Walt Whitman's *Leaves of Grass* in his handwriting, just as they had at first seized some of Blake's drawings at the Warren Gallery. But he would have none of it.

No, for God's sake leave my unfortunate name alone just now. . . . No, the trouble is, once the police attack you, you are entirely at their mercy—so there it is.

Still—and though he was longing to be south again and to be in 'some sort of a place of our own'—it was 'really very nice here—an old inn with garden quiet and shady, where one can sit all day if one likes.'

VII

Till nearly the end of September the Lawrences stayed in Germany—or rather moved in a quiet way between Bavaria and Austria. Rottach with its lake—'so sunny and still'—where they had friends: Villach yet once more, with its full, swift river by which one could sit and watch the people and the swallows and feel like an old veteran—and from which now and again one could visit Munich if one felt like it. Till with October in sight it seemed the easiest and wisest thing to slip back to Bandol.

After collecting themselves at the Hotel Beau Rivage they found a little villa right on the sea, with a balcony looking seaward for Lawrence. Just at first he was in bed there, then up again, and always up and down. As usual in his letters home, each period in bed was no more than 'a little bout,' only to be expected in the process of getting straight again. He insisted on having the bedroom to himself, and strictly forbade Frieda to come in until after five o'clock each morning, when he should have got over his first and worst fit of coughing. She might come in then, with the big yellow cat pushing through the door before her to jump on to Lawrence's bed.

He passed day after day of a serene autumn on the balcony watching the sea and the dreamlike islands and the Mediterranean fishing boats going about their ages, old business. And in that sight his heart was at home—at home as it had never been in New Mexico. Men out there of his own order of consciousness were in touch with the unknown life of the cosmos, and they partook of that life the more profoundly because they measured themselves as men in conflict against it, therein becoming something more than men. Hope could not die out of the world so long as there was this. The wasted end of our epoch, even if it were faint as a filament wavering in air, would endure and would be joined to the beginning of a new epoch—when the time was ripe. When that time arrives Lawrence will come into his own, but much death and destruction may lie between. For the present, if even half the eyes that feast daily on the sight of the Mediterranean could look at the fishing fleet with the eyes of Lawrence, the new era might begin at once. Yet, to find it as Lawrence found it, all his savage pilgrimage was necessary, and was not too much. For days at a stretch he was sunk far into himself in a state of passivity such as he had never known before, not writing even letters, not reading nor even painting. For the first time I ceased to hear from him.

But out of this state of passivity came poems which may well prove to be his finest,[1] as Frieda declares that they are.

[1] These are not yet published.

And he cannot have been passive for so very long on end, as *Apocalypse* belongs to that winter, and he turned out also various articles of a popular nature, such as 'The Risen Lord,' which to his surprise was published in *Everyman* without cuts. He was glad to hear in December that the *Obscenity* pamphlet had sold over 6000. It was almost as if the tide was turning in his favour. If he could get at the people over the heads of the literary cliques, he believed, the tide *would* turn. Though he was not pleased with his health he still did not think he was worse. It was chiefly that he could not walk. First Paris and then Germany had been bad for him. He must be patient and his strength would come back. He grew to like the place so much that it was often discussed whether they should take on the Beau Soleil as a permanency or find another villa in the neighbourhood. They had a good cook, and Lawrence had great belief in the power of lying low. In the middle of January he felt so much better that once more he could see himself and Frieda going for summer to New Mexico and making their home at Bandol each winter. Frieda's younger daughter came out to stay and acted as a sort of secretary to Lawrence. Though he would not be treated as an invalid he could do with a little practical help along lines which were not Frieda's. Or perhaps it was chiefly that the girl might feel happier if she felt useful, to which end he insisted on giving her a small salary.

His friends were far more anxious than he, and before the end of January he was persuaded to see a doctor from England in whom both Koteliansky and Gertler had great confidence—Gertler with good reason, as he had himself suffered from pulmonary trouble, had been attended by this doctor and was now in good health. Lawrence therefore had himself examined.

The diagnosis was acute bronchitis aggravated by the

lungs, the treatment recommended was two months of sanatorium treatment.

When we heard that Lawrence had agreed to this it was at first as if we were hearing his death sentence. Lawrence in a sanatorium! Yet I told myself that he must be taking the doctor's advice, not in any spirit of despair but in the determination to follow what was declared to be the speediest road to recovery. He hated this way, but after all it might not be so bad as he had thought, and he was tired of not getting better. Of one thing we felt sure, Lawrence would not have consented to go if he had thought he was in real danger. And though he might well be worse than he thought himself, somehow one believed that Lawrence would not die.

Writing to tell Ada about it, he was as simple and as reticent as a schoolboy, and as hopefully comforting. She had wanted to come out again to see him, but he said not to come till he was better and walking about, as he would be soon. It would be too annoying to have to cope with sanatorium rules about visitors twice weekly, and the rest of it. He did not truly want to see Ada just then.

On February 3rd he went into the Sanatorium Ad Astra at Vence, and Frieda to the Villa Robermond a little higher up the hill. Then of course Lawrence had visitors. Mr. H. G. Wells calling from his villa not far away, was among them. Also the Aga Khan with his bride. His Highness had been so charmed with Lawrence's pictures when he saw them in London that he had the idea of showing them in a private gallery in Paris. As a result of his call at Vence, which was found very enjoyable, Lawrence telegraphed to the Warren Gallery to hold the pictures (now restored by the police) instead of sending them to him at Vence as had been arranged.

On the day after his arrival he wrote to assure Ada that it was 'quite nice and not alarming,' that he thought he

would 'be all right,' and that he had a balcony from which
he could see the coast-line and Cannes five miles off. Next
week, 'all being well,' he would be going down to lunch.

He endured the sanatorium life for three weeks, then he
decided that he would endure it no longer. It was not the
regimen that was too much for him. Of that he could be
entirely patient. But the necessarily mechanical ordering of
an institution was what his spirit could not bear and retain
its courage. If he was to live he might not stay longer,
equally if he was to die it must not be there.

Unaided, to the surprise of those who were with him, he
packed his things and without help walked up the rough and
stony hill path to the Robermond villa. And that night, as
every night at the Sanatorium, he refused to let anybody help
him with his toilet.

What remains is not for me to tell. I know only that
Lawrence—physically the ghost of what he had been, a mere
handful of a man—fought death to the last, and at the last
accepted what had to be with the simplicity of the brave. He
gave orders that his funeral, if he died, was to be of the
cheapest description. Yet he went on hoping that he would
not die. At home we did not, could not, believe that he
would. He bore with fortitude the severe pain—for now
it seems that his malady was developing into tubercular menin-
gitis. His mind stayed clear and composed. He would not
permit injections for deadening the pain, though he would
swallow an opiate.

For the onlookers, particularly for Huxley who was there,
it was merely terrible to see the light withdrawn from those
bright and daring eyes by the nature of the struggle. But to
Frieda, Lawrence's courage was more vivid even than his
suffering. 'Had you seen his splendid fight to the last,' she
wrote to me soon after, 'and his courageous dying it would
have given you courage, it was inspiring.'

It ended within two days of his move to the Villa Robermond. On the 2nd of March, 1930, in his forty-fifth year, died this great English writer and Englishman of destiny. He did more than make his mark on his generation; he marked a way out. For the honour and material success which would have come, and which he would have enjoyed and handled well, he lived not long enough. But all the more he was victorious. Against terrific odds he did his work, held to his belief and lived his life richly. When we in London heard of his death, it was the sense of our own failure that came home to us,—that and the sense of Lawrence's potency in death as in life. He needed, and needs now, no funeral oration. His emblem, the phoenix, has not played him false. If it be true of any man it is true of him, what he said himself—'the dead don't die. They look on and help.'

INDEX

293